URBAN COMPETITIVENESS

Policies for dynamic cities

Edited by Iain Begg

The POLICY
PRESS

First published in Great Britain in February 2002 by

The Policy Press
34 Tyndall's Park Road
Bristol BS8 1PY
UK

Tel +44 (0)117 954 6800
Fax +44 (0)117 973 7308
e-mail tpp@bristol.ac.uk
www.policypress.org.uk

British Library Cataloguing in Publication Data

A catalogue record for this book is available from the British Library

ISBN 1 86134 357 4 paperback

A hardcover version of this book is also available

Iain Begg is Professor of Economics at the European Institute, within the Business School at South Bank University.

Cover design by Qube Design Associates, Bristol.

Photograph on front cover by Simon McMaster

Printed and bound in Great Britain by Hobbs the Printers Ltd, Southampton.

Contents

List of tables and figures

Tables

Figures

Box

Acknowledgements

Tlis book is one of a series of publications emerging from the CITIES: Competitiveness and Cohesion Research Programme funded by the British Economic and Social Research Council (ESRC). The programme, which was also generously supported by the Department of Transport, Local Government and the Regions (DTLR), consists of 23 projects in 25 universities. It was launched in 1997 and will complete its work during 2002. This volume brings together early fruits of the work of the entire Programme and incorporates findings from several of the projects on one of the core themes, as well as two specially commissioned chapters on North American experience. More details of the Cities Programme can be found on our website http://cwis.livjm.ac.uk/cities

Any volume of this sort relies on the cooperation of the authors and, above all, of the people who work behind the scenes to turn the raw material into the finished product, and we are grateful to all of them. Particular thanks are due to Sarah Plant, Corinna Gannon and Dermot Hodson at South Bank University, for their efforts in organising a workshop at which first drafts of the chapters were presented and contributing to the editing process; and to Dawn Rushen, Karen Bowler, Helen Bolton and their colleagues at The Policy Press for the efficient manner in which they handled the production of the book.

The research that underpins much of this volume would, quite simply, not have happened without financial support, and we are indebted to the ESRC and the DTLR for funding it. If the results do not live up to expectations, blame us.

Iain Begg
South Bank University, London

Michael Parkinson
Director ESRC Cities Programme
Liverpool John Moores University

January 2002

Foreword

The British government believes that cities are central to the competitiveness of our economy and we have introduced many policies designed to improve their performance. Yet the concept remains elusive and its determinants are poorly understood.

We know that cities compete. We also know that how well they fare matters for the overall health of the economy. A recent Treasury paper on productivity in the UK has highlighted the strong links that exist between the economic performance of cities and their regions (HM Treasury, 2001, 'Productivity in the UK: 3 – The regional dimension', November). We know, too, that the policies implemented by different tiers of government play a significant part in shaping competitiveness. But it is often difficult to judge which policies make a difference and in what ways.

It is, therefore, a great pleasure for me to introduce this volume in which established and younger researchers put forward new ideas on how to assess and encourage the competitiveness of cities. The research provides a wealth of new ideas on how to promote more competitive cities and identifies many innovative ideas for policy makers.

The book draws extensively on a major investment made by the Economic and Social Research Council in its Cities Programme during the past five years. My Department was very happy to support that Programme. I am glad to see its many ideas now emerging. I look forward to a lively debate about the ideas and proposals that the Programme – and this book in particular – have generated.

Lord Falconer of Thoroton
Minister of State for Housing, Planning and Regeneration
Department for Transport, Local Government and the Regions

ONE

Introduction

Iain Begg

In contrast to earlier epochs when land or minerals were the primary sources of wealth, it is urban activities that today are the principal foundations of economic prosperity. Cities that are able to facilitate the achievement by producers of high and rising levels of productivity are national assets, while those that are beset by problems of congestion, dysfunctional factor markets or social unrest risk can have a detrimental effect on the national economy. There are, consequently, compelling reasons for investigating the competitive position of cities and for trying to understand how the 'competitiveness' or 'performance' of cities can be enhanced.

A research programme launched in 1997 by the British Economic and Social Research Council (ESRC) had as one of its core themes the elucidation of the processes that shape urban competitiveness. The Cities: Competitiveness and Cohesion programme – which, for reasons we can only speculate about, opted *not* to have CCCP as its acronym – also sought to investigate social cohesion in cities and to try to understand the linkages between the two themes. The programme comprised four large projects that undertook integrated case studies of major British urban areas (London, Bristol, the Liverpool/Manchester conurbations and the central belt of Scotland) and a variety of projects looking at more specialised topics.[1] As part of the research programme, there were regular meetings of a 'theme group' on competitiveness which provided the opportunity for researchers from different projects as well as interested specialists not directly involved with the programme to meet and to develop thinking on the topic. The present volume grew out of these deliberations.

Competitiveness is, plainly, a sought after condition. But it is also a poorly understood concept, notwithstanding the fact that policy makers invest considerable amounts of time and resources in trying to promote it. The US, for example, has a Competitiveness Commission; under the auspices of the European Commission prominent business leaders came together to form a Competitiveness Advisory Group; and the UK has had a succession of competitiveness White Papers over the last decade. Impelled, above all, by the work of Michael Porter (1990), the expression 'competitive advantage' has leapt from business schools, through discourse on national economic performance, to acquire pride of place in many a local economic development strategy document.

Many influential economists are, however, profoundly sceptical about the notion of competitiveness, taking the view that it is relevant only to businesses and that intervention by policy makers is usually aimed at distorting free trade and preventing competition for mercantilist reasons. Although the locality, region or country may obtain a short-term advantage, such market distortions are considered ultimately to be counterproductive, in so far as they result in a sub-optimal allocation of resources (Krugman, 1996a, 1996b). At the urban level, subsidies to developers and inward investors, selective relaxation of planning controls, or decisions on infrastructure investment could, indeed, result in a zero- or even negative-sum gain. Yet it is undeniable that some cities in ostensibly similar circumstances 'perform' significantly better than others. This implies that if the laggards can catch up with the leaders, then large gains can be achieved. The latter viewpoint suggests that the game should prove to be positive-sum.

The chapters in this volume all explore competitiveness from different vantage points. Much of the underlying research emanates from the ESRC research programme and this volume presents findings from several of the projects. This work is complemented by two studies that draw on North American experience. No attempt has been made either to impose a common definition of competitiveness or framework of analysis. Instead, the individual chapters elucidate different facets of the subject and present analyses that reflect the authors' interests. Nevertheless, a number of common themes can be discerned and the different chapters offer both contrasting and complementary views on what constitutes competitiveness and how policy can support it. This introduction discusses the meaning of competitiveness, presents an overview of the volume and of the content of individual chapters, and concludes by identifying policy issues.

Definitions

'Competitiveness' has much in common with the proverbial elephant: we know one when we see one, but have great difficulty describing it. Indeed, in a 1998 reissue of his book *The competitive advantage of nations*, Porter, in commenting on how it was received, observes that 'what became clear ... was that there was no accepted definition of competitiveness' (Porter,

1998, p xii). It manifestly concerns the performance of economies and can, at one level, be equated with the trajectory of the economy on 'outcome' variables such as the level of, or change in, value added, employment or the incomes of the population. Inputs into the productive process give a second perspective: if they are defective, deficient or unduly costly, or if conditions inhibit their effective use, competitiveness will suffer. These factors determine a large part of the costs of doing business in a particular location.

It does not, however, follow that the most competitive place is bound to be the one that has the lowest costs. On the one hand, low costs can be achieved by cutting corners or tolerating conditions that would be considered unacceptable elsewhere (such as severe environmental degradation or exploitation of labour), so that it is a squeeze on input costs rather than high productivity that gives the location its edge. On the other hand, a competitive economy can be considered to be one that raises the standard of living of its residents and workforce. A definition that has gained favour in the OECD is, therefore, that competitiveness for a country is the degree to which it can, under free and fair market conditions, produce goods and services which meet the test of international markets, while simultaneously maintaining and expanding the real incomes of its people over the long term.

Globalisation may be a much abused term, equally subject to conceptual uncertainty, but there is little doubt that nations, regions and cities do compete with one another (Duffy, 1995). But, as the contributions to Jensen-Butler et al (1997) make clear, the various forms of internationalisation (of goods, services, investment and information flows) have had a profound effect on productive structures. London, today, finds itself in competition with New York, Tokyo, Frankfurt and Paris for the most advanced business services. In the emerging high technology sectors, the competition is often among (mainly) smaller cities associated with leading universities and located in several countries, rather than with domestic rivals.

In an idealised market system, adjustment would be instantaneous and it could be argued that the whole competitiveness agenda is a false one. Yet the evidence of protracted imbalance between successful and declining cities and the resulting problems is persuasive. To put it a different way: location matters, and some cities manifestly offer a better mix of attributes for business than others. A third approach, consequently, is to consider the stock of assets and, to extend the logic of the balance sheet metaphor, liabilities – widely defined – that constitute the environment in which economic activity takes place. These will include both the tangible, in the form of physical assets or measurable variables, and more amorphous traits such as image, the quality of governance, and social and cultural features.

Many influences on urban competitiveness reflect national and international economic conditions that are beyond the direct influence of the individual city. They include macroeconomic variables (such as the exchange rate and the interest rate) and major structural changes in the economy (for example, the long-run shifts towards the service sector or the trends associated with globalisation such as transnational investment flows and changing patterns of international specialisation). But many characteristics of what I have called elsewhere (Begg, 1999) the 'business environment' are very much within the sphere of influence of the city, however difficult they might be to transform. Together, they shape the attractiveness of a city to investors and thus the prospects for successful economic performance.

Because cities typically comprise different bundles of assets from those in nations and have fewer policy levers to pull (or that can be pulled on their behalf), some care is needed in identifying specifically urban aspects of competitiveness. There is only a limited literature on this topic, although Kresl (1995) and the various contributors to the special issue of *Urban Studies* - vol 36, no 5/6, published in May 1999 – provide a range of insights. The new material in this volume extends the debate on this important issue.

Structure of the volume

All the chapters in this book are based on recent, empirically focused research projects. The balance between conceptual, empirical and policy analyses varies, but all the chapters draw on project findings that covered each of these. The first section of the book focuses primarily on conceptual discussion, including the exploration of the significance of new technologies, the links between social cohesion and competitiveness, and the role of property markets as 'shaping factors' that help to explain divergences in economic performance.

The section begins with a chapter by Bill Lever in which he examines how the global shift towards a more knowledge intensive productive system affects urban competitiveness. He argues that, whereas more traditional economic activities can relocate quite readily, promoting the knowledge sectors requires greater attention to be given to improving those aspects of the urban context which affect the quality of life. For Lever, cultural and environmental factors will be especially significant, but fresh thought on the role of housing markets is also needed. The shift towards the knowledge economy also raises difficult policy questions about how active the public sector should be in promoting knowledge creation and by intervening in the urban development process. The French approach of constructing technopoles, for example, is one which Lever explores.

Martin Boddy, in Chapter Three, looks at the social underpinnings of urban competitiveness and asks how the pursuit of the latter affects social cohesion. The links between social cohesion and competitiveness were a key research question in the development of the ESRC 'Cities' programme, and Boddy shows that there are subtle and difficult issues to confront. He suggests that a lack of social cohesion may not impede competitiveness unduly, but equally that even where cities 'perform' well there tends to be an obstinate persistence of diverse forms of social exclusion. The policy implication is that more active measures are needed to ensure that the fruits of prosperity are more equitably distributed.

Gareth Potts provides a complementary view in Chapter Four, in which he assesses different facets of the urban social fabric. His central aim is to offer a holistic framework for debating and researching wider links between the competitiveness of firms in cities and the various aspects of 'social inclusion', 'social capital' and 'social cohesion'. The chapter points to important links between social conditions and urban concentrations of similar and related firms, especially in knowledge intensive activities.

Chapter Five, by Ken Gibb, Daniel Mackay and Michael White, draws on the literature, and some Scottish evidence from a recent project funded by Insignia Richard Ellis, to examine critically the role of property as a 'shaper' of urban economic competitiveness. They focus, especially, on the nature of market failure in the property market and illustrate the questions raised by the discussion of the literature with evidence from the Scottish property sector. The chapter also appraises a framework adopted by Scottish Enterprise – the publicly funded economic development agency – which is operationalised in its *RAPID* property market intervention programme.

In Part II of the volume, the emphasis shifts to empirical studies in which the authors try to draw out inferences both from broad trends in urban change and from the experience of individual cities. Chapter Six, by Iain Begg, Barry Moore and Yener Altunbas, looks at the long-term evolution of British cities. Using data from the 1950s onwards, they show that there have been systematic and persistent trends in urban Britain in which the major conurbations have been the main losers, while smaller cities in the south of the country and new towns have been the main beneficiaries.

Nick Bailey, Iain Docherty and Ivan Turok in Chapter Seven provide detailed empirical analysis of the competitive positions of Edinburgh and Glasgow, and try to relate the two Scottish cities to their English counterparts. They assemble a range of indicators on output, new firm creation, and the labour and property markets. Their analysis presents a sharp contrast between the more successful Edinburgh and the continuing problems facing Glasgow, although they end on an optimistic note for the latter.

Chapter Eight, by James Simmie, James Sennett and Peter Wood, examines innovation and its impact on the competitive position of urban regions. Using survey data, they find that the London area stands out as an area with a high rate of innovation. Key factors have been the presence of Heathrow airport, which facilitates knowledge flows that underpin innovation, and the supply of skilled and qualified labour.

Measuring competitiveness is not easy, not least because of the slippery nature of the concept and diverse views on how it should be advanced. Despite the problems, there is plainly a demand from urban policy makers for techniques to measure competitiveness, so that the two methodologies for assessing it put forward by Iain Deas and Benito Giordano in Chapter Nine, and by Peter Kresl in Chapter Ten, are valuable additions to the policy toolbox. Both chapters outline the approach and apply it to case study cities, with Deas and Giordano testing theirs on the English conurbations, while Kresl looks at Montreal.

Deas and Giordano adopt a two-pronged approach to derive indicators of competitiveness. They look, first, at the 'assets' of the city, which they define in terms of a range of socio-economic indicators. They then examine various 'outcome' variables that provide evidence on how well a city has been performing. At the heart of the methodology is the presumption that cities with superior asset endowments should, other things being equal, attain better results. In their application of the approach to the English conurbations, Deas and Giordano show that some, such as Manchester, have achieved more than might have been expected from a relatively poor asset base, while others have suffered the double whammy of poor assets and a disappointing performance.

Kresl's methodology is to construct both quantitative and qualitative measures of a city's standing. He selects key output measures that reveal how well a city is 'performing', but stresses the importance of putting that performance in perspective by looking at the city's main characteristics and thus its prospects. By exemplifying the method for Montreal, a city which has been substantially transformed in recent years, Kresl draws attention to the policy choices and developments that have been critical in the transformation of the city. The approach can, therefore, be seen to have useful diagnostic properties as well as allowing comparisons.

In Part III of the volume, the emphasis is more on policy issues. Chapter Eleven, by Philip Cooke, Clare Davies and Rob Wilson, also looks at the questions of clustering and networking, but with the emphasis on linkages between cities as opposed to companies. Their key finding is that, in a context where growth and sustainability seem to be in opposition, conflict between them may be moderated through the development of urban networks. They maintain that partnership and collaboration among hitherto competing jurisdictions is the central factor in urban networks. They offer the possibility of groups of urban centres, located distantly from major metropolitan areas, cooperating and generating a 'city effect' or economies of agglomeration, to counter the 'urban overload' or agglomeration diseconomies that giant cities often suffer from. If new 'city-effect' facilities can be provided by networks pooling funding and expertise, to be able to afford a collective facility that individual towns would not be able to afford, then this is an example of the positive functioning of the urban networks idea.

Ned Hill and Jeremy Nowak in Chapter Twelve put forward a number of propositions for achieving better urban governance, and by this means finding a way to improve the prospects for the least promising cities. They exemplify their approach by looking at one of the US's most distressed cities: Camden in New Jersey. Their research draws extensively on interviews with practitioners in different US cities and they offer six propositions, offset by six obstacles to be overcome, for achieving their aims. Part of the fascination of their chapter is that it highlights the pronounced differences in what can be done, relative to the UK, as a result of the distinctive institutional framework for urban administration. Yet in their discussion of neighbourhoods (another theme that features prominently in the ESRC 'Cities' programme), and of planning challenges, they echo many of the issues that surface in the British discourse.

The last chapter, by Glen Bramley and Christine Lambert, explores the links between planning policy and urban competitiveness and identifies a range of shortcomings in the British system. They highlight the contradictions between policy stances that favour business development, while failing to provide adequately for the supporting infrastructure or complementary housing. In part, this is the result of a compartmentalisation of policy and of academic study of planning. To remedy this they put forward a framework for analysis which tries to integrate planning and broader approaches to economic development.

Lessons for policy

Together, the chapters in this volume offer a wide range of insights into economic development policy and the options for improving urban competitiveness that are taken up further in the Conclusions. Both Boddy and Potts argue, from different standpoints, that competitiveness and cohesion should not be treated separately, and that a more radical agenda for urban development should have people and genuine equality of opportunity at its heart. Urban competitiveness can gain from and, in turn, influence the local social fabric in various ways. Social ties can affect the efficient working of business and labour market networks in cities, but are not always without their dis-benefits in terms of economic efficiency and equal access to different areas and groups.

One of the strongest conclusions that emerges from the various contributions to this volume is that boosting or restoring the competitiveness of a city which is in difficulty is an extremely challenging and time-consuming business. Part of the explanation is that cities are subject to long-run pressures for change as described by Lever. This emerges not only from the evidence of persistent patterns presented in the overview of urban Britain by Begg, Moore and Altunbas, but also from case studies that place other cities in context. Thus, despite all the favourable publicity that Glasgow has secured in recent years, and the vast policy effort over several decades, Bailey, Docherty and Turok suggest that it is really only since the mid-1990s that they find signs that Glasgow's competitiveness has improved. Similarly, Deas and Giordano find few reasons for optimism about Merseyside despite the effort that has gone into its regeneration, especially since the Toxteth riots in the early 1980s, while Hill and Nowak paint a sombre picture about the prospects for Camden, New Jersey.

There are, clearly, parallels between the two approaches to assessing competitiveness outlined in Chapters Nine and Ten in that they go beyond looking at obvious and limited sets of outcome variables. As a result they provide a richer means of appraising the competitiveness of a city. Both are, however, rather demanding in data, although they are likely to be especially useful to policy makers who want to engage in benchmarking exercises to help in formulating economic development strategies.

Equally, the story that Kresl tells about the Montreal revival and of the role in it of well-conceived governance, and the more tentative findings by Deas and Giordano about Manchester having achieved more than expected given its weak asset base, suggest that there is no inevitability about processes affecting competitiveness. What is, nevertheless, clear is that for a city to break out of a cycle of relative decline requires concerted action by different 'stakeholders'.

The links between land-use planning and competitiveness are difficult to judge. Land and property are generally seen as part of the set of hard assets that underpin the competitive position of cities and are viewed as 'drivers' of urban economic competitiveness. The chapter by Gibb, Mackay and White sees these drivers as central to the enhancement of the 'physical business environment' of cities and regions. It also recognises that the land and property markets can, and often do, fail to provide optimal outcomes. Well known and visible examples of this market failure would include spatial externalities, vacant and derelict land and volatile property market cycles.

Economic development strategies frequently target inward investment and, as Bramley and Lambert point out, the assembly of appropriate sites is often a key contribution by the locality. Yet, the same authorities may, for various reasons, resist the expansion of housing that would be the concomitant of increased economic activity and this can lead to a dangerous imbalance in otherwise competitive urban economies. As an illustration, Cooke, Davies and Wilson argue that in innovative environments such as the knowledge-intensive economic centres of Oxford and Cambridge, pressures to reconcile sustainability with economic dynamism have led to calls for a new concept of 'planning for growth' rather than traditional 'planning for containment'. Simmie, Sennett and Wood also note the impact that planning has had on clusters of innovative firms in South East England.

Hill and Nowak point out that in the US, where the fiscal resources of the urban authority depend on the local tax base, problems tend to be compounded and can lead to prolonged vicious cycles of decline in distressed urban areas. Although the fact that the bulk of local government financing comes from central government means British cities do not face the same threats, there is a wider issue for policy. This is that so long as the different components of policy lack an integrated framework, cities will be vulnerable to inconsistencies in decision making.

Networking between cities, as analysed by Cooke, Davies and Wilson, offers one way of achieving such policy integration. More attention to the balance between social cohesion and competitive priorities is another. At the same time, it is abundantly clear that a single policy formula is not the answer. What worked for Montreal will not necessarily be a solution for Liverpool, Glasgow or Camden, New Jersey. Indeed, a key point implicit in the methodologies developed by Kresl and by Deas and Giordano is that it is vital to understand what is distinctive about the particular city in order to arrive at sensible policy proposals. Equally, as Begg, Moore and Altunbas stress, cities form part of an urban system in which specialisation inevitably occurs. It follows that not all cities can hope to acquire the attributes that Simmie, Sennett and Wood find to have been central to the success of the London Metropolitan region in becoming so successful in fostering innovation.

These are just some of the many policy issues that surround the conceptualisation, measurement and choice of strategies to enhance urban competitiveness.

Notes

[1] For more details, see the programme website at http://www.livjm.ac.uk/cities

References

Begg I. (1999) 'Cities and competitiveness', *Urban Studies*, vol 36, no 5/6, pp 795-809.

Duffy, H. (1995) *Competitive cities: Succeeding in the global economy*, London: Spon.

Jensen-Butler, C., Schacher, A. and van Weesep, J. (eds) (1997) *European cities in competition*, Aldershot: Avebury.

Kresl, P. (1995) 'The determinants of urban competitiveness', in P. Kresl and G. Gappert, (eds.), *North American cities and the global economy: Challenges and opportunities*, Urban Affairs Annual Review, no 44, London: Sage Publications.

Krugman, P. (1996a) 'Making sense of the competitiveness debate', *Oxford Review Of Economic Policy* 12, pp 17-25.

Krugman, P. (1996b) *Pop internationalism*, Cambridge, MA: MIT Press.

Porter, M.E. (1990, 1998) *The competitive advantage of nations*, London: Macmillan.

TWO

The knowledge base and the competitive city

William F. Lever

Introduction

As the world's economy becomes increasingly globalised, nation states have had to reassess their comparative and competitive advantage. The patterns of production and trade in manufactured goods have shifted towards the new international division of labour, in which multinational enterprises have sought locations in areas of low labour cost, typically in the newly industrialised countries (NICs) and subsequently in the less developed countries (LDCs) (Daniels and Lever, 1996). As more of the world's economy has been engaged in services, the new, international division of labour (Coffey and Bailly, 1992) has emerged, again capitalising on low labour costs in the LDCs in sectors such as data processing and global tourism (Howland, 1996). Against this background the developed nations have had to consider in which sectors they retain a competitive advantage and how this competitive advantage can be sustained. The answer generally has been that governments should work to develop the 'knowledge-based economy'. Typical of such views is the UK's White Paper, *Our competitive future: Building the knowledge driven economy* (DTI, 1998). Such documents argue that "all businesses, large and small, new and established, in manufacturing and services, low and high technology, urban and rural located, will need to marshall their knowledge and skills to satisfy customers, exploit market opportunities and meet society's aspirations for a better environment" (DTI, 1998, p 6). In March 2000, the European Council of Ministers indicated the importance of transforming the European Union economy into one based on knowledge in order to sustain its competitiveness against other major trade blocks such as North America, South East Asia and, prospectively, China, up to 2010 and thereafter.

The term 'knowledge' as used in these reports can be defined in several ways (OECD, 1995; DTI, 1998). There is technical knowledge, which contributes to the development of new products and new processes. There is customer-base knowledge, which covers new markets, consumer choice and tastes and fashions. There is knowledge that relates to financial inputs to the production process. Lastly, there is knowledge as human capital in the form of skills. All of these types of knowledge are accessible to policy intervention, and the reports list a series of government strategies to increase and improve the knowledge base. The objective of such interventions is usually to facilitate, in some way, the research and development that increases knowledge. Malecki (1997) describes the role of research and development in generating innovation, through the linear model. The linear model assumes that knowledge is generated through research, which advances concepts and findings through scientific methods of induction or deduction. While generally true, it has been pointed out that advances in knowledge may involve feedback loops, reiterations, paradigm shifts and intuitive leaps that do not form a single linear path. However, the linear model tends to be the one that guides policy. The implications of the linear model for public policy are clear. If the level of research and development is increased, a corresponding increase in innovation should (eventually) follow. Carrying the argument one stage further, since it is basic research from which innovation ultimately flows, government science and industrial policy must include measures aimed at achieving an appropriate balance between basic and applied research (Ronayne, 1984). The linear model is also an outcome of the neoclassical framework which finds 'market failure' in basic research (Smith, 1995). The type of knowledge which flows from this intervention is characterised by high risk, indivisibilities (and often large minimum scale) and difficulties in appropriating (monopolising) the returns or benefits. Thus governments must engage in, or subsidise, basic research and create property rights in the 'intellectual property' that result via patents and other means.

The simple linear model linking research and development to general knowledge, firm specific knowledge and innovation, however, has now been challenged. Work by Myers and Rosenbloom (1996), and Malecki (1997), shows the extensive range of feedback loops and circuits within the innovation process, but all may be regarded as forms of knowledge.

A further distinction is made between knowledge that is tacit or articulate and knowledge that is standardised or codified. The latter may readily be transmitted through journal articles, project reports or prototypes, whereas the former has a higher degree of uncertainty and the precise meaning is more interpretative and less easily conveyed through a standardised medium. As a consequence, when knowledge is more tacit in nature, face-to-face interaction and communication are important and geographic proximity may promote commercial activity (von Hipple, 1994). That is, the less codified and articulated the knowledge, the greater the degree of centralisation in geographic organisation.

Knowledge and city economies

Much of the debate about knowledge as an element of competitive advantage has, in policy terms at least, been conducted at the national level, probably because government assistance to research and development tends to take the form of national programmes such as the UK's Foresight programme. However, studies of urban competitiveness have also stressed the role of the quality of local knowledge (Knight, 1995). As society becomes increasingly knowledge-based, the nature of city development changes because activities in the knowledge sector are becoming more important and requiring very specific conditions and environments. These are very different from those required by community-based activities, which are declining, and knowledge-based activities, which are expanding in cities out of the necessity of being in close proximity to knowledge resources (Knight and Stanback, 1970). Advances in communications and informatics are making it easier for activities in the production sector to be uncoupled from those in the knowledge sector, but activities in the knowledge sector are culturally based and very difficult to transplant. Production can now be monitored and the costs are quality controlled over long distances. If city development and growth are to be more orientated towards activities in the knowledge sector, greater attention will have to be given to improving those factors which determine the quality of life, factors which are more cultural and environmental than those in the production sector.

While early studies of the impact of telecommunications on urban development tended to stress the 'levelling out' of access to information, especially from satellite technology, more recent studies have taken the alternative view that the advantage conferred by access to knowledge will be spatially very uneven (Graham, 1999). There are two reasons for this. The technology of knowledge transfer is by no means ubiquitous and the access to local concentrations of such technology may be crucial. Second, and perhaps more important, is the relevance of knowledge and information transferred face-to-face. Routine information is easily transferred but high quality, confidential information, particularly in financial services, but also in creative design and product innovation, must be low risk, error free and unambiguous. In terms of defining the knowledge base as an important element in urban competitiveness it is useful to distinguish between tacit and codified knowledge. Codified knowledge is widely available, through the Internet for example, and might comprise lists and details of input suppliers, business services and potential markets. While valuable, it confers little competitive advantage as it is geographically widely available and accessible to all or most enterprises. Competitiveness, at the establishment level, is only enhanced by access to tacit knowledge. This has a much greater value because it is conveyed, often face-to-face, in ways that reduce the risk of mistake or deliberate misrepresentation. The participants in the knowledge exchange have trust in one another and value the information transmitted as being more reliable as a basis for investment. Recent examples of deliberate deceit in financial services, such as the events which led to the collapse of Barings Bank, and the trading of derivatives, have shown the importance of avoiding risk and building confidence between business partners. The fact that tacit knowledge often has to be transmitted face-to-face means that it is not ubiquitous. Locations which best facilitate person-to-person contacts will have their competitiveness improved as a consequence. These considerations have led to an increase in, rather than a lessening of, the spatial concentration of knowledge processing in a small number of highly connected cities (Budd, 1995; Warf, 1995).

Measuring the knowledge base

While the relationship between the knowledge base and economic growth and development is well acknowledged, measuring the relationship is much less easy. One attempt at the European scale was made by Cheshire and Carbonaro (1996). Several alternatively specified multiple regression models were developed to explain income growth in the period 1979-90 for 117 Functional Urban Regions (FURs). The independent variables were of several types including measures of population size and growth, the impact of European integration on market potential (defined in terms of access to population weighted by spending power), economic structural variables (agriculture, coalmining, port activities) linked to European Union Objective 1 and 2 status, national dummies and, significantly for the measurement of the knowledge base, the number of research and development (R&D) establishments per million inhabitants. In all models this last variable is found to be significant at the one per cent level of confidence. There are therefore increasing returns to scale in the concentration of human capital employed in R&D. This suggests that localised knowledge spillovers and dynamic increasing returns to knowledge do in part 'explain' differentials in economic growth. The study, however, fails to establish an unambiguous causal link because of multi-collinearity between the variables. R&D may well be linked to the national dummies (high in Germany, low in Belgium) and to income changes and investment, which act as intervening variables in GDP change.

A similar study of cities in the US (Kresl and Singh, 1999) produces a similar finding. First, using the number of research centres per million workforce, the study is able to correlate research with competitive success measured by the relative growth of retail sales, manufacturing value added and business service receipts, in 1977-92. A second variable, the engineering and research component of the labour force, is found to have a stronger relationship with competitiveness. The study cites Denver as a case of high competitiveness linked to both measures of research and knowledge followed by cities such as San Francisco, San Diego and Boston. At the other end of the scale come Milwaukee, Cleveland and St Louis. The classification of cities on this criterion is argued to reflect how successfully they have transformed their economies, minimising the impact of the collapse of sectors such as foodstuffs, chemicals and engineering and capitalising on the growth of the new economy sectors such as data processing, finance and personal services. An alternative approach to measuring the knowledge base in competitiveness across a number of cities was employed by Knight (1995) and Drewett et al (1988) for the European Commission. The studies pointed to the growing concentration of science-based techno-industrial activities in the core axis of Western Europe but, unlike the other studies, sought to distinguish between the various types of knowledge such as research and development, international finance, administrative headquarters of high level organisations, multinational corporations and non-governmental organisations. Other types of knowledge of a socio-cultural nature are less formalised and more widely dispersed. Twenty cities were asked to evaluate the relative importance of the various types of knowledge in city economic growth and the relative measures are shown in Table 2.1. The cities were also asked to indicate the importance of any elements that they felt were lacking and needed to be added to the knowledge base for each type of knowledge resource. Recognition that elements of the intellectual infrastructure such as university programmes, libraries, research facilities and cultural institutions were missing was acknowledged by at least half of the cities surveyed.

Table 2.1: Knowledge resources: importance to a city's comparative advantages

Type of nnowledge	Importance
Science and technology (universities, R&D)	4.7
Commerce, banking, insurance	3.7
Industry and production know-how	3.7
Arts and culture	3.6
Administration and coordination (international and national)	3.3
Creativity	3.2

Note: insignificant = 0: very important = 6.

Source: EC/FAST study: The future of European cities

Measuring the quantum of knowledge

All these studies have made a theoretical or an empirical linkage between levels of local knowledge, be it quantitative or qualitative, and the competitive success of the local urban economic system. However, it has proved difficult to find unambiguous measures of the quantity of knowledge. Unlike other factors of production, capital, labour and space, for which absolute measures are easily available, knowledge cannot be measured in finite, discrete amounts. Consequently, studies which seek to measure the quantity (and quality) of knowledge in a local economy, and to assess its relationship with competitiveness, have been forced to use proxies or complementary indicators. Similarly, when policy makers set out to enhance the knowledge base, the absence of an objective categoric measure of knowledge makes it difficult for them to measure their progress to set objectives, or to assess the relative efficiencies of different policy interventions. In this respect it is more difficult for policy makers to benchmark the development and supply of knowledge than it is to audit labour skills, capital availability or space provision.

In terms of Feldman's (2000) distinction between tacit and codified knowledge, it is particularly difficult to measure the former. Using data on the results of publicly supported R&D projects in the European Union, Feldman and Lichtenberg (1998) construct several indicators of tacitness based on the degree to which projects result in prototypes, which might be easily transferred to others, or result in know-how that is knowledge, which is less able to be transmitted. The results indicate that the more tacit the knowledge generated by the R&D, the greater the extent of geographic and administrative centralisation of the R&D activities.

In the absence of such objective measures, two approaches have been taken to measure correlates of knowledge – we term them 'inputs' and 'outputs'. Input measures are defined as the necessary preconditions for the generation or transmission of knowledge. We can identify five such measures: i) measures of telematic infrastructure, ii) measures of education, usually in the form of graduates in the workforce, iii) the existence of R&D establishments, iv) measures of the connectivity of local airports, given that knowledge is most successfully transmitted face-to-face, which requires a high speed facility with which to move people, and v) measures of fairs, expositions and conferences as means of conveying information whether commercial, academic or creative.

Outputs are measures of the product of knowledge in forms that are transferable and utilisable. We can identify four such measures: i) patents, in that most countries have a system of patenting innovations to protect intellectual property rights; ii) publications in academic and scholarly journals as a means of signalling new knowledge, validated by peer review and an editorial process; iii) new firm formation rates, although the great majority of new enterprises do not depend upon innovation and its commercial application; and iv) measures of creativity. These are less easy to quantify and tend to use counts of workers engaged in creative activities.

These various measures incorporate elements of both tacit and codified knowledge. Measures involving or implying face-to-face contact, such as airport connectivities, trade fairs and conferences, are clearly more closely related to tacit knowledge, whereas publications and patents are codified.

Input measures

Measures of telematic infrastructure

As facilitators of the interactive functioning and development of global cities, convergent media, telecommunications and computing grids (known collectively as telematics), are the basic integrating infrastructures that underpin intensely interconnected planetary urban networks. Inter-urban telecommunications networks (both fibreoptic and satellite) comprise a vital set of hubs, spokes and tunnel effects, linking urban economies together into 'real' or 'near real time' systems of interaction, which substantially reconfigure both space and time barriers within and between them (de Roo, 1994). Such knowledge technologies help to integrate distant financial markets, service industries, corporate locations and media industries with virtual instantaneity and rapidly increasing sophistication.

Their dynamics mean that the very small geographical areas of the main global finance, and corporate and media capitals, dominate the emerging global political economy of telecommunications to a degree that is rarely recognised because of the dominance of national figures in available data (Graham, 1999).

Two sources of data help demonstrate this dominance. First, we can see how the economic sectors, which are overwhelmingly located in global cities, tend to dominate international communications flows as a whole. For example, over 80 per cent of international data flows are taken up by the communications flows of the financial services sector (Sussman, 1997). Over 50 per cent of all long distance calls in the US are taken up by only five per cent of all telephone customers, largely transnational corporations whose control functions still cluster in the global metropolitan areas of the nation.

There is also a small amount of available data on the dominance of national telecommunications patterns by particular global cities. Finnie (1998), for example, found that about 55 per cent of all international private telecommunications circuits that terminate in the UK do so in London and about 75 per cent of all advanced data traffic generated in France come from within the Paris region.

In an attempt to measure urban competitiveness conferred by access to telecommunications, Finnie ranked 25 global cities on an aggregate score based upon price, the choice of operators/providers and the availability of high quality, advanced and sophisticated systems (such as dark fibre systems which are dedicated and wideband). Table 2.2 shows how the ranking is dominated by five US cities, followed by London. Cities which are currently experiencing a proliferation of urban fibre infrastructures following recent liberalisation came next (Stockholm, Paris, Sydney, Hong Kong, Frankfurt and Amsterdam). The remainder trailed further behind because of lack of competition (choice), higher prices and the absence of the most sophisticated services. Perhaps significantly, Moscow (24) and Beijing (25) were ranked last with scores of 134 and 105 respectively.

Measures of education

Studies of the competitiveness of cities have tended to use numbers of students in higher education as a measure of the knowledge base. Such studies are somewhat ambiguous because there is no guarantee that students will remain in the local economy (and many do not as the older historical universities such as Oxford and Cambridge attract students on quality grounds, and accept they will be lost on graduation). However

Table 2.2: Ranked scores of global cities by competitiveness in telecommunications infrastructure (1998)

Rank	City	Total	Tariff	Choice	Availability
1	New York	438	148	182	108
2	Chicago	428	154	166	108
3	Los Angeles	428	152	168	108
4	San Francisco	425	149	168	108
5	Atlanta	409	141	160	108
6	London	391	131	161	99
7	Stockholm	386	129	149	108
8	Toronto	361	123	148	90
9	Paris	337	118	129	90
10	Sydney	331	123	118	90
11	Hong Kong	328	107	149	72
12	Frankfurt	321	78	135	108
13	Amsterdam	308	100	118	90
14	Tokyo	300	77	133	90
15	Brussels	294	97	107	90

Source: Finnie (1998, p 21)

the use of student numbers also gives a second dimension to the knowledge base because of the assumed generation of pure new knowledge in universities which may find a commercial take-up in the local science park or high technology small firm sector. However, a number of major science locations owe their origins to spin-offs from local universities: examples would include Silicon Valley close to Berkeley, the Cambridge Science Park and the Montpellier 'technopole' in France. The link between the size of the local university and the growth of the local economy has been stressed in a number of studies seeking to measure competitive success (see, also, the chapter by Cooke, Davies and Wilson in this volume).

One such study (McGregor et al, 1997) covered 24 European cities (excluding capitals) to measure the competitive advantage of Glasgow within that group. The top ten ranked cities are shown in Table 2.3. The list shows the tendency for large southern European cities (eg Barcelona, Naples, Milan, Valencia, Bologna, Marseilles) to predominate in the ranking based on the size of the student body. However, the definition of 'university' differs from one country to another, which lends further ambiguity to this measure.

Research and development establishments

There is an intuitive relationship between the generation of knowledge through R&D and economic competitiveness. The work of Cheshire and Carbonaro (1996) has already been cited in which, in a multiple regression model of 117 European cities, the number of R&D establishments belonging to the largest Fortune 500 companies per million inhabitants was used as an independent variable. It was found to be a significant predictor of economic growth in all three models used. The fact that the models performed better with powers of the variable rather than absolute values suggests that clusters of R&D establishment achieve considerable economies of scale over single establishments. In some cases the advantage of such clusters represents sharing of information but, such is the nature of the competitive advantage of innovation, it is more likely that the advantage is based upon shared services, access to a pool of highly qualified (graduate and technical) labour, the clustering of government contracts (in defence procurement for example) and the activities of property developers in marketing 'science parks'. (Simmie, Sennett and Wood, this volume).

The relationship between concentrations of R&D establishments and economic growth is mediated by their sectoral composition. The OECD standard employs R&D strictly defined according to the Frascati manual to identify high technology industries (OECD, 1995). This definition defines research and experimental development to 'comprise creative work undertaken on a systematic basis in order to increase the stock of

Table 2.3: Numbers of students (000s) in higher education

Rank	City	Number 1996
1	Barcelona	131.0
2	Milan	115.6
3	Naples	100.0
4	Munich	84.5
5	Valencia	68.3
6	Cologne	63.0
7	Bologna	59.1
8	Lille	58.4
9	Marseilles	56.0
10	Manchester	52.1

Source: World of Learning, 1997

knowledge, including knowledge of man, culture and society, and to use this stock of knowledge to devise new applications' (p 29). Explicitly excluded from R&D are education and training, scientific and technical information services, routine testing and analysis, specialised medical care, and production and related technical activities. A number of activities are recognised as the boundaries of R&D such as postgraduate studies, industrial design and trial production, some aspects of which are classified as R&D while others are excluded. On the basis of this definition industries can be classified in terms of their R&D intensity. Table 2.4 shows how R&D clusters are most likely to occur in aerospace, pharmaceuticals, computers, communications equipment and scientific instruments.

It has been argued that although R&D is important in increasing the knowledge base, it does not confer an advantage on the local economy as the benefits may rapidly be transported elsewhere intracorporately (Gibb, 1985). However, some studies have been able to measure the impact that R&D establishments do have locally. Smith (1995), for example, was able to demonstrate the extent of local linkages between 111 high technology plants in Oxfordshire and the local (South East England) economy while

Table 2.4: Industries by R&D intensity

Industry	Intensity
High intensity	8.1
Aerospace	12.4
Pharmaceuticals	11.9
Computers, office equipment	11.0
Communications equipment	9.0
Scientific instruments	6.4
Medium intensity	2.5
Motor vehicles	3.4
Chemicals other than drugs	2.0
Non-electrical machinery	2.0
Plastics	1.2
Low intensity	0.5
Food, drink	0.3
Petroleum refining	1.0
Iron and steel	0.7
Paper and printing	0.3
Textiles	0.3

Source: OECD (1995)

Segal, Quince and Wickstead undertook a similar survey of the Cambridgeshire high technology cluster (Segal, 1986).

Airports

We have already stressed that where knowledge is transferred interpersonally, access to high-speed personal transport is important, and this leads to measures of connectivity of city airports. A study by Buursink (1994), for example, identifies cities with consular offices and embassies, as 'Europoles' and then measures the connectivity of their airport(s) to other airports by scheduled flights. He argues that:

> the most indispensable attribute of a Eurocity is, without doubt, an airport which is an important node in international air traffic, in particular in intraEuropean traffic. A city that is to be considered as a commercial centre of European scale cannot do without an airport offering frequent and fast connections with other main centres in Europe. (p 6)

Table 2.5 shows the pre-eminence of the London and Paris airports in Europe. Two further trends are noticeable – the impact of the opening up of Central and Eastern Europe on airports such as Frankfurt, Munich, Dusseldorf and Vienna and the growth of some very actively marketed national hub airports such as Copenhagen and Milan. The study also shows the increasing connectivity of East European airports such as Prague, Warsaw and even Riga, following liberalisation.

Fairs, expositions, conferences

Formal events for the exchange of knowledge of various types are also used as a measure of the knowledge base although the advantage accruing to the location of such events is less clear. A study by Rubalcaba-Bermejo and Cuadrado-Roura (1995) spells out the economic advantages of holding fairs and exhibitions: these include enhanced knowledge, increased competitive power, growth in trade and cultural exchange. The study develops an ambitious regression model to explain the level of fairs and exhibitions activity (in terms of space, number of visitors and number of foreign visitors). High levels of activity are explained by local population size, rental levels, local per capita income, infrastructure, tradition and even weather. The study develops a composite index of the scale of fairs and exhibitions activity, which generates a hierarchy of provision. Table

Table 2.5: European airports and their connectivity

City	Connections	Change 1991-93
London	98	0
Paris	91	+1
Frankfurt	84	+14
Amsterdam	75	0
Zurich	70	+3
Brussels	65	+5
Copenhagen	64	+5
Munich	57	+11
Milan	47	+6
Dusseldorf	44	+6
Vienna	43	+5
Geneva	38	+3

Source: ABC World Airways Guide 1996

2.6 shows that the leading cities belong to three groups – the topmost leaders of which are London and Paris, outstanding fair-hosting cities such as Milan and Birmingham, and leading German cities such as Frankfurt and Cologne whose success stems from both size and internationalisation (in the absence of Berlin).

Output measures

Patents

The process by which innovations, whether new products, new processes or even new concepts are registered, in order to protect the innovators' intellectual property rights and to benefit from their commercial application, offers a potentially fruitful avenue for the measurement of knowledge. The volume of patents, and their location, should give some indication of the 'amount' of new knowledge over time. In practice, rather less use has been made of this source than might have been expected, for two reasons. First, different nation states have different legal systems of patent registration, which makes an international comparative analysis difficult. Second, patent information does not include data on commercial application, it merely records the new knowledge. Useful as this may be, it does not measure the economic comparative advantage of innovation. Patents are, in their very nature, privately held so that they do not convey

Table 2.6: Major exhibition centres in Europe

Rank	City	Fairs	Visitors (000s)
I	Paris	98	5,230
2	London	136	2,606
3	Milan	46	2,972
4	Birmingham	80	1,684
5	Frankfurt	22	1,251
6	Cologne	22	1,210
7	Hannover	17	1,893
8	Bologna	15	1,395
9	Munich	18	1,333
10	Barcelona	36	1,703
11	Madrid	42	1,536
12	Dusseldorf	17	1,358

Source: Feria database

an advantage to the wider local economy beyond that of the innovator. David and Faray (1995) make this distinction between public information, which is completely codified (patents, copyrights), and fully disclosed knowledge in the form of scientific papers.

One detailed study of patents within a single national context is that by Gershuny and Miles (1983) in the UK, which covered some 2,300 registered patents. The spatial distribution showed a clear bias in favour of the South East region in a way that suggested that i) affluent regions have a patents Location Quotient above 1.0, ii) that proximity to central government also improves the amount of regional knowledge through the process of procurement, and iii) patents do correlate with levels of regional R&D.

Slightly less formalised than patents are listings of new developments in trade journals, which can be locality-based. These represent the public (or semi-public) announcements of commercial applications of inventions and discoveries.

Published papers

A second measure of knowledge output is the volume of academic and scientific papers in refereed journals. The measures developed by Matthiessen and Schwarz (1999) have the merit that the spatial origins of the authors can be used to locate this knowledge base and the knowledge can be divided into subsets such as medicine, computer science, natural sciences and engineering. It is a measure of output that is based on the quantity of local research. However, the benefit rapidly extends beyond the local economy for, as David and Faray indicate, the act of publication means that the knowledge quickly passes into the global domain. Table 2.7 shows the leading European research centres based on publications listed in the Science Citation Index, both in terms of absolute numbers, for the period 1994-96, and in terms of a ratio to local population size. The large European capitals (London, Paris, Berlin, Moscow and the Randstadt) figure prominently on the absolute measure, but on the relative measure smaller university cities (Oxford, Cambridge, Bristol, Geneva and Basel) head the rankings. While this is an interesting measure of the knowledge base it does appear to exhibit an Anglophone bias with its emphasis on British, Dutch, Swiss and Scandinavian authorship.

Dividing up the papers by discipline reveals an interesting division between the medical sciences and biology (London, Paris, Edinburgh, Manchester, Amsterdam and Stockholm) and the physical sciences (Moscow, St Petersburg, Paris, Geneva, Warsaw and Berlin). The paper then goes on to differentiate between 'complete' research centres, ranked hierarchically by size from London ('extremely large') to cities such as Aachen, Hamburg, Lyon, Prague ('small') and cities in which only a limited range of disciplines are represented such as Birmingham (engineering), St Petersburg (geosciences and nuclear physics), Budapest (computer sciences) and Geneva (nuclear physics, because of the location of the Centre Européene de Recherche Nucleare).

Table 2.7: Research centres in Europe

Rank	Published papers 1994-96		Rank	papers per 000	
I	London	64,742	I	Cambridge	81
2	Paris	45,752	2	Oxford-Reading	41
3	Moscow	39,903	3	Geneva	29
4	Randstadt	36,158	4	Basel	20
5	Copenhagen	21,631	5	Bristol-Cardiff	15
6	Stockholm	20,195	6	Zurich	13
7	Berlin	19,872	7	Stockholm	12
8	Oxford-Reading	18,876	8	Helsinki	12
9	Edinburgh Glasgow	18,688	9	Copenhagen	11
10	Manchester-Liverpool	17,764	10	Randstadt	10
11	Cambridge	16,230	11	Munich	10
12	Madrid	15,947	12	Edinburgh-Glasgow	10

New firm formation rates

If innovations flowing from the knowledge base lead to economic advantage, then the rate at which new enterprises are created should be a measure of this advantage. However the manner in which statistics are compiled may make international comparisons difficult; it is often the case that new enterprises are recorded when they first cross some tax liability threshold based on turnover for example (Keeble and Wever, 1987). More crucially, a large proportion of registered new businesses do not reflect innovation but are small wealth-consuming, consumer service outlets which confer no economic advantage, except very marginally through the quality-of-life dimension. Nevertheless some studies (eg Lever et al, 1990) have used new, firm formation rates per 10,000 population as a measure of economic performance. There are substantial differences, for example, between Amsterdam (30), Milan (25) and Turin (23) with high rates and Lille (4), Bremen (4), Hamburg (5) and Lyons (5) with low rates, although there must be a suspicion that national recording practices account for some of the difference.

Creativity

An increasing interest has developed in the contribution which creativity, the creative arts and innovation can make to postmodernist urban economies. Measuring creativity, as a special form of knowledge is difficult. Hall (1998), in a wide-ranging historical review, indicates that several cities (Athens, Paris, Vienna, London, Berlin, Los Angeles) have at one time achieved a peak of cultural creativity in the arts, music, architecture, literature and film – but without accurate measures. In a more detailed study Hall refers to Pratt's work on the economic impact of the creative sector in London's economy (Pratt, 1997; Hall, 2000). Pratt estimates that 4.5 per cent of all employees in Britain are in the cultural industries but of this total, one quarter was in London. London in 1994 had a location quotient above 1.0 in all the cultural industries and between 4.0 and 5.0 in sectors such as advertising, film production, radio and television and publishing, although various factors had led to a lessening of this concentration by the early 1990s (Hall, 2000). Comparative studies are less easy to undertake, but Boyle et al (1996) were able to measure the contribution of the cultural creative sectors to the economic regeneration of three cities, Detroit, Birmingham and Sheffield.

———

Conclusion

It seems inarguable that the comparative advantage and competitiveness of cities and nation states in the developed world will be based on the knowledge base. Measuring the amount of knowledge in a local or national economy, however, is far from easy. This is particularly true of tacit knowledge as distinct from codified knowledge, which is more routine in nature and more easily available. Tacit knowledge, which includes creativity, innovation and networks of human capital, is more difficult to evaluate because it raises questions of reliability, confidentiality and non-linearity. There are several problems, not only in the measurement of the quantity and quality of the local urban knowledge base, but in measuring the relationship between the knowledge base and economic growth and development. Measures of the knowledge base such as the number of research and development establishments, the level of expenditure on R&D, the numbers of academic papers and patents, and the existence and size of universities, do correlate with economic growth and competitiveness. However, as it is extremely expensive to generate new knowledge, the competitive advantage conferred by this knowledge is likely to be limited to the private enterprises that generate it. Where the knowledge is generated in the public sector (as in the case of universities or public R&D establishments), its dissemination raises difficult issues. Such knowledge may be made widely available on ethical grounds, as in the case of the human genome programme, or it may be offered to the highest bidder. It is rare, however, for the existence of such knowledge to fuel the economic competitiveness and growth of the whole of the local, urban economy. Knowledge does appear to be spatially clustered but, as Simmie, Sennett and Wood point out in Chapter Eight of this volume, network clusters of knowledge may exist but their rationale is not the exchange of knowledge between enterprises. It is, rather, the existence of shared positive external economies such as qualified labour, appropriate commercial property, sympathetic land use planning and a high quality of life, culture and amenities.

Government intervention, both local and national, to stimulate the knowledge base in order to enhance competitiveness, has had to confront these difficulties. The British government has focused upon education, in particular in measuring the quality of research through the Research Assessment Exercise in the 1990s upon which departmental funding is in part based, and increasing university student numbers (see also Chapter Nine by Deas and Giordano). In fostering research and development the government has sought, not to increase spending on public establishments, but help to the private sector to increase spending through grant assistance, tax breaks and government contracts. In the belief that a high rate of new firm formation reflects the commercial application of new knowledge, the government has tried to help new businesses come into being through grant aid, the provision of advice on start-ups and a reduction in bureaucracy. In order to facilitate the supply of telecommunications infrastructure it has turned to privatisation, competition and deregulation in order to increase greatly the number of suppliers and the range of services, and lower prices.

Most of this intervention has been at the national scale. Enhancing urban competitiveness by public sector intervention is less common. The government has recognised the importance of particular localities in knowledge creation and has sought to help areas such as the Cambridge Science Park, the M4 corridor and West Lothian, which have high concentrations of knowledge-based enterprises. It has stopped short of the French approach of designating 'technopoles' such as Sophia Antipolis, Montpellier and Toulouse. Local government in Britain has sought to develop 'knowledge-based development' strategies although this often reduces to little more than ensuring that, if possible, high quality land and space is available for the new enterprises, and working on the local quality of life through the housing market and leisure facilities. While it is difficult to measure absolutely the quality and quantity of knowledge available within urban economies, there is evidence that it does correlate with economic growth, and we must assume, therefore, that the size of the knowledge base is positively related to urban competitiveness.

References

Boyle, M., Findlay, A., LeLievre, E. and Paddison, R. (1996) 'World cities and the limits to global', *International Journal of Urban and Regional Research*, vol 20, pp 498–517.

Budd, L. (1995) 'Globalisation, territory and strategic alliances of different financial centres', *Urban Studies*, vol 32, pp 345–60.

Buursink, J. (1994) *Euroservices and Euroairports: The position of East European cities as Eurocities*, paper presented to the 'Cities on the eve of the 21st century' conference, Lille.

Cheshire, P.C. and Carbonaro, G. (1996) 'Urban economic growth in Europe: testing theory and policy prescriptions', *Urban Studies*, vol 33, pp 1111–28.

Coffey, W. J. and Bailly, A. S. (1992) 'Producer services and systems of flexible production', *Urban Studies*, vol 29, pp 857-68.

Daniels, P.W. and Lever, W. F. (1996) *The global economy in transition*, Harlow: Addison Wesley Longman.

David, P. A. and Faray, D. (1995) 'Accessing and expanding the science and technology base', *STI Review*, no 16, pp 13-68.

de Roo, P. (1994) 'La métropolité', in A. Sallez (ed) *Les villes, lieux l'Europe*, Mouchy: DATAR, pp 9-17.

DTI (Department of Trade and Industry) (1998) *Our competitive future: Building the knowledge driven economy*, Cmnd 4176, London: DTI.

Drewett, R., Knight, R. and Schubert, U. (1988) *The future of European cities: The role of science and technology*, FAST-Monitir Prospective Dossier No 4, DG XII, Brussels: European Commission.

Feldman, M.P. (2000) 'Location and innovation: the new economic geography of innovation, spillovers and agglomeration', in G. L. Clark, M. P. Feldman and M. S. Gertler (eds), *The Oxford handbook of economic geography*, Oxford: Oxford University Press, pp 371-94.

Feldman, M. P. and Lichtenberg, F. R. (1998) 'The interaction between public and private R and D investment: crosscountry evidence from the European community's R and D information service', *Annales D'Economie et de Statistique,* no 49-50, pp 199-222.

Finnie, G. (1998) 'Wired cities', *Communications Week International*, 18 May, pp 19-22.

Gershuny, J. I. and Miles, I. D. (1983) *The new service economy*, London: Francis Pinter.

Gibb, J. M. (ed) (1985) *Science parks and innovation centres: Their economic and social impact*, Amsterdam: Elsevier.

Graham, S. (1999) 'Global grids of glass: on global cities, telecommunications and planetary networks', *Urban Studies*, vol 36, pp 929-50.

Hall, P. (1998) *Cities in civilisation: Culture, technology and urban order*, London: Wiedenfeld and Nicolson.

Hall, P. (2000) 'Creative cities and economic development, *Urban Studies*, vol 37, pp 639-51.

Howland, M. (1996) 'Producer services and competition from offshore: US data entry and banking', in P. W. Daniels and W. F. Lever (eds), *The global economy in transition*, Harlow: Addison Wesley Longman, pp 310-27.

Keeble, D. and Wever, E. (1987) *New firms and regional development in Europe*, London: Croom Helm.

Kline, S. J., Rosenberg, N. (1986) 'An overview of innovation', in R. Landau and N. Rosenberg (eds) *The positive sum strategy*, Washington DC: National Academy Press, pp 275-305.

Knight, A.K. and T.M. Stanback (1970) *The metropolitan economy: The process of employment expansion*, New York, NY: Columbia University Press.

Knight, R.V. (1995) 'Knowledge-based development: policy and planning implications for cities', *Urban Studies*, vol 32, pp 225-60.

Kresl, P.K. and B. Singh (1999) 'Competitiveness and the urban economy: twenty four large US metropolitan areas', *Urban Studies*, vol 36, pp 1017-28.

Lever, W. F., McGregor, A. and Paddison, R. (1990) *City audit: Comparative European urban performance data*, Glasgow: CURR/TERU, University of Glasgow.

Malecki, E. J. (1997) *Technology and economic development: The dynamics of local, regional and national competitiveness*, Harlow: Addison Wesley Longman.

Matthiessen, G.W. and Schwarz, A.W. (1999) 'Scientific centres in Europe: an analysis of research strength and patterns of specialisation based on bibliographic indicators, *Urban Studies*, vol 36, pp 453-78.

McGregor, A., Lever, W. F. and Simpson, E. (1997) *Competitive cities: A statistical analysis of Glasgow's economic performance*, Glasgow: University of Glasgow.

Myers, M.B. and Rosenbloom, R.S. (1996) 'Rethinking the role of industrial research', in R.S. Rosenbloom and W.J. Spencer (eds), *Engines in innovation: US industrial research at the end of an era*, Boston, MA: Harvard Business School, pp 209-28.

OECD (Organisation for Economic Co-operation and Development) (1995) *Industry and technology, scoreboard of indicators*, Paris: OECD.

Pratt, A. (1997) *The cultural industries sector: Its definition and character from secondary sources on employment and trade, Britain, 1984–91*, Research Papers on Environmental and Spatial Analysis No 41, London: London School of Economics and Political Science.

Ronayne, J. (1984) *Science in government*, Oxford: Blackwell.

Rubalcaba-Bermejo, R. and Cuadrado-Roura, J.R. (1995) 'Urban hierarchies and territorial competition in Europe: exploring the role of fairs and exhibitions', *Urban Studies*, vol 32, pp 379-400.

Segal, N.S. (1986) 'Universities and technological entrepreneurship in Britain: Some implications of the Cambridge phenomenon', *Technovation*, no 4, pp 189-204.

Smith, K. (1995) 'Interactions in knowledge systems: foundations, policy implications and empirical methods', *STI Review*, no 16, pp 69-102.

Sussman, G. (1997) *Communications, technology and politics in the information age*, London: Sage.

von Hipple, E. (1994) 'Sticky information and the locus of problem solving: implications for innovation', *Management Science*, no 40, pp 429-39.

Warf, B. (1995) 'Telecommunications and the changing geographies of knowledge transmission in the late twentieth century', *Urban Studies*, vol 32, pp 361-78.

THREE

Linking competitiveness and cohesion

Martin Boddy

Economic competitiveness and social exclusion lie at the heart of the UK government's urban policy agenda, underpinning policy initiatives at national, regional and local levels. The two themes have been extensively researched, although usually separately and with few attempts to link them. The two issues were also prominent in the ESRC 'Cities' research programme with a particular focus on the important issue of the relationship *between* competitiveness and cohesion, posing the question as to 'how cities develop and mobilise distinctive economic assets to secure competitive advantage and how these processes impact upon and are influenced by social cohesion ...'. This raises the question of the nature and the direction of the possible relationship between competitiveness and cohesion, problematising:

> ... the extent to which social cohesion (and absence of exclusion) ... impact the competitive advantage of places ... can widespread, positive linkages between social and economic progress in cities be identified? Conversely, does widespread, concentrated disadvantage impose costs in relation to image, dampened demand, poverty traps, lower labour market efficiency, sub-optimal uses of public and private spaces and higher costs in dealing with drugs, crime and poorer health? In short, can research provide new insights in respect to the often stated assertion that promoting social cohesion and combating exclusion is not merely a redistributive activity but also contributes to economic competitiveness by mobilising skills, creativity and active citizenship? (ESRC, 1996)

It is this relationship between cohesion and competitiveness that this chapter tries to explore. Before addressing this set of issues more directly, it is important to try to pin down a few definitions.

Social cohesion, social exclusion, social inclusion: towards definitions

Social cohesion and social exclusion are now widely used concepts both in research and in the policy arena in the UK. Like ideas of 'community' however, they have acquired multiple and fuzzy meanings – perhaps as Atkinson (1998) suggests, this being the reason for their proliferation. At the same time, as with many such terms, there are important issues being discussed in the name of cohesion and exclusion and one cannot simply dismiss what they try to capture. For while some have suggested they represent simply a relabelling of earlier debates around now less fashionable concepts of poverty and deprivation (Levitas, 1996, 1998), many would argue that while true to some extent, there are important ways in which debates, both academic and policy, have developed and moved forwards, as outlined below.

It is commonly suggested that the term 'social exclusion' originated in continental Europe: in France it was used to refer to those who did not fall within the state social insurance scheme (Lenoir, 1974) extended later to emphasise unemployment (Paugham, 1993, referred to in Burchardt et al, 1999). It gained wider currency in discussions of social policy around the European Commission with some suggesting it perhaps represented a more palatable alternative to 'poverty'. Again, however, later usage has emphasised the differences between poverty, defined more narrowly as lack of money or material possessions and social exclusion, the latter suggesting that individuals are in some way cut off from active engagement with some dimension(s) of 'normal society' (Atkinson, 1998; Burchardt et al, 1999). Thus Giddens writing in *The third way* (1998, p 104), argues that 'Exclusion is not about graduations of inequality, but about mechanisms that act to detach groups of people from the social mainstream'. Meanwhile in the policy arena the new Labour government in the UK, first elected in 1997 under Tony Blair, was quick to establish a Social Exclusion Unit within the Cabinet Office to address the fact that 'Over the past twenty years hundreds of poor neighbourhoods have seen their basic quality of life become increasingly detached from the rest of society' (SEU, 2001).

Social exclusion in this sense goes well beyond simple notions of poverty, emphasising broader ideas of 'deprivation'. Again, this has much in common with earlier definitions of multiple deprivation. Earlier definitions of poverty as relative deprivation also used measures of the resources required to participate in mainstream society in defining poverty thresholds (Townsend, 1979), elaborated in later studies of poverty and social exclusion (Gordon et al, 2000). In a descriptive sense social exclusion clearly does overlap with ideas of multiple deprivation and with more sophisticated approaches to the definition of poverty.

It has also, however, been argued that social exclusion goes beyond the purely descriptive and captures notions of process or causal mechanisms – Giddens' idea of 'mechanisms' identified above is a case in point, while Berghman (1995) sees social exclusion as a dynamic process rather than a state or outcome. This focuses attention on the idea that there are active processes or mechanisms of exclusion which in turn generate outcomes on a range of different dimensions in terms of poverty, deprivation or disadvantage. This emphasises the need to focus on 'the factors and processes by which people find themselves unable to participate in society and the economy or are cut off from the life chances available to the mainstream of society' (Hills, 1999). Building on Atkinson (1998) and Burchardt et al (1999), Hills (1999, pp 5-6) stresses five aspects of social exclusion:

- *Relativity*: people are excluded from a particular society, as opposed to a focus on ability to purchase an 'absolute' basket of goods.
- *Multi-dimensionality*: income and consumption are central, but so are other aspects of participation such as ability to carry out socially valued activity (not just paid work), political involvement and social interaction.
- *Agency*: someone or something or some process is responsible for exclusion or inclusion occurring, while inability to control major aspects of one's life is an important aspect of being excluded.
- *Dynamics*: such processes occur over time with long-lasting or cumulative effects. Duration in particular states matters and so do prospects for the future.
- *Multi-layered*: exclusion operates at different levels – individual, household, community/neighbourhood, institutions.

While emphasising the importance of process and causal mechanisms, empirical research, seeking to operationalise ideas of social exclusion, has focused on what can be seen as the outcomes of processes of social exclusion. Outcomes of social exclusion are seen in patterns of unemployment, health, school performance and so on. Individual indicators have been combined in more comprehensive attempts to map out different dimensions of exclusion. Howarth et al (1999) set out some 50 indicators as a basis for monitoring progress across a wide range of social and economic dimensions – referring to these as indicators of 'poverty and exclusion'. The Department of the Environment, Transport and Regions commissioned work to draw up 'indices of deprivation', drawing on a wide range of information sources, extending earlier indices based on population census data (DETR, 2000a). The new indicators have been widely used in a policy context as a basis for identifying geographical concentrations of deprivation (for example, DETR, 2000b) and have been made widely available both as individual indicators and combined in an overall index of deprivation (National Statistics, 2001).

Other work has drawn in a number of UK survey-based data sets to develop comprehensive analyses of the outcomes of exclusion. Studies have typically sought to identify and to measure different dimensions of exclusion, captured by different sets of indicators. The 1999 Poverty and Social Exclusion Survey (Gordon et al, 2000) which followed up a sub-sample of the UK General Household Survey, explored four dimensions of exclusion: exclusion from the labour market; exclusion from services both in the home and outside; exclusion from social relations through non-participation in common social activities, isolation and lack of support mechanisms and disengagement from civic activities; and exclusion from adequate income or resources (poverty of impoverishment as such).

Other studies have drawn on longitudinal and cohort-based surveys to examine different dimensions of exclusion (Machin, 1998; Hobcraft, 1998, 2000; Burchardt et al, 1999; Hills, 1999; Sparkes, 1999). Burchardt et al (1999) use the British Household Panel Survey (BHPS) to measure social exclusion over the period 1991-95. They define social exclusion on the basis that:

> An individual is socially excluded if (a) he or she is geographically resident in a society and (b) he or she does not participate in the normal activities of citizens in that society. (p 230)

They then identify five more detailed dimensions of exclusion, which they use as the basis for operationalising social exclusion in terms of different variables in the survey data. In similar fashion to Gordon et al (2000), they identify:

- *Consumption activity*: being able to consume at least up to some minimum level of the goods and services that are considered normal for the society.
- *Savings activity*: accumulated savings, pension entitlements, or owning property.

- *Production activity*: engaging in an economically or socially valued activity such as paid work, education or training, retirement over state pension age, or looking after a family.
- *Political activity*: engaging in some collective effort to improve or protect the immediate or wider social or physical environment.
- *Social activity*: engaging in significant social interaction with family or friends and identifying with a cultural group or community (Burchardt et al, 1999, p 230).

Importantly, these studies have also started to look at different facets of the dynamics of exclusion, examining the extent to which exclusion at the individual level persists over time or is more transitory; relating exclusion in adult life to childhood contexts and experiences; and looking at intergenerational patterns of exclusion. Thus it has been suggested that while for a proportion of individuals or households, exclusion is a temporary state, for the great majority it is persistent over time (Hills, 1999). Intergenerational mobility in terms of earnings and education is limited to a significant degree (Machin, 1998). There are also strong links between social exclusion in adulthood and childhood experiences which are an important factor in maintaining such immobility. Hobcraft (1998, 2000) has shown that childhood poverty, family disruption, contact with the police and educational test scores are powerful predictors of social exclusion later in life. Educational qualifications show a clear and strong relationship with a wide range of measures of adult disadvantage at the ages of 23 and 33. Childhood poverty has particularly strong effects, being the clearest predictor of negative adult outcomes even controlling for other factors – Hobcraft refers to 'the pervasive legacy of childhood poverty in later life' (2000, p 34). Such work has identified in some detail the outcomes of social exclusion, linkages between different dimensions and the dynamics of exclusion over time in a descriptive sense. This in turn starts to point to some of the processes and causal mechanisms driving exclusionary outcomes. It also, usefully, starts to provide pointers in terms of policy approach (Hills, 1999).

Here, since 1997, Labour governments have placed a strong emphasis in policy on 'welfare to work', giving particular weight to exclusion from paid work as a central tenet of policy direction. Broader policy objectives on educational standards and school performance, and measures addressed more generally to poverty and lack of resources through, for example, tax credits for working families and the introduction of a minimum wage, recognise the importance of other dimensions of exclusion.

There are connotations in the broader definitions of exclusion described earlier, particularly linking the role of the density, variety or quality of social contacts with processes of socialisation or the breakdown of socialisation processes. This in turn is seen as impacting on individual values, attitudes and behaviour seen in, for example, propensity to crime or attachment to paid work. Here Giddens' term 'structuration' is perhaps more helpful than the standard term 'socialisation' – structuration emphasises the way in which social processes are constantly and actively made and remade in an active and contested fashion rather than the more passive notion whereby individuals are socialised or programmed by contact with family, peers, the educational system, worlds of work or non-work (Giddens, 1976, 1979).

Here we are moving towards difficult territory, closer to earlier and, in some contexts, discredited debates around the underclass or cycles of deprivation – discredited because they can be seen as blaming the victim or their family or immediate community context. Concepts of power embedded in Giddens' idea of structuration provide a counter to this, however. This approach to definition also emphasises again that social exclusion refers not simply to material exclusion from, say, paid work. The qualitative connotations around the nature of social contacts and social activities of the socially excluded have already been noted.

Linking exclusion to the idea of structuration suggests that social exclusion also has something to do with norms, rules and values – and the disconnection of the socially excluded from the norms, rules and values of what might be called the 'socially included' for which, perhaps uncomfortably, read 'mainstream society'. It might be argued, and rightly so, that there is clearly no one single set of social norms, rules and values, but the notion of social exclusion does of necessity carry some connotations of dominant, or mainstream – otherwise the question of 'exclusion from what?' is left begging. Burchardt et al (1999), in defining social exclusion, argue the same point: exclusion from the 'normal activities' of a particular society implies some definition of the norm. Burchardt et al attempt to make reasonable assumptions based on the variables available in the BHPS data. Gordon et al (2000), developing earlier work, measure 'deprivation' on the basis of items which at least 50 per cent of adults surveyed considered necessities of life that all adults should be able to afford.

This has hopefully brought us closer to an understanding of the idea of social exclusion. The ESRC 'Cities' programme in fact refers to 'social cohesion'. In discussing cohesion, however, the programme outline quoted earlier seems to imply that 'cohesion' represents the opposite of '. It also goes on to refer to the effects of 'widespread concentrated disadvantage' and problems of crime, drugs and health. There would seem to be some conflation or confusion here between social cohesion and what might be better described as social inclusion. Inclusion and cohesion obviously relate, and cohesion is frequently used in a loose sense to mean inclusion. Social cohesion can perhaps, however, best be seen as a property of society or particular social groups as a whole – a system property. Social inclusion is then, more precisely, the opposite of social exclusion and refers to the participation of individuals in the normal activities of society and the extent to which they are attached to, for example, the labour market, housing market or social activities.

Cohesion, as referred to here, is a more elusive term. It is perhaps strong when there is not only a high level of individual-level inclusion in the normal activities of society (with social activities perhaps a particularly important dimension), but also strong attachment to shared norms, rules and values. Social cohesion as such may then serve to combat social exclusion, and in turn mitigate poverty, deprivation and disadvantage.

There is common ground here as well with some versions at least of social capital and the work of Becker (1964), Coleman (1988), Fukuyama (1995) writing on trust, and Putnam (1995, 2000). The 'social' and 'political' dimensions of exclusion as defined by Burchardt et al (1999) and Gordon et al's (2000) dimension of 'exclusion from social relations' in particular, have much in common with ideas of social capital – 'bowling alone' in Putnam's terms would clearly score low in terms of social inclusion or active participation in normal social activities. Active citizenship and political attachment and participation as incorporated by, for example, Gordon et al and Burchardt, have also been seen as indicators of the stock of social capital in particular communities or societies (Putnam, 2000).

One qualification before moving on, however. It is usually implied that social cohesion is 'a good thing' and lack of cohesion bad. It needs to be noted that social cohesion may not necessarily be as benign or beneficial as implied so far. A highly cohesive community may itself be exclusionary of others – it is a question of scale and boundaries. And it might be questioned whether lack of cohesion is necessarily reflected in social exclusion – with the attendant negative consequences for individuals and society (or simply others). A set of individuals may lack social cohesion but be well off and consider themselves to be, both materially and in other respects.

It is also important to distinguish social cohesion as discussed here, from two related sets of ideas. There is a tendency as well to use notions of social cohesion (and social capital) at the institutional or organisational level. Social cohesion from this perspective has been used to refer to the prevalence of networks, collaboration, partnership working, institutional capacity or institutional thickness (Amin and Thrift, 1995). In this sense it is used to express something about the quality of institutional processes, processes of representation or of governance. Here again, trust, collaboration, mutuality, 'joined-upness' even, are seen as desirable attributes. And social cohesion is here, in a sense, the obverse of fragmentation. There are links, again, to the individual level – social cohesion and social capital in the sense of active citizenship, political participation, shared norms and values, can be seen as supporting or facilitating organisational or institutional level cohesion and the quality of governance. The different levels relate – but one needs to be wary of sliding between them unwittingly. It would seem to be unhelpful to refer to processes and linkage at the organisational or institutional level in terms of social cohesion.

Second, there are parallels as well with ideas from social economics and institutional economics, which emphasise non-market or 'social' attributes. Social networks and trust are seen as the bases for collaboration, the exchange of tacit knowledge or 'un-traded interdependencies' and which can therefore be the basis for innovation and competitive advantage (Boddy, 1999; Braczyk et al, 1998; Storper, 1997). Again, this is simply noted in order to emphasise both the parallels but also the important differences between this and the ideas of social inclusion and exclusion, and of social cohesion discussed earlier. And again, it is important to avoid conflating the two.

Social exclusion and competitiveness

Having attempted to clarify definitions of social exclusion it is important to note that competitiveness itself is, of course, not unproblematic in conceptual terms (the remainder of the chapter refers to 'exclusion' and by implication 'inclusion' rather than cohesion as such). Given, however, that there has been more exploration of the term and a greater degree of discussion, if not agreement, around alternative meanings (Boddy, 1999a, 1999b, contributions to *Urban Studies* vol 36, no 5/6, 1999, and other chapters in this volume, notably those by Kresl and by Deas and Giordano), it is not intended to pursue this side of the debate here at length. Competitiveness at a simple level, whether at the level of individual enterprises or national economic units, can be taken to mean performance in terms of output, productivity, investment, surplus or profit and, possibly, employment. At the level of the city or region one might include population and employment growth and the attraction of population, jobs and investment.

What, then, of the relationship between exclusion and competitiveness? There would seem to be two main questions we can ask about the relationship between the two:

1. Does social exclusion impact adversely on competitiveness and economic growth – and does social inclusion enhance competitiveness and growth?
2. Do competitive success and economic growth necessarily combat social exclusion – or can they impact adversely on social inclusion?

It should be said at the outset that the evidence-base from which to attempt to answer these questions is limited. The discussion presented here is, therefore, of necessity somewhat speculative.

Does social exclusion impact adversely on competitiveness and economic growth?

Looking first at the question of the possible impacts of social exclusion on competitiveness, this is to some extent the business case for concern over social exclusion as opposed to the social justice case. Does social exclusion pose a threat to competitiveness and business success? The logic of the economic case is fairly easy to state. This evidence is, however, as suggested above, more limited one way or another.

Taking the logical case first, it can be argued that high levels of social exclusion might have some or all of the following adverse impacts:

- In relation to business activities, the image or anticipated costs associated with social exclusion depress levels of private sector investment.
- Similarly, in relation to individuals and households, the image or anticipated costs, and the expectations in terms of quality of life, crime, schooling and so on (Rogerson, 1999) may deter or drive out the better off, more skilled, more 'conventionally socialised' households.
- Social exclusion generates increased costs in terms of health services, social care, policing, drug-related services, insurance. These impact as direct costs or through levels of local taxation on businesses and households, as Hill and Nowak (this volume) show so graphically for Camden New Jersey.

- Labour market exclusion, ill health and disability, poor levels of education and skills (including 'life' and transferable skills) lead to labour market inefficiency and under-utilisation of potential human resources.
- Spatially concentrated poverty, unemployment and workless households increase the likelihood that individuals will experience poverty and unemployment. 'Neighbourhood effects' thus increase the overall incidence of poverty and social exclusion.
- Some combination of the above effects tip localised neighbourhoods over the threshold into a spiral of decline and disinvestment, exacerbating a range of problems and further threatening competitiveness.
- Social exclusion impacts adversely on active citizenship, presenting obstacles to regeneration and undermining governance structures.

One has, however, to go a step further to make the connection between competitiveness and social exclusion. From the perspective of individual cities, high levels of social exclusion, with the effects outlined here, could clearly, in theory at least, impact adversely on competitiveness and economic growth.

From the perspective of the economy as a whole, if the effects of social exclusion in one location simply shift investment to an alternative location, then the overall impact of social exclusion may be redistributive as between places and local populations, but it will not impact on output as a whole. From a wider, macroeconomic perspective, one would therefore have to argue that social exclusion impacted adversely in terms of efficiency and/ or utilisation of potential resources at the level of the economy as a whole. This might be the case if, for example, the effects of social exclusion led to sub-optimal patterns of location across the national economy as a whole, or to overheating and congestion costs in the more favoured locations. This would be compounded if lack of demand in less favoured locations led to deterioration in the stock of physical assets such as housing and infrastructure and of human capital in the form of skills and recent experience of paid work. Some commentators have argued anecdotally that overheating in the south of the country had by 1999-2000 indeed pushed up business costs and impacted on productivity. Others have drawn attention to the scale of residential abandonment and deterioration of urban infrastructure, albeit in relatively focused neighbourhoods (Power and Mumford, 1999; Power 2000). This is analogous to earlier arguments in favour of spatial economic policy in the UK (Kaldor, 1970).

For the UK at least, evidence of adverse effects of social exclusion of the type outlined above is fairly limited. There may well be differences between urban areas with contrasting levels of 'exclusion' as measured, for example, by unemployment or indices of deprivation. Bristol, for example, a relative buoyant urban area with unemployment below the national average (based on the travel to work area) has only 5 wards out of 34 in the worst 10 per cent as measured by the government's Index of Deprivation 2000 (ONS, 2001). Liverpool, on the other hand, with unemployment nearly twice that national level, has 25 out of its 33 wards in the worst 10 per cent. Both cities were studied in detail as case studies in the ESRC research programme. In the case of Bristol, there was no apparent evidence that business investment has been deterred in any part of the city by these sorts of factors. Businesses questioned in the course of the Bristol case study did not see social problems as any form of deterrent to investment and expansion in the city. There has been major investment immediately adjacent to pockets of concentrated deprivation in the urban core. Lack of investment adjacent to other pockets of deprivation on the city's outer estates, particularly on its southern fringe, was seen as reflecting problems of accessibility and availability of suitable greenfield sites compared with the booming north fringe adjacent to the M4/M5 motorway intersection and high speed rail line, rather than issues associated with social exclusion (Boddy et al, 1999a).

In places such as Liverpool, where social exclusion as measured by indices of deprivation is considerably more widespread, the effects may be stronger. It seems more likely that they shape the geography of business investment within urban areas – although here again, even in the less prosperous urban areas, there are examples of business investment, residential development and redevelopment close to areas with high levels of deprivation. The UK, generally, has not seen the wholesale out-migration of businesses, people and jobs evident, for example, in US cities such as Detroit (Farley et al, 2000; O'Connor et al, 2000; see also the chapter by Hill and Nowak in this volume). Levels of unemployment and social deprivation in less buoyant urban areas in the UK to a large extent reflect long-term structural decline in their economic base, coupled with the locational preferences of the expanding service sector and other elements of the 'new economy' that have on balance favoured the South of England. How far social exclusion in these more peripheral urban areas deters investment or affects the availability of staff with key professional, technical or managerial skills is, however, hard to determine. Studies of business location preferences in the M4 corridor indicate that businesses compare the image and quality of life associated with cities such as Liverpool, Glasgow or Swansea unfavourably with places such as Bristol, Reading or Oxford. Factors such as crime and education also figure in indicators of quality of life (Rogerson, 1999). It is hard, however, to disentangle what might be the specific effects of different levels of social exclusion from the combined effect of more general locational factors.

Does competitive success and economic growth impact adversely on social exclusion?

Turning the question the other way round, we can speculate on the possible impacts of competitive success on social exclusion. It is very widely argued that economic growth and competitive strength are prerequisites if problems of poverty, inequality and social deprivation are to be addressed. It may be, however, that competitive success and economic growth themselves tend to exacerbate social exclusion. If so, there are clearly implications in terms of policy. Increasing social exclusion may be seen as a cost to be borne. It might, alternatively, lead to questioning of the simple pursuit of economic growth and competitive strength divorced from issues of social equity or sustainability. Ultimately, growing social exclusion may have negative impacts on competitive strength.

Again, however, the evidence is limited – particularly in the sense of establishing any causal linkage between competitive success and any exacerbation of social exclusion. But there is evidence of increasing polarisation and a worsening of a range of indicators of social exclusion, against an overall background of continuing economic growth:

There is some evidence of increasing polarisation in terms of household incomes at the national level in the 1980s and 1990s. Net incomes of the lowest earning 10 per cent of households fell by 8 per cent between 1979 and 1994-95. Net incomes of the best-off 10 per cent rose by 68 per cent (Hills, 1998). Households on less than 40 per cent of the average rose from 7.3 million to 8.4 million between 1995 and 1998 (Howarth et al, 1999).

There is some evidence as well of an increase in relative rates of unemployment between best and worst wards or neighbourhoods within urban areas – a steepening of the curve from highest to lowest. The Joseph Rowntree Foundation Inquiry into income and wealth (1995) found that the already wide gap between the best and worst wards within urban areas had widened between the 1981 and 1991 censuses of population. This is borne out by a range of local studies (Sheffield City Council, 1997; Pacione, 1997).

In the social housing sector, high and increasing rents combined with means tested housing benefits were, until recently, encouraging the formation of benefit-only ghettos. Poor housing and neighbourhood conditions lead to those households that can, exiting the social housing sector.

More generally, monitoring of 50 different indicators of poverty and deprivation carried out for the Joseph Rowntree Foundation has found that while 15 had improved, most have either remained unchanged or deteriorated in recent years, despite (modest) continuing year on year economic growth in the UK (Howarth et al, 1999). Even though unemployment has continued to fall, numbers of long-term workless households have remained at over 2 million continuously since 1995. In terms of health, the long-term ill rose from 3 million to 3.6 million between 1991 and 1998. And local government districts where mortality rates were more than 10 per cent above the average increased from 28 per cent in 1991 to 39 per cent by 1998 (Howarth et al, 1999).

There is growing evidence as well, as suggested by figures on household income quoted earlier, that children in particular suffer disproportionately from social exclusion (Robson et al, 2000). Deterioration in household incomes among the poor impacted in particular on children – the proportion of all children growing up in households with less than half the average income grew from 10 per cent in 1979 to 32 per cent by 1994-95 (DSS, 1995).

Income Support beneficiaries are also proportionately more concentrated among families with children than among the population as a whole. Child poverty has continued to become more polarised, with levels strikingly concentrated in the more urban areas. This suggests that social deprivation has impacted most severely on families with young children in the larger urban areas and that it is the young who have suffered most severely from social exclusion.

In terms of education, moreover, there is a particular and increasing concentration of children from poor households underperforming in schools (Robson et al, 2000). It is also notable that performance appears to grow worse at later stages of schooling: the relative underperformance of urban areas becomes progressively poorer as between ages 6, 10 and 15 (Table 3.1). Further, there is a consistently worse performance in more urban areas and (with the sole exception of Leeds) within core cities as against the overall conurbations.

Evidence of concentrations of children in poor households (Table 3.2) and of performance in assessment tests and exams is of particular concern given that these are the strongest indicators of the likelihood of social exclusion on multiple dimensions later in life (Hobcraft, 1998, 2000; Sparkes, 1999).

There is clear evidence, then, of persistent and in some respects increasing

Table 3.1: Educational performance by settlement type

	% pupils aged 6 with <Level 3 SAT, 1998	% pupils aged 10 with <Level 4 SAT, 1998	% 15 year old pupils with no/low GCSEs, 1997
Categories			
Inner London	21.8	11.3	8.8
Main metropolitan areas	19.3	10.0	10.9
Large cities	22.8	11.0	8.8
Other metropolitan areas	18.1	8.9	8.1
Industrial	17.8	8.7	6.3
Outer London	17.6	7.3	6.2
Small cities	20.1	9.7	7.9
New towns	17.3	7.7	5.9
Resort/retirement areas	17.5	7.5	5.2
Mixed urban/rural areas	14.4	5.8	3.9
Remote rural	15.4	6.7	4.0
England	17.5	8.1	6.4
Conurbations			
Greater London (Inner London)	19.1 (21.8)	8.7 (11.3)	7.0 (8.8)
Greater Manchester (Manchester)	18.0 (23.0)	8.2 (10.8)	8.0 (14.6)
Merseyside (Liverpool)	16.1 (17.8)	7.9 (10. 3)	10.0 (12.5)
South Yorkshire (Sheffield)	19.5 (19.2)	10.6 (11.3)	10.2 (10.3)
Tyne & Wear (Newcastle upon Tyne)	18.1 (17.6)	8.8 (12.7)	9.6 (14.7)
West Midlands (Birmingham)	20.0 (20.3)	9.8 (10.1)	8.2 (9.5)
West Yorkshire (Leeds)	18.2 (17.2)	10.1 (7.6)	9.4 (9.3)
Cleveland (Middlesbrough)	17.5 (20.6)	8.9 (8.6)	8.4 (14.7)

Note: The core cities of the conurbations are shown in brackets.

Source: Robson et al (2000)

polarisation and social exclusion, though evidence that this is in any way linked to competitiveness, economic growth or competitive strength is lacking. The scale of poverty and deprivation is generally worse in economically less successful cities with generalised lack of demand for labour.

Table 3.2: Child poverty by city type

Categories	% population Income Support claimants, 1996	% children in Income Support households, 1996
Inner London	23.5	49.1
Main metropolitan areas	20.0	37.6
Large cities	16.5	32.9
Other metropolitan	15.4	30.2
Industrial	12.0	24.3
Outer London	13.3	29.2
Small cities	13.3	26.2
New towns	11.8	24.8
Resort/retirement areas	11.7	23.1
Mixed Urban/rural areas	7.3	14.0
Remote rural	9.0	15.8
England	12.8	25.7
Conurbations		
Greater London (Inner London)	17.2 (23.5)	36.8 (49.1)
Greater Manchester (Manchester)	16.1 (27.5)	31.0 (47.0)
Merseyside (Liverpool)	21.6 (27.4)	40.9 (19.1)
South Yorkshire (Sheffield)	15.6 (16.2)	30.4 (29.0)
Tyne & Wear (Newcastle-on-Tyne)	17.8 (19.1)	33.0 (36.0)
West Midlands (Birmingham)	17.4 (20.6)	34.4 (40.5)
West Yorkshire (Leeds)	13.9 (13.3)	27.9 (25.2)
Cleveland (Middlesbrough)	16.0 (20.7)	31.5 (39.5)

Note: The core cities of the conurbations shown in brackets.

Source: Derived from Indices of Deprivation 2000 (DETR, 2000)

There is clear evidence of the persistence of spatially concentrated poverty and deprivation within the economically more successful urban areas. Bristol and Swindon, for example, in the buoyant M4 growth corridor, both have a number of wards in the worst 10 per cent nationally as measured by both the 1991 and 2000 DETR index of deprivation. This is not the same as arguing that it is economic success that is actually generating or maintaining social exclusion in any overall sense. It seems to demonstrate, rather, that processes and patterns of concentrated deprivation persist despite economic success, suggesting that certain problems of social exclusion are beyond the reach of conventional regeneration policies.

One important qualification to this is that it would appear that patterns of economic restructuring and labour market change in more buoyant urban economies are themselves generating increasing polarisation within the labour market and an increasing concentration of employment in relatively low paid jobs within the urban economy, particularly in the service sector (IER, 1999). As Hills (1998) notes: 'The gap between high and low pay grew rapidly, partly linked to increasing premiums for skills and qualifications, in turn linked to technological change.' The labour market is tending to polarise into the relatively more skilled and better paid on the one hand – the 'knowledge workers' – and those who service the urban population or perform routinised service occupations for the business sector on the other.

Social-spatial polarisation in more successful places like Bristol may also be generated through the interaction of housing markets and 'markets' for schooling. Test results and exam performance in Bristol demonstrates increasing polarisation in the public education sector in terms of school performance. Patterns of outwards migration suggest that better off households, those able to move, have increasingly, over recent years, developed patterns of movement and residential preference which have exacerbated this. In the case of Bristol, this has involved patterns of movement both within the city, avoiding the south of the city and favouring the north. It has also encouraged demand in areas of new greenfield development on or beyond the urban fringe where school performance is in some cases spectacularly better. This pattern of residential preference is reinforced in terms of inwards migration from outside of the city–region. It is further exacerbated in the case of Bristol by the very high proportion of children who are educated in the city's private school sector. Those who can afford private education do; those who can't but who can afford to move into the catchment areas of the better schools do; and those who can do neither are stuck.

Low levels of educational attainment, and related social and life skills, are major sources of social exclusion, including later exclusion from the labour market and employment opportunities, and a wide range of other indicators of exclusion (Machin, 1998; Sparkes, 1999; Hobcraft, 2000). This provides strong evidence that educational performance and school outcomes are, to a significant degree, affected by the social and economic characteristics of the neighbourhood in which individual schools are located. Issues of individual school performance and teaching quality highlighted by UK governments and their advisors in recent years can therefore only be a partial response to the evident educational underperformance in particular cities and neighbourhoods.

Conclusion

It has been possible here to explore some of the definitional issues around social exclusion and to clarify some of the conceptual terrain. It has been possible also to start to explore the relationship between social exclusion and economic competitiveness. As noted above, however, the evidence-base from which to explore the relationship between the two in empirical terms remains weak and the relationship itself, is complex. It is not as yet possible to provide very satisfactory responses to the questions posed.

By way of conclusion, in the case of the UK there is little evidence that social exclusion has major adverse impacts on economic competitiveness, business investment and economic growth as between different urban areas. Structural change in the economic base of cities and the differential impact of this, depending on the historical endowment of different urban areas in terms of industrial structure, has been the main determinant of competitive strength in recent decades. Social exclusion may have steered investment patterns within particular urban areas to some extent but evidence suggests that this has only happened to a limited degree – business investment in UK cities is in many cases concentrated close to areas with high concentrations of poverty and social deprivation. At the level of urban areas as a whole and their relative competitive strength, beyond the impact of structural change already noted, it is hard to disentangle any effects of social exclusion from the combination of general locational factors impacting on business investment.

Evidence on the impacts of competitiveness on social exclusion is equally limited, if not more so. Again, however, despite continuous if modest economic growth over recent decades, there remains persistent and in many respects worsening social deprivation and polarisation of economic and social circumstances within UK cities. Spatially concentrated poverty and deprivation persists in UK cities, and the gap between the best and the worst areas would appear to have widened in recent years. Levels of social exclusion and social deprivation in absolute terms are clearly, as one would expect, higher and more generalised in the less economically buoyant urban areas such as Glasgow or Liverpool. On the other hand, there are persistent spatial concentrations of social deprivation and social exclusion in more buoyant urban areas such as Bristol. Structural change within the labour market and the impacts of the educational system would appear to be two sets of processes that contribute to such persistent polarisation. They also suggest that competitive success and economic growth, while it may trickle down to some extent, does not inherently operate to decrease differentials in terms of economic and social circumstances – and may in fact exacerbate them. From a policy perspective, this suggests that active measures are needed to link all sections of the community and all neighbourhoods within urban areas to the benefits of competitiveness and economic growth.

References

Amin, A. and Thrift, N. (1995) 'Globalisation, institutional "thickness" and the local economy', in P. Healey, S. Cameron, S. Davoudi, S. Graham and A. Madani Pour (eds) *Managing cities: The new urban context*, London: Wiley.

Atkinson, A. (1998) 'Social exclusion, poverty and unemployment', in A. Atkinson, and J. Hills (eds) *Exclusion, employment and opportunity*, CASE Paper No 4, London: London School of Economics and Political Science, pp 1-20.

Becker, G. (1964) *Human capital, a theoretical and empirical analysis, with special reference to education*, New York, NY: Columbia University Press.

Berghman, J. (1995) 'Social exclusion in Europe: policy context and analytical framework', in G. Room (ed) *Beyond the threshold: The measurement and analysis of social exclusion*, Bristol: The Policy Press.

Boddy, M. (1999a) 'Geographical economics and urban competitiveness: a critique', *Urban Studies*, vol 36, no 5/6, pp 811-42.

Boddy, M. (1999b) 'Cities and competition: definitions and issues', *Business briefing: World urban economic development*, World Competitive Cities Congress, 19-21 May, Washington, DC.

Boddy, M. (2000) 'Technology, innovation and regional economic development in the State of Victoria', *Environment and Planning C: Government and Policy*, no 18, pp 301-19.

Boddy, M., Lambert, C., French, S. and Smith, I. (1999) *Bristol Business Survey: Central and north Bristol, Bristol Integrated City Study*, Working Paper 6, Mimeo; Bristol: School for Policy Studies, University of Bristol.

Braczyk, H.-J., Cooke, P. and Heidenreich, M. (1998) *Regional innovation systems*, London: UCL Press.

Brown, P. (1995) 'Cultural capital and social exclusion: some observations on recent trends in education, employment and the labour market', *Work, Employment & Society*, vol 9, no 1, pp 29-51.

Burchardt, T., Le Grand, J. and Piachaud, D. (1999) 'Social exclusion in Britain, 1991-95', *Social Policy and Administration*, vol 33, no 3, pp 227-44.

Coleman, J. (1988) 'Social capital in the creation of human capital', *American Journal of Sociology*, vol 94, supplement S95-120.

DETR (Department of the Environment, Transport and the Regions) (2000a) *Indices of Deprivation 2000*, Research Regeneration Summary No 31, London: DETR.

DETR (2000b) *Our towns and cities: The future*, London: DETR.

DSS (Department for Social Security) (1995) *Households Below Average Incomes 1994/95*, London: HMSO.

ESRC (Economic and Social Research Council) (1996) 'ESRC research programme, cities, competitiveness and cohesion: programme description/specification', Swindon: ESRC.

Farley, R., Danziger, S. and Holzer, H. (2000) *Detroit divided*, New York, NY: Russell Sage Foundation.

Fukuyama, F. (1995) *Trust: The social virtues and the creation of prosperity*, London: Hamish Hamilton.

Giddens, A. (1976) *New rules of sociological method*, London: Hutchinson.

Giddens, A. (1979) *Central problems in social theory: Action, structure and contradiction in social analysis*, London: Macmillan.

Giddens, A. (1998) *The third way: The renewal of social democracy*, Cambridge: Polity Press.

Gordon, D., Adelman, L., Ashworth, K. (2000) *Poverty and social exclusion in Britain*, York: Joseph Rowntree Foundation.

Hobcraft, J. (1998) 'Intergenerational and life course transmission of social exclusion: influences of child poverty, family disruption and contact with the police', CASE Paper No 15, London: London School of Economics and Political Science.

Hills, J. (1998) *Income and wealth: The latest evidence*, York: Joseph Rowntree Foundation.

Hills, J. (1999) *Social exclusion, income dynamics and public policy*, CASE Paper No 129, London: London School of Economics and Political Science.

Hobcraft, J. (2000) *The roles of schooling and educational qualifications in the emergence of adult social exclusion*, CASE Paper No 43, London: London School of Economics and Political Science.

Howarth, C., Kenway, P., Palmer, G. and Miorelli, R. (1999) *Monitoring poverty and social exclusion 1999*, York: Joseph Rowntree Foundation.

IER (Institute for Employment Research) (1999) *Review of the economy and employment 1998/99: Labour market assessment*, Warwick: Institute for Employment Research, University of Warwick.

Joseph Rowntree Foundation (1995) *Income and wealth: Report of the JRF inquiry group, vols 1 and 2*, York: Joseph Rowntree Foundation.

Kaldor, N. (1970) 'The case for regional policy', *Scottish Journal of Political Economy*, vol 17, pp 337-48.

Lenoir, R. (1974) *Les exclus*, Paris: Seuil.

Levitas, R. (1996) 'The concept of social exclusion and the new Durkheimian hegemony', *Critical Social Policy*, no 46, pp 5-20.

Levitas, R. (1998) *The inclusive society? Social exclusion and New Labour*, Basingstoke: Macmillan.

Machin, S. (1998) 'Childhood disadvantage and intergenerational transmissions of economic status', in A. Atkinson and J. Hills (eds), *Exclusion, Employment and Opportunity*, CASE Paper No 4, London: London School of Economics and Political Science, pp 56-64.

National Statistics (2001) http://www.statistics.gov.uk

O'Connor, A., Tilly, C. and Bobo, L. (eds) (2000) *Urban inequality: Evidence from four cities*, New York, NY: Russell Sage Foundation.

Pacione, M. (ed) (1997) *Britain's cities*, London: Routledge.

Power, A. (1999) *Estates on the edge,* London: Routledge.

Power, A. (2000) 'Poor areas and social exclusion', CASE Paper No 35, London: London School of Economics and Political Science.

Power, A. and Mumford, K. (1999) *The slow death of great cities: Urban abandonment or urban renaissance*, York: Joseph Rowntree Foundation.

Putnam, R. (1995) 'Tuning in, tuning out: The strange disappearance of social capital in America', *PS: Political Science & Politics*, vol 28, no 4, pp 664–83.

Putnam, R. (2000) *Bowling alone: The collapse and revival of American community*, New York, NY: Simon & Schuster.

Robson, B., Parkinson, M., Boddy, M. and Maclennan, D. (2000) *The state of English cities*, London: DETR.

Rogerson, R. (1999) 'Quality of life and city competitiveness', *Urban Studies*, vol 36, no 5/6, pp 969–86.

Social Exclusion Unit (2001) *A new commitment to neighbourhood renewal: National strategy action plan*, London: Cabinet Office.

Sparkes, J. (1999) *Schools, education and social exclusion*, CASE Paper No 29, London: London School of Economics and Political Science.

Sheffield City Council (1997) 'Sheffield trends: An annual compilation of indicators for Sheffield, statistical supplement'.

Storper, M. (1997) *The regional world*, New York, NY: Guilford.

Townsend, P. (1979) *Poverty in the United Kingdom*, London: Allen and Lane/Penguin Books.

Wilson, R.A. (2000) *Projections of occupations and qualifications 1999/2000*, Sheffield: DEE.

FOUR

Competitiveness and the social fabric: links and tensions in cities

Gareth Potts

Introduction

Political and academic interest in many Western countries has increasingly focused upon the terms 'economic competitiveness' and what, for ease of use I refer to here as the 'local social fabric' (social inclusion, social capital and social cohesion). This chapter explores the linkages between competitiveness and this fabric. In so doing the aim is to highlight how each of the four terms are conceptually useful, highlighting their salience for urban areas. It also aims to elucidate how a better understanding of social issues can enrich debate about competitiveness.

An important theme in analysis of competitiveness is 'clusters' of competing and collaborating firms. Immediately, this creates an opening for study of how social capital (in its sense of trust ties and shared norms) might underpin inter-firm relations. Other dimensions of the interplay between the social fabric and competitiveness are also of interest and several of these are taken up in the subsequent sections of this chapter.

Section one notes that much is already known about such relationships but stresses that the considerable body of work tends to overlook the inherently exclusive nature of social ties and the issue of wider spatial disparities and policies to overcome these. Section two looks at the importance of social ties to labour markets, notably in relation to highly localised concentrations of firms and supporting institutions. Section three concentrates on work quality (pay and conditions) and egalitarianism, rather than just having/obtaining work (inclusion/capital) and the absence of social unrest (cohesion) per se, and examines whether areas with high productivity firms tend also to be the home for the greatest inequality. The fourth section considers how work-life issues bear on social inclusion, while the penultimate section looks at the role of education in social cohesion. The last section considers the ways in which businesses can benefit from low crime and social order (cohesion) and, to some extent, can seek to influence these through corporate community efforts.

Clusters and business networks

The widespread interest in the gains that can accrue from clustering of particular forms of economic activity has prompted a search for elucidation of the factors that stimulate and sustain such clusters. Work on industrial districts, innovative *milieux* and social capital has, arguably, cast the greatest light on social ties and shared norms in localised business clusters/networks – albeit often using areas whose history and industrial structure are highly atypical. Ties of trust can underpin market-based and informal connections between firms – indeed, ties can occur in the development of new products and processes where prices do not yet exist. Physical proximity (face-to-face contact) between key actors in firms, although it does not guarantee such relations, can certainly help, especially if it is complemented by cultural proximity (such as shared values, levels of education and attitudes to learning and innovation). Ties of trust and shared norms can also perform an informal (less costly) social control function against unethical business practices such as worker poaching, late payment, sale of defective goods, insider-trading and so on.

Networks consequently play a pivotal role in the emergence of clusters. They can also have an important influence on the dynamics of economic growth and often grow stronger – possibly in exponential fashion. Thus, the *milieux* literature notes how two entities (usually manufacturer/service provider and customer) can, through dialogue, improve the product/service offered and/or its use. Trust is also something that can be built up. Through learning-by-doing and the build-up of trust, networks grow stronger. The use of word-of-mouth to recommend companies to potential customers can also be exponential in nature (Camagni, 1991; Scott and Storper, 1992; Stanley, 1992; Amin and Thrift, 1994; Gertler, 1995; Maillat, 1995; Bramanti and Ratti, 1997; Portes, 1998).

The above use of the term 'social' is not intended to indicate ties whose origins lie outside the workplace. However, in a few cases, business and social/family networks have been seen to overlap considerably (possibly further reinforced by various other characteristics and local identities). Examples here include the social capital work of Putnam (1993) on Italian city-regions, Coleman (1988) on the Jewish-dominated New York diamond market and O'Connor et al (1999) on the 'urban village' lifestyles seen in Manchester's nightclub scene. Where such strong non-work social ties are absent competitive gains can still be fostered by constructing ties of trust within the business sphere (see Cohen and Fields, 2000, on Silicon Valley).

Pitfalls of the network approach

Strong social ties do not, however, always or unambiguously support competitiveness. There is evidence from the *milieux* writers that business networks can become introspective and tied in to particular technological trajectories – even to the extent that they stifle innovation (Camagni, 1991; Grabher, 1993). From the social capital camp, Portes (1998) has also noted how, in certain localised (immigrant) networks, family and friends may parasitically seek (and receive) jobs and loans from business owners. To remain competitive, firms need to find the best supply-chain ties and partners – not those they most like or feel obliged to help. This latter leads into the fact that solutions in regard to *milieux*/districts have been seen to lie in seeking non-local avenues – including worker in-migration and foreign direct investment. However, what has received less attention in the clamour to study and recreate clusters is the exclusivity of networks – an exclusivity that may occur for different reasons.

For instance, Porter (1995, 1997), when discussing competitive strategies for US inner-city firms, suggests the importance of forging links with customers and suppliers from wider city-region clusters (thereby benefiting from their dynamism). Yet, as has been argued, networks are inherently cumulative or exponential in nature and so, by definition, create greater division between members and non-members. This interpretation of networks thus differs from, but reinforces, the better known concerns of social capital writers (see Portes and Landolt, 1996) about the exclusivity of certain ethnic business communities. Thus, where there is unequal access to networks or to customers, the inequality between those that are 'in' and those that are 'out' seems certain to intensify without some form of corrective intervention such as efforts to award public contracts to suitable firms. There is the further question here, asked by Andersen (1999), about whether an expanded social economy (this includes cooperative and other mutual forms including credit unions and Local Exchange Trading Systems) can 'reinsert itself into the wider economy (p 142). It may well be that such activity's social and/or economic value lies more in its ability to foster cohesion in areas that might otherwise be swamped by crime, disorder and apathy. Certainly, despite their laudable social aims, such businesses have largely proven uncompetitive with mainstream capitalist firms (Birchall, 1997; Hausman, 1998; Olin Wright, 1998). Understanding social economy-mainstream economy relationships is important to competitiveness, local social fabric research and debate.

Another consequence of policies that encourage clusters is that they are often portrayed as alternatives to redistributive spatial economic policy. Indeed, in the US and the UK, the latter policies have been heavily downgraded. The case for spatial policy can be made on a number of levels (see, for example, Martin, 1993): equality of opportunity; environmental protection; alleviation of inflationary pressure on core areas; and spillovers (stimulation of periphery region demand for goods and services in the core regions that fund such policy). Against this, the main concern is not to disrupt existing or emerging growth centres – notably through restrictive land-use planning. If inclusion and cohesion are accepted as valid policy objectives, urban and regional, it would make sense to implement policies to highlight and develop existing or emerging clusters in less favoured regions, or to give them preferential treatment in terms of money available for supporting clusters and local economic development more generally. These considerations need to be kept firmly in mind at a time of increased political devolution in many states, especially if devolution of fiscal responsibilities lessens redistribution between urban regions. Finally, the clusters/networking preoccupation of so many local economic development policies risks obscuring national-level (pre-competitive) collaboration – notably support for collectivised training and basic research[1].

Getting work: labour markets and social ties

Intensification of competition has influenced, and been influenced by, significant changes in the labour markets of advanced economies. The rise of dual-career couples who need the security of having various employment opportunities within easy commuting distances is an important characteristic of contemporary labour markets. Increasingly flexible forms of employment contract have become the norm in many sectors, including high-wage ones. Contract lengths have shortened and periods of unemployment have become more frequent – particularly for the less skilled and unskilled. As part of the growth in contracting-out, human resource management is also increasingly outsourced to recruitment agencies.

At the bottom end of the labour market, cities and poorer regions serve as increasingly important sources of flexible, cheap non-unionised (often female) labour – a legacy of de-industrialisation, unskilled immigration and shifting gender relations. Such 'dis-integration' of the labour market also creates new demands in terms of information flows about labour market opportunities and in terms of knowledge of workers elsewhere in the labour market (Burchell et al, 1999; Peck and Theodore, 1999; Walker, 1999). One of the earliest social capital writers, the US economist Glenn Loury, noted (1977) the lack of information on job opportunities that faced many young black workers in US inner cities because so few were already in work in such areas[2].

From the perspective of competitiveness, such changes are of interest for a number of reasons. For example, the benefits for firms of co-location may partly depend on the co-location of workers, while social ties often play a part in the recruitment process. Such social ties are particularly important to competitiveness in tight labour markets – companies need to explore every avenue possible to find additional workers (such as the semi-retired or women who may be considering returning to the workforce after having children). For employers eager to have such routes into the labour market, one strategy is to forge ties with trusted intermediaries who can comment on worker suitability, such as churches or community organisations. Similarly, current employees may recommend people they have worked or trained with (or, more rarely, non-professional friends or acquaintances).

Equally, from the perspective of workers, such ties are much more valued in areas and periods of high un/under-employment (Granovetter, 1973; Porter, 1997; Waldinger, 1997; Newman, 1999). Community links may be especially important in deprived areas where many workers will lack a formal work history and so need references that are more based upon their character than their work history (Porter, 1995). More commonly, companies might introduce reward schemes for existing employees who introduce new workers to the company (so-called 'find-a-friend' schemes). As part of the increased contracting out process referred to earlier, it is recruitment agencies that increasingly need to have such networks rather than the firms themselves. So, for example, there is some evidence from Chicago (see Peck and Theodore, 1999) of hiring halls and day-labour contractors moving to the poorest parts of the inner cities.

As with business networks, labour market ties may also have adverse effects on competitiveness and social inclusion. Worker cliques may create disciplinary problems and family ties may serve as impediments to promotion of non-family employees (Granovetter, 1973; Waldinger, 1997; Newman, 1999). Moreover, access to networks cannot guarantee jobs for all if there is deficient demand for labour in the wider urban economy and will not offset wider material inequalities in terms of pay and working conditions (Donnison, 1998). Thus, the strong political and academic focus on improving the social capital of individuals/neighbourhoods ought not to close off discussion of wider national spatial policy that seeks to create a more even distribution of employment. There is further overlap with the previous section in that, as Patterson (1998) notes, employee/firm networks can grow exponentially as those in work move between firms – thereby raising the potentially exclusive aspects that can accompany exponential network development. Finally, it is also important that companies are aware that word-of-mouth recruitment can reproduce social/racial homogeneity (see CRE, 1999) – possibly with direct (failure to make use of available talent) and indirect (social order) impacts upon competitiveness. This is particularly pertinent for cities – given their greater preponderance of racially and socially diverse populations.

Intervention by the state to offset unequal access to social ties into the labour market (and to job opportunities in general) has included dispersal of individuals to areas of higher *suitable* job opportunities elsewhere in the metropolitan area[3], assistance for out-commuting by inner-city workers, workplace integration efforts and subsidised transport (Sawicki and Moody, 1996; Newman, 1999; Silver, 2000). Not all such activity needs to be by the state, and there is US evidence of employment agencies that profit from recruiting inner-city workers and finding them work in expanding suburban industry (Peck and Theodore, 1999). From the perspective of social cohesion, travel-to-work type measures have the benefit that they do not threaten to break up existing residential communities/neighbourhoods.

Work quality and egalitarianism

Competitiveness and (in)equality

It can be argued that the 'real competitiveness issue' is not, in contrast to what Krugman (1996) says, simply that displaced workers (and those with fixed investments in a particular area/country) maximise their comparative advantages. It is also about equity and workers' positions. As trade and factor flows become increasingly international, inequalities between territorial units may become greater. Workers faced with strong competition from overseas don't simply always move into the most productive domestic sectors, but may find themselves lowering their *real* living standards to compete with lower unit costs elsewhere – domestic inequality being the result. In the longer term such competitors may supplant these workers in a global productivity league table. Walker (1999) notes how the considerable industrial restructuring in the US since the 1970s has, allied to underinvestment and a diminution of the power of labour unions and of state welfare entitlements, seen an increase in jobs in unskilled personal and business services or low-wage manufacturing.

But, as he stresses, such inequality is not a *necessary* condition of free trade or capitalism. The point here is that public investment in basic research and a strong educational system do not constitute the sort of state intervention rejected by Porter and Krugman. Such investment means workers under pressure from lower cost competition may move into newer, higher skilled, more productive work. Indeed, some economists such as Atkinson (1998) see inequality as a form of exclusion. It is also pertinent to point out that investment that upgrades the economy of one city does not automatically damage its neighbours. Rather, such investment can lead to an improvement in the productivity levels of all, thereby obviating the risk of a zero-sum game or a descent into competitive short-term cost cutting.

Support for strong forms of equality have been made on intrinsic grounds – notably greater community, trust (Bowles and Gintis, 1998) and longevity (Wilkinson, 1997) although full equality of outcome is (not unreasonably) usually dismissed as being unlikely to promote self-respect (Hausman and Macpherson, 1996). This need not be at the expense of competitiveness, as a more economic case for equality also exists. Economists typically stress that anything approaching full equality of outcome would destroy incentives (Hausman and Macpherson, 1996) but that there may well still be *extrinsic* gains in greater equality such as increased productivity and reduced crime and disorder (Glyn and Miliband, 1994; Bowles and Gintis, 1998). Wilkinson (1997) found compelling evidence that it is the direct and indirect effects of differences in *relative* social position that account for the (economically costly) health disadvantage seen among lower socio-economic groups.

A degree of social support for redistribution such as that seen in the Scandinavian welfare states (see Esping-Andersen, 1990) can also help to ensure that workers in demand internationally are happy to stay in their country of origin. In this case, mechanisms for encouraging a greater sense of cohesion need to be discussed more within local social fabric discourses, while also keeping competitiveness aims in mind. To satisfy investors (increasingly able to invest money internationally) there must also be greater *profit* in equality. A key question for students of urban and regional issues is, therefore, whether increased political devolution may increase urban and regional identities, fostering a greater interest in egalitarianism, while, at the same time, creating the conditions for a more productive local economy.

Localised inequality

Atkinson (1998) suggests that the opportunities for social mobility, not just work quality, are important aspects of inclusion – that is, even if (by definition) all cannot rise to the most senior jobs, at least there should be no structural barriers to suitably talented and motivated individuals from doing so. However, labour market polarisation of the sort referred to earlier makes it unlikely that many individuals will be able to bridge the divide. This will be exacerbated if the polarisation is inter-regional or international – that is, if the next step up the job ladder requires geographical relocation (with all its detrimental effects on community, identity, social ties and so on – the sorts of things espoused in the local social fabric literature).

Of particular interest here is the fact that labour market polarisation is *particularly* likely to occur in hi-tech areas where new high value-added industry occurs in a hitherto underdeveloped area (Crang and Martin, 1991) or de-industrialised setting. Indeed, in large urban regions such as the 'Boston–Route 128' area and London, economic success and decline exist in relative proximity. Polarisation is also marked in those successful urban economies that see a *glut* of often-illegal and unskilled immigrants.[4] The US, particularly New York and Los Angeles, offers the best examples owing to the proximity of its (often-porous) border to Latin America. The problem for those interested in the local social fabric is that poor labour market conditions for many (through offering cheap services to business and residents) can constitute a competitive advantage (Sassen, 1994; Bates, 1996; Peck and Theodore, 1999; Walker, 1999). There is some evidence (Porter, 1997) that while poor immigrant workers often have lower expectations in regard to work conditions, some individuals with poor work offset it through social ties. For example, those with wealthy spouses/partners (or other social support networks) are less likely to be concerned about poor jobs. While such work may constitute the best use of unskilled workers, it does not offer the sort of jobs that, if inclusion is to be meaningful, economic development policy and general education policy should be encouraging.

The possibility for achieving greater redistribution through local-level political activity, such as the various Living Wage movements in the US (see Merrifield, 2000), is also an important focus for local social fabric debates. Certainly, many of the most competitive local economies are firmly embedded in certain cities or urban-regions and so offer some hope that local unions/worker coalitions might be easily organised and might have a high chance of success in securing better pay/conditions without compromising (and, conceivably, enhancing) competitiveness. On the other hand, labour militancy has been eroded in many countries by companies deliberately seeking out non-unionised labour, by anti-union legislation, by the decline of union membership with deindustrialisation, and by the rise of non-unionised service sectors. There is also initial (US) evidence to suggest that the nature of contingent work and/or depressed labour markets are very detrimental to the old workplace-based unionism – contacts are needed more but harder to achieve (Peck and Theodore, 1999; Walker, 1999; Sennett, 2000). The strategies and successes of collective labour action in non-unionised areas is also something that needs to be considered – such as whether labour unions and other social movements seek to link into their social networks to gain strength and increased membership[5].

Employment and the wider social fabric

Work-life balances

Work clearly has the potential to affect the sorts of wider social networks referred to earlier – an impact that has not been picked up in the local social fabric literature. Unsurprisingly, workers in tight labour markets (particularly if these are unionised) are more likely to benefit from freedom in terms of hours worked – such as part-time and job-share arrangements or working from home. Work-life balances may also include sensitivity to cultural differences (for example, allowing minority ethnic workers time off for prayer or religious holidays) and to family/personal crises. It may include regular (daytime) working hours and recognition of the importance of work as a key site through which workers arrange their social lives – for example, providing time and physical space for workers to socialise at work. Poor pay and/or working conditions may, as a result, not only undermine social support mechanisms, such as those that facilitate recruitment (Etzioni, 1998; Newman, 1999; Purcell et al, 1999; Heery and Salmon, 2000), but also have a damaging effect on the flexibility and thus competitiveness of the local labour market.

The interplay between the labour market and competitiveness will also be influenced by other social factors, notably around the area of social, community and political engagement. Examples include whether pay conditions and long or uncertain working hours[6] affect workers' ability to form social ties, to join various associations and to take an interest in the education of themselves and/or their children – all of which may have potential economic benefits. Such networking might be particularly important perhaps for high growth areas with lots of new young in-movers/workers. Another interesting question is whether social networks are less important for highly skilled workers who may be able to purchase personal/ancillary services. As the corollary to this, how important are informal (mutual-aid type) channels for less wealthy workers and to what extent might work-life imbalances have a negative effect on such ties? Finally, to what extent are unions taking up such issues and with what success?

Complexities around 'welfare-to-work' concepts of inclusion

Social inclusion debates, particularly among politicians, have tended to favour paid employment (formal or informal) as the main channel to promote inclusion. Some have, however, argued that this devalues unpaid work undertaken by those on benefits (Levitas, 1996; Lister, 1998). Such work may be beneficial to communities and/or local economies in terms of developing social ties and trust norms, and could consequently justify state subsidy (see also Chanan, 1999). This is not to suggest that inclusion in paid employment is not desirable and important. For many people, work is the central locus of their social life and the source of friendships. What is being suggested is that the picture is more complex and that local knowledge needs to be brought to bear on such complexities – and research undertaken where such knowledge is lacking.

A similar point can be made about certain types of informal economic activity. Informal personal services (such as household repairs) are not undertaken solely to supplement social security payments or to substitute for jobs in the formal economy. Indeed, unemployed workers are more likely to be excluded from this sort of activity due to other aspects of exclusion. These include: their lower likelihood of owning a car and work tools; reduced social ties to those with money; lack of skills and confidence; and to their greater fear of being reported (if their earnings exceed social security limits (Williams, 2000). Ultimately, this merely reiterates the need for debate and research to focus upon securing a greater number and more geographically even distribution of jobs in the formal economy at varying spatial scales.

Where employers face a shortage of suitable workers it may be that the characteristics of potential workers (rather than, say, the quality of education and training) are a causal factor. For example, Mann (1999) notes changes in the behaviour of the poor (notably the rise in teenage parents, family break-up and single mothers) that increase unemployment and other forms of *ex*clusion. However, he also notes that causality may run in two directions – that is, such changes need to be set within the context of wider economic changes (notably a long-standing lack of overall employment opportunities). He gives the example of how the negative effect of poor employment opportunities on the masculine identities of working-class men seriously erodes their ability to act as responsible 'father figures'. Likewise, Newman (1999) asserts that 'we rarely read about the importance of work opportunities as a means of cutting down on teenage pregnancy (p 119).

Educational inclusion and economic competitiveness

School mix and social order

Shortcomings in education in many areas of Britain have allowed inequalities of opportunity to emerge within the state-funded education system. The quality of education also has implications for both competitiveness and cohesion/inclusion, and in forestalling economically costly disorder, especially in cities. For example, a report on the city of Bradford – which was afflicted by race-related riots in the summer of 2001 – by a recent head of the UK's Commission for Racial Equality, saw part of local social order problems as lying in the 'virtual apartheid' of the city's school system (Ouseley, 2001, p 14). Similar comments were to be heard in the other two cities affected by riots in this period (Oldham and Burnley, both in North West England)[7]. Indeed, social unrest has almost invariably been an urban phenomenon – due to sizeable concentrations of ethnic minorities and unemployment or poor quality jobs. As Johnson (1999) is at pains to stress in a UK context, inclusion discourse must focus not just on 'failing schools' (a term favoured by the New Labour government), but also upon 'failing cities'[8]. He defines these as being where large areas are hit by deindustrialisation and social decay (the latter likely to prove unpopular with staff).

The difficulty for competitiveness may come where any local education authority unilaterally introduces policies (including radical measures such as 'busing') aimed at social or racial/ethnic mix objectives that risk pushing residents to move away. Higher skilled parents may want (and be able to afford) schools where pupils are not from minority groups or from less advantaged backgrounds and might seek residence elsewhere, undermining the local skills base. Certainly, 'white flight' to the suburbs was intensified by court busing orders in, notably, south Boston in the 1970s and Detroit in the 1990s. Even city-region level integration efforts (that is bigger school board districts) may simply precipitate further movement into the self-exclusion of the private sector or to other areas (Fainstein, 1996; McCrate, 1998).

Social mix and educational standards

Social mixing in schools can nevertheless yield advantages in terms of educational attainment, again with potential knock-on benefits for competitiveness. Evidence from Scotland suggests that schools with a sufficiently high level of pupils from advantaged homes can raise the performance of pupils from less advantaged backgrounds (Cowie and Croxford, 1996; Willms, 1996). However, such systems cannot be created where competitive internal markets operate within the state education system (as seen in the UK), or with a planning system that does not seek to impose social mix through distribution for affordable housing (seen in many nations). Since the late 1980s state schooling in the UK has seen greater information on school performance, greater choice of school for parents and the attachment of schools' funding to their pupil numbers. All of this means that, effectively, schools compete for pupils and parents compete for places, both engendering a risk of polarisation between localities.

This quasi-market has had a strong urban dimension to it. Concerns about ensuring parental choice alongside an equitable and transparent schools admissions procedure are 'particularly acute in the large conurbations' (West et al, 1998, p 11). Such areas, owing to their size, can offer more diversity, yet this can open up more inequality. Wealthier parents are more endowed with the resources to find and transport their children to schools in other parts of the region and to buy homes near those oversubscribed schools that operate a 'catchment area' policy[9]. Moreover, urban areas are more likely to have parents and pupils whose first language is not English and who may also fare less well in admission interviews (Social Exclusion Unit, 1998; West et al, 1998; Johnson, 1999; Sparkes, 1999; Gibson and Asthana, 2000). It is regrettable, then, that in the UK at least the education research community and the urban studies community have so little contact.

Social order and corporate community ties

The competitive advantages of cohesion

Cohesion, in the senses of both order and low crime, is clearly important for business eager to lure suitably skilled workers, investors and tourists. Such firms *may* be able to market their area's peacefulness and/or its success at reducing crime and social order problems. This could be particularly valuable in cities where external *perceptions* of crime or order in certain places exceed the actual level – a good example here being Mayor Guiliani's 'zero tolerance' policing policy and its effects on crime and, in turn, perceptions of New York. Marketing could conceivably even include mention of organisational membership and civic engagement more generally[10]. Even areas without such engagement may be able to promote themselves as places of tolerance and cosmopolitanism (see Cohen and Fields, 2000, on Silicon Valley). Evidence suggests that imagery of social cohesion is often used by city marketers (albeit not in so sophisticated a fashion as to include more detailed information such as civic engagement) (Griffiths, 1998; Hall, 1998; MacCannell, 1999; Short and Kim, 1999).

Social unrest, especially in urban areas, can impose significant costs upon businesses. The unrest witnessed in UK cities in the summer of 2001 and in the past resulted in costs and considerable anxiety in the business communities affected. Disorder has been more likely to be urban due to the intersection of large and concentrated racial groups and the sorts of poor labour market conditions referred to above – although policing styles have also been important factors too. To forestall such problems and prevent loss of competitiveness, sensitive policy development is required. Social order is, for instance, more likely to be achieved where there are good employment opportunities for all, and if social institutions, such as schools, foster social tolerance. Davis (1998), for example, notes how the Los Angeles mid-city riot in 1992 was driven primarily by hunger – in turn due to poor working opportunities and off-licences and markets that greatly overcharged for poor quality merchandise (service exclusion). In discussing this same city he also notes how structural unemployment and non-white invasion of hitherto white neighbourhoods have precipitated a series of racist attacks by violent groups. It is also worth noting that some of the most economically distressed areas will be ones with little business activity. If urban economies are to be regenerated or stimulated and are to improve their competitive positions, institutions and initiatives need to be put in place that make it unlikely that disorder will occur.

US research suggests that crime against business is a particularly strong burden upon companies in areas of high and concentrated deprivation – notably, inner cities and large public housing estates/projects (Porter, 1995, 1997; Inc., 2000). Crime against business is, of course, a broad category and includes commercial burglary, theft from offices, vehicle theft, vandalism, theft by staff, attacks against staff/customers, and violence in the evening economy (pubs and nightclubs). There are also less direct effects – such as the effect of the drugs economy on crime and the social fabric more generally, and crime against workers (as residents).

While the impact of crime on business competitiveness is complex, solutions based purely on law enforcement or security will not necessarily work. Building up social capital can help to lessen crime against business – from vigilant neighbours, through to localised inter-firm partnerships (using pagers or radios) who notify each other of potential threats (shoplifting teams, troublesome customers and so on), and through which the police can disseminate information on crime/criminals. Firms in clearly delimited areas such as shopping centres and business parks also often collaborate to support 'Business Watches' and/or shared contributions to a local security presence (Fainstein and Gray, 1996; McIntosh et al, 1998). Seemingly minor measures of these sorts can combine to improve the business environment in a way that boosts the overall competitiveness of a city.

Again, however, activity against business crime *may* simply see crime displaced to (and possibly intensified upon) other (usually less affluent) companies, areas or individuals. There may also be displacement through wealthier workers extracting themselves from crime and disorder by living in suburban/gated communities thereby lowering the chances of suffering crime. Gated communities are particularly a US phenomenon (see Blakely and Synder, 1997), but moving to low crime areas does (consciously or otherwise) constitute a form of what Levitas has rightly termed self-exclusion (in Le Grand, 1999). In both instances, equality of opportunity should be taken to mean that public resources need to be focused doubly upon the needier areas.

Corporate community relations

Pressures upon companies to engage with their 'communities' for competitive advantage are of two main sorts. First, cuts to state welfare in the last two decades in many Western nations have seen corporations increasingly being asked to assume such activity. In addition, the emergence of 'globalisation' as a major social and environmental concern has also seen many of the major corporations facing international pressure to be more aware of their external environments (human and/or physical). However, such 'communities' are often on a national or international scale and so not pursued further here (McIntosh et al, 1998; Burke 1999).

Second, urban disorder in the US and UK was a prime mover in the emergence of strategic corporate community engagement on a significant scale (Barnekov et al, 1989). Examples of such engagement include; seconding staff to urban regeneration partnerships, charitable donations, free use of company space for community organisations, work experience placements for school pupils, efforts to recruit local workers, and sponsorship of local projects more generally (public art and so on). Certainly, there is some limited evidence that a positive role and image in their local communities may help companies to minimise crime against them (Porter, 1995, 1997) and that efforts to deal with local labour market exclusion can reap benefits. For example, the major French hypermarket chain Auchan had gang warfare outside one of its supermarkets. It subsequently hired the (unemployed) gang leaders as security guards and provided retail space for several community-owned boutiques. Previously frightened customers returned in considerable numbers (McIntosh et al, 1998).

The corporate sector can also contribute in a variety of ways to the social cohesion in a city by appropriate human resource management. A good image for recruiting able/committed workers may be important on two levels. The first of these is the recruitment of the increasing (though still small) number of graduates concerned with potential employers' general position on corporate social responsibility. Staff secondment is increasingly seen as an additional method for developing staff confidence and their presentational and management skills, but can also support the development of social structures that contribute to the underlying competitiveness. For example, there has been a modest increase recently in corporate interest in encouraging staff secondment (usually part-time) to local voluntary organisations. Targets include seeking to enhance the employability of the long-term unemployed and offenders (help with reading, CV preparation, interview techniques and so on), and helping with local schools (reading support for pupils, managerial support for teachers). The second human resource reason is at a much more geographically localised and lower skill level. With this latter, firms are more concerned with availability and and/or cheapness – local transport vagaries, routes and timetables often placing an increased premium upon worker proximity (Porter, 1995, 1997; McIntosh et al, 1998; Burke, 1999).

Exhortations to such activity, by Porter and those in the corporate community-relations field, fail to highlight the downside to such activity – in particular geographical unevenness. These writers offer useful conceptual frameworks for looking at such relations but err strongly on the side of overemphasising the possibilities. Clearly, areas with major social problems may well face such problems partly because of sustained absence of economic activity – thus, there are likely to be fewer firms able to offer community support of various sorts.

Conclusions

The term competitiveness, although ultimately concerned with productivity, is shorthand for the myriad of constituent processes that underpin it – processes that need to be elaborated. Similarly, the 'local social fabric' terms have lacked clarity and kept more radical concerns off the agenda. The conceptual framework offered in this chapter is one that can be employed by those eager to ensure wealth creation is maximised, and by those for whom more egalitarian concerns are paramount. The principal areas for taking forward links and tensions between competitiveness and the (expanded) local social fabric are included in Table 4.1. Although this chapter has endeavoured to be as wide-ranging as possible, it makes no claim to be to be all encompassing and there are many other facets of the relationship between the social fabric and competitiveness that could fruitfully be researched.

In considering these issues, the importance of cities and urban-regions has become apparent – in terms of clusters, networks, labour markets, social order and education. It has also been stressed that the answer to 'urban problems' are often likely to lie at higher spatial levels – through union activity, transfer payments and regulations. Indeed, the economic and/or social cases for inter-territorial distribution and cross-territorial regulation need to receive increased consideration when moves to greater political decentralisation are being seen in so many nations. This does not mean, however, that cities and regions cannot serve as policy laboratories in which the various linkages and putative policy responses can be more extensively analysed.

Table 4.1: Competitiveness and the local social fabric: taking research, debate and policy forward

Theme	Extending research and/or debates
Clusters and business networks	• Understanding network exponentiality and policies to lessen/offset this. • Understanding relationships between the social and mainstream economies. • Policy that seeks to develop existing or emerging clusters in less-favoured areas. • Fate of regional economic policy in fiscally devolved nations. • Need to ascertain when local clustering is preferable to national clustering.
Getting work: labour markets and social ties	• Spatial policy to ensure greater equality of labour market opportunity. • Employer treatment of workers with identical skills but different nationality, ethnicity or sexuality. • Employer efforts to increase the numbers of applications from minority groups. • Factors determining the level and sector representation of business ownership among minority groups.
Work quality and egalitarianism	• Mechanisms for encouraging a greater sense of understanding and support for egalitarianism – eg citizenship education, compulsory military service and school integration. • Mechanisms to ensure widespread share ownership and for discussing the future of state ownership. • Effects of increased devolution upon local interest in egalitarianism. • Economic development policy and general education policy efforts to eradicate poor jobs. • The possibility for achieving greater redistribution through local-level political activity. • Strategies and successes of collective labour action in non-unionised areas and for international action.
Employment and the wider social fabric	• Effects of pay and long/uncertain hours upon workers' social, familial and civic engagement. • Importance for different types of worker of social networks versus bought services. • Value/importance of unpaid work by those on benefits. • Impact of informal personal services on the formal economy. • Involvement of the unemployed in the informal economy. • Changes in the behaviour of the poor and its effects upon labour market exclusion. • Effect of long-term unemployment upon potential labour force characteristics.

Table 4.1: contd.../

Theme	Extending research and/or debates
Educational inclusion and economic competitiveness	• Effects of the educational quasi-market and the housing market upon equality of educational opportunity. • Opportunities and need for social and racial mixing within schools. • Schools that teach about different religions and encourage pupil community service. • Need to consider evidence on busing from the US and the governance implications. • Effects of economic success/failure upon school results and teacher recruitment. • Effects of social and racial/ethnic mixing in schools upon educational attainment and tolerance/ understanding, respectively. • Mechanisms to help parents and pupils unfamiliar with the *lingua franca*.
Social order and corporate community ties	• Extent to which place marketers use information on local social fabric issues. • Need to consider places less able to fund marketing and with greater crime problems. • Inter-territorial spillovers of crime. • Identification of the underlying causes of urban disorder and places that are more likely to be vulnerable to disorder. • Consideration of institutions and initiatives that make it unlikely that disorder will occur in the first instance. • Inegalitarian displacement effects of anti-crime measures. • Need to highlight best practice in corporate-community relations. • Need to highlight the benefits to firms of such activity. • Need to consider how resources saved might be redirected to needier areas. • Danger of overemphasising the possibilities for privatist solutions to social problems. • Establishment of which schools lack corporate involvement and which areas/groups lack links into local employers. • Consideration of how all places can consult more widely on proposed developments and concede power-of-veto to local populations.

Acknowledgements

Particular thanks are due to Aidan While (Hull) who read two versions of the chapter and offered extremely insightful comments. Thanks also to the following for kindly offering lengthy comments upon early versions of this work: Balihar Sanghera (Novosibirsk); Laura Smethurst (Essex); Alan Murie (Birmingham); and Peter Tierhorst (Amsterdam). Comments on early versions were also kindly made by Dave Byrne (Durham), Pete North and Iain Begg (both South Bank). Lastly, thanks to Linda Croxford (Edinburgh), Margaret Maden (formerly Keele) and Anne West (LSE) for pointing me to useful education research.

Notes

[1] The UK Department of Trade and Industry has, for example, recently identified nine 'agri-business' clusters in different regions.

[2] The absence of work in these areas can of course also be exclusory in that it may affect equality of opportunity by denying local youth role models to encourage positive attitudes to working and looking for work (Wilson, 1999).

[3] A celebrated example here is the (small-scale) Gautreux project in Chicago that has seen those moved out from inner-city projects substantially improving their chances of finding a job (see Dreier and Moberg, 1996).

[4] Immigration can of course benefit competitiveness without constituting a labour market glut – immigrants' arrival is mostly driven by economic demand for labour (the danger only comes when workers keep coming as a downturn occurs).

[5] Recent work by Nicholls (2001) on Los Angeles is interesting here in noting how unions in that city have linked in with churches and community groups as a means of coordinating labour protest among contingent (non-unionised) immigrant workers. Thus social struggles may manage social ties in the way that firms might.

[6] Such as the growth of night working that is in typically urban activities such as security, nightclubs, taxis and all-night supermarkets (Kreitzman, 1999; Harkness, 1999).

[7] Such segregation is often, in turn, bound up with segregation in access to social rented housing (see Ratcliffe, 2001).

[8] Despite the strength of the argument, the use of the term 'failing city' appears to constitute the sort of exclusionary labelling that Johnson is keen to avoid.

[9] This latter may be partly responsible for the rise in lengthy commutes by workers (see Larson, 1998; Benito and Oswald, 1999) – the stressfulness of which may, conceivably, affect worker productivity.

[10] Such engagement and other social ties may of course also be valuable in *retaining* skilled workers too.

Bibliography

Amin, A. and Thrift, N. (1994) 'Living in the global', in A. Amin and N. Thrift (eds), *Globalisation, institutions and regional development in Europe*, Oxford: Oxford University Press.

Andersen, J. (1999) 'Social and system integration and the underclass', in I. Gough, and G. Olofsson (eds) *Capitalism and social cohesion*, Basingstoke: Macmillan Press.

Atkinson, A. (1998) 'Poverty, social exclusion and the British empirical tradition', Thanks-Offering to Britain lecture at the British Academy, London, 22 October.

Barnekov, T., Boyle, R. and Rich, D. (1989) *Privatism and urban policy in Britain and the United States*, Oxford: Oxford University Press.

Bates, T. (1996) 'The political economy of urban poverty in the 21st century: How progress and public policy generate rising poverty', *The Review of Black Political Economy*, Fall/Winter.

Benito, A. and Oswald, A. (1999) *Commuting in Great Britain in the 1990s*, Warwick: Department of Economics, University of Warwick.

Birchall, J. (1997) *Co-operation in Europe, the international co-operative movement*, Manchester: Manchester University Press.

Blakely, J. and Synder, M. (1997) *Fortress America: Gated communities in the United States*, Lincoln, NE: Brookings.

Bowles, S. and Gintis, H. (eds) (1998) *Recasting egalitarianism: New rules for communities, states and markets*, London: Verso.

Bramanti, A. and Ratti, R. (1997) 'The multi-faced dimensions of local development', in R. Ratti, A. Bramanti and R. Gordon (eds) *The dynamics of innovative regions: The GREMI approach*, Aldershot: Ashgate.

Burchell, B., Day, D., Hudson, M., Ladipo, D., Mankelow, R., Nolan, J.P., Reed, H., Wickert, I.C. and Wilkinson, S.F. (1999) *Job insecurity and work intensification: Flexibility and the changing boundaries of work*, York: Joseph Rowntree Foundation.

Burke, E. (1999) *Corporate-community relations: The principle of the neighbour of choice*, Wesport, CO: Praeger.

Camagni, R. (1991) 'Introduction: From the local 'milieu' to innovation through co-operation networks', in R. Camagni (ed) *Innovation networks: Spatial perspectives*, London: Belhaven Press.

Chanan, G. (1999) 'Employment policy and the social economy: Promise and misconceptions', *Local Economy*, February.

Cohen, S. and Fields, G. (2000) 'Social capital and capital gains: An examination of social capital in Silicon Valley', in M. Kenney (ed) *Understanding Silicon Valley: The anatomy of an entrepreneurial region*, Stanford, CA: Stanford University Press.

Coleman, J. (1988) 'Social capital in the creation of human capital', *American Journal of Sociology*, vol 94.

Cowie, M. and Croxford, L. (1996) 'The effectiveness of Grampian secondary schools, report to Grampian Education Authority', Centre for Educational Sociology, Edinburgh University.

Crang, P. and Martin, R. (1991) 'Mrs Thatcher's vision of the "new Britain" and the other sides of the Cambridge phenomenon', *Environment and Planning D: Society and Space*, vol 9, pp 91-116.

CRE (Commission for Racial Equality) (1999) *Racial equality means business: Case studies*, London: CRE.

Davis, M. (1998) *Ecology of fear: Los Angeles and the imagination of disaster*, London: Picador.

De Souza Briggs, X. (1997) 'Social capital and the cities: Advice to change agents', *National Civic Review*, vol 86 no 2, pp 111-17.

Donnison, D. (1998), 'The sociology of knowledge', *Prospect*, p 11, January.

Dreier, P. and Moberg, D. (1996) 'Moving from the "hood": The mixed success of integrating suburbia', *The American Prospect*, issue 24, Winter.

Esping-Andersen, G. (1990) *The three worlds of welfare capitalism*, Cambridge: Polity Press.

Etzioni, A. (1998), 'A communitarian perspective on sustainable communities', in D. Warburton (ed) *Community and sustainable development: participation in the future*, London: Earthscan.

Fainstein, S. (1996) 'Justice, politics and the creation of urban space', in A. Merrifield and E. Swyngedouw (eds) *The urbanization of injustice*, London: Lawrence and Wishart.

Fainstein, S. (2001) 'Competitiveness, cohesion and governance: their implications for social justice', *International Journal of Urban and Regional Research*, vol 25, no 4, pp 884-8.

Fainstein, S. and Gray, M. (1996), 'Economic development strategies for the inner city: The need for governmental intervention', *The Review of Black Political Economy*, Fall/Winter.

Gertler, M. (1995) 'Being there: proximity, organisation and culture in the development and adoption of advanced manufacturing technologies', *Economic Geography*, vol 71, no 1, pp 1-26.

Goldberg, D. (2000) 'The new segregation', in D. Bell and A. Haddour (eds) *City visions*, London: Prentice Hall.

Gibson, A. and Asthana, S. (2000) 'What's in a number? Commentary on Gorard and Fitz's "Investigating the determinants of segregation between schools"', *Research Papers in Education*, vol 15, no 2.

Glyn, A. and Miliband, D. (eds) (1994) *Paying for inequality: The economic cost of social injustice*, London: Rivers Oram Press,.

Grabher, G. (1993) 'Re-discovering the social in the economics of inter-firm relations', in G. Grabher (ed) *The embedded firm: On the socioeconomics of industrial networks*, London: Routledge.

Granovetter, M. (1973) 'The strength of weak ties', *American Journal of Sociology*, vol 78.

Griffiths, R. (1998) 'Making sameness: place marketing and the new urban entrepreneurialism', in N. Oatley (ed) *Cities, economic competition and urban policy*, London: Paul Chapman Publishing.

Hall, T. (1998) *Urban geography*, London: Routledge.

Harkness, S. (1999) 'Working 9 to 5?', in P. Gregg, and J. Wadsworth (eds) *The state of working Britain*, Manchester: Manchester University Press.

Hausman, D. and MacPherson, M. (1996) *Economic analysis and moral philosophy*, Cambridge: Cambridge University Press.

Hausman, D. (1998) 'Problems with supply-side egalitarianism', in S. Bowles and H. Gintis (eds) *Recasting egalitarianism: New rules for communities, states and markets*, London: Verso.

Heery, E. and Salmon, J. (2000) 'The insecurity thesis', in E. Heery and J. Salmon (eds) *The insecure workforce*, London: Routledge.

Inc. (2000) The Inner City 100 Almanac, *Inc.*, special issue on the Inner-City 100, p 78, May.

Johnson, M. (1999) *Failing school, failing city: The reality of inner-city education*, Charlbury: Jon Carpenter.

Kreitzman, L. (1999) *The 24 hour society*, London: Profile Books.

Krugman, P. (1996) *Pop internationalism*, London: MIT Press.

Larson, J. (1998) 'Surviving commuting', *American Demographics*, July

Le Grand, J. (1999) 'Beyond the Pale', Analysis, Radio 4, 5 April.

Levitas, R. (1996) 'The concept of social exclusion and the new Durkheimian hegemony', *Critical Social Policy*, vol 16, pp 5-20.

Lister, R. (1998) 'From equality to social inclusion: New Labour and the welfare state, *Critical Social Policy*, vol 18, pp 215-25.

Loury, G. (1977) 'A dynamic theory of racial income differences', in P. Wallace and A. Lamond (eds) *Women, minorities and employment discrimination*, Lexington, VA: D.C. Heath.

Maccannell, D. (1999) 'New urbanism' and its discontents', in J. Copjec and M. Sorkin (eds) *Giving ground: The politics of propinquity*, London: Verso.

McCrate, E. (1998) 'Which norms? How much gain?: two reasons to limit markets,' in S. Bowles and H. Gintis (eds) *Recasting egalitarianism: New rules for communities, states and markets*, London: Verso.

McIntosh, M., Leipziger, D., Jones, K. and Coleman, G. (1998) *Businesses and communities, in corporate citizenship: Successful strategies for responsible companies*, London: Financial Times/Pitman Publishing.

Maillat, D. (1995) 'Territorial dynamics, innovative milieux and regional policy', *Entrepreneurship and Regional Development*, vol 7.

Mann, K. (1999) 'Critical reflections on the "underclass" and poverty', in I. Gough and G. Olofsson (eds) *Capitalism and social cohesion*, Basingstoke: Macmillan.

Martin, R. (1993) 'Reviving the economic case for regional policy', in R. Harrison and M. Hart (eds) *Spatial policy in a divided nation*, London: Jessica Kingsley Publishers.

Merrifield, A. (2000) 'Living-wage activism in the American city', *Social Text 62*, vol 18, no1.

Newman, K. (1999) *No shame in my game: The working poor in the inner city*, New York, NY: Vintage Books.

Nicholls, W. (2001) 'The territorial turn in progressive urban politics: The case of Los Angeles', paper presented to International Sociological Association Research Committee on Regional and Urban Development (RC21) Conference: 'Social inequality, redistributive justice and the city', Amsterdam, the Netherlands, 15-17 June (contact walternicholls@email.com).

O'Connor, J., Raffo, C.V. and Lovatt, A. (1999) *Cultural entrepreneurs and the city: Risk, learning and the competitive city*, World Urban Economic Development, London: World Markets Research Centre.

Olin Wright, E. (1998) 'Equality, community and "Efficient redistribution"', in S. Bowles, and H. Gintis (eds) *Recasting egalitarianism: New rules for communities, states and markets*, London: Verso.

Ouseley, H. (2001) *Community pride, not prejudice: Making diversity work in Bradford*, Bradford: Bradford Vision.

Patterson, O. (1998) 'Affirmative action: Opening up workplace networks to Afro-Americans', *The Brookings Review*, vol 16, no 2, pp 17-23.

Peck, J. and Theodore, N. (1999) 'Contingent Chicago: restructuring the spaces of contemporary labour', Royal Geographical Society /Institute of British Geographers, Economic Geography Research Group Working Paper 99/03.

Porter, M. (1995) 'The competitive advantage of the inner–city', *Harvard Business Review*, pp 55-71, May–June.

Porter, M. (1997) 'New strategies for inner–city economic development', *Economic Development Quarterly*, vol 11, no 1, pp 11-27.

Portes, A. and Landolt, P. (1996) 'The downside of social capital', *The American Prospect*, issue 26, May–June.

Portes, A. (1998) 'Social capital: its origins and applications in modern sociology', *Annual Review of Sociology*, vol 24.

Potts G. (2002: forthcoming) 'Regional policy and the regionalisation of university–industry inks', *European Planning Studies*.

Purcell, K., Hogarth, T. and Simm, C. (1999) *Whose flexibility?: The costs and benefits of non-standard working arrangements and contractual relations*, York: York Publishing Services/ Joseph Rowntree Foundation.

Putnam, R. (1993) 'The prosperous community: social capital and public life', *The American Prospect*, Issue 13, Spring.

Ratcliffe, P. (2001) *Breaking down the barriers: Improving Asian access to social rented housing*, London: Chartered Institute of Housing.

Sassen, S. (1994) *Cities in a world economy*, London: Pine Forge Press.

Sawicki, D. and Moody, M. (1996) 'Deja-vu all over again: Porter's model of inner city redevelopment', *The Review Of Black Political Economy*, vol 24, no 2/3, Fall/Winter, p 75.

Scott, A. and Storper, M. (1992) 'Regional development reconsidered', in H. Ernste and V. Meier (eds) *Regional development and contemporary industrial response: Extending flexible specialisation*, London: Belhaven Press.

Sennett, R. (1999) *The corrosion of character: The personal consequences of work in the new capitalism*, London: Norton.

Short, J. and Kim, Y. (1999) *Globalisation and the city*, Harlow: Longman.

Silver, H. (2000) 'Social exclusion and social capital', paper to 12th Annual Meeting of the Society for the Advancement of Socio-Economics (SASE) 'Citizenship and Exclusion', London School of Economics and Political Science, 7-10 July.

Social Exclusion Unit (1998) *Truancy and school exclusion*, Cm 3957, London: The Stationery Office.

Sparkes, J. (1999) 'Schools, education and social exclusion', CASE Paper No 29, London: Centre for the Analysis of Social Exclusion, London School of Economics and Political Science.

Stanley, C. (1992) 'Cultural contradictions in the legitimation of market practice: paradox in the regulation of the city', in L. Budd and S. Whimster, *Global finance and urban living: A study of metropolitan change*, London: Routledge.

Waldinger, R. (1997) *Social capital or social closure? Immigrant networks in the labour market*, Working Paper 26, Los Angeles, CA: Lewis Centre for Regional Policy Studies, University of California.

Walker, R. (1999) 'Putting capital in its place: globalisation and the prospects for labour', *Geoforum*, vol 30, pp 263-84.

West, A., Pennett, H. and Noden, P. (1998) 'School admissions: increasing equity, accountability and transparency', *British Journal of Educational Studies*, vol 46, no 2, pp 188-200.

Wilkinson, R. (1997) 'Socioeconomic determinants of health: health inequalities: relative or absolute material standards?', *British Medical Journal*, vol 314, pp 591-5.

Willms, J. (1996) 'School choice and community segregation: findings from Scotland', in A. Kerckhoff (ed) *Generating social stratification: Towards a new research agenda*, Boulder, CO: Westfield Press, pp 133-51.

Williams, C. (2000) 'Informal employment: implications for work and welfare', paper presented to Local Economy Policy Unit (LEPU) seminar on 'Precarious Work: Coping With The Informal Economy', South Bank University, London, 5 April.

Wilson, W. (1999) 'When work disappears: new implications for race and urban poverty in the global economy', *Ethnic and Racial Studies*, vol 22, no 3, pp 479-99.

FIVE

The property sector and its role in shaping urban competitiveness: a selective review of literature and evidence[1]

Kenneth Gibb, Daniel Mackay and Michael White

Introduction

This chapter examines the literature and new qualitative evidence on property market research within the Central Scotland region. It is primarily concerned with the way in which industrial land and city office markets contribute to, or detract from, urban economic competitiveness. Land and property are generally seen as part of the set of hard assets and are typically viewed as 'drivers' of urban economic competitiveness (Begg, 1999). Scottish Enterprise (SEN – the agency that promotes economic development in Scotland) considers these drivers as central to the enhancement of the 'physical business environment' of cities and regions (1996).

These aims have to be located in a wider understanding of the fundamental questions they relate to, namely:

- What is urban economic competitiveness?
- How should one conceptualise the urban economy?
- How can urban land and property markets be conceptualised?

In addition, however, public agencies intervene in land and property markets and, like analysts, they have a relatively well or poorly developed framework with which to conceptualise the property market. In particular, the focus is typically on the demand for property as a derived demand of wider business demand (according to the property industry) or as a relatively unproblematic factor market (urban analysts) that may or may not operate efficiently (Ball et al, 1998). In Scotland, for instance, policy is increasingly guided by a market failure framework. As with the 'big' concepts highlighted above, this market failure framework has to be critically assessed. In this chapter we draw on a selective review of the literature augmented by evidence from various Scottish sources, including recent research for Insignia Richard Ellis[2].

The structure of the chapter is as follows. The second section looks more closely at the way property and land markets are conceptualised, distinguishing the real estate economics textbook view from a range of institutional perspectives. Section three begins with a discussion of urban economic competitiveness and the role of property. It then goes on to examine the 'hard asset' view of property as a driver of urban economic competitiveness. Finally, in section three, the views of key actors within the Scottish property sector are consulted. A wider perspective on property markets and competitiveness is suggested: one that is more complex than that suggested by the hard asset/driver type framework. The fourth section returns to the Scottish Enterprise conceptualisation and looks critically at both what it conceives of as market failure and sets out a wider perspective on market failure. The final section concludes by summarising and revisiting the main themes of the paper.

Conceptualising the property market

In urban economic competitiveness models such as that proposed by Begg (1999), which is discussed in the next section, the property sector is viewed implicitly as an urban asset (or liability if the sector is not working well) playing the role of a 'shaping factor'. This is in sharp contrast to the views of key actors in the property sector whose perspective is more narrow and endogenous. The main missing link is, of course, the property research literature. In this section we draw on core work carried out on urban property markets in order to contrast different conceptualisations of the market. Although the way the property market (more usually, the property development market) operates is contested by the different perspectives, to divide the literature between economic and institutional perspectives, as is done in this section, is rather artificial. There is, in fact, both considerable commonality between the two perspectives and extensive variety within either viewpoint (Ball et al, 1998).

Economic approaches

Two recent textbooks capture the essence of recent developments in land and property economics. DiPasquale and Wheaton (1996) in the US and Ball, Lizieri and MacGregor (1998) in the UK both employ a similar multi-sector model of the land and property market. These models are useful because they demonstrate the interdependence of the occupier or space market with the property investment market and in turn between these markets and the development and land markets. The occupier markets are largely influenced by derived demand considerations (for instance, manufacturing output is argued to drive demand for industrial space, although office demand will also be a function of space per employee considerations). The property investment market, which is based on the rents achievable in the occupier market (and related capital values), has to make competitive returns in the context of a global capital market. The land market involves competing land uses and a range of physical and policy constraints (see also the chapter by Bramley and Lambert in this volume) on the availability of supply. However, occupier rents (and their expected values) shape developer demand for land, along with factors such as the cost of finance.

These models are useful because they highlight the subtle interdependencies between parts of the property system with the real and financial economies. The property sector is also defined in the economics literature in terms of its special characteristics: durability, spatial fixity, market thinness, heterogeneity, (stock) supply inelasticity, and extensive state intervention in the land and construction markets. In turn, these features of commodity complexity combine to create a number of stylised facts about urban property markets, which include the following:

- *Durability* means that markets for rented property and for owner-occupation can develop in parallel. There is a danger that one assumes that property markets are wholly rented, when in fact owner-occupation is often important in specific sub-sectors and at the margin at different points in the property cycle. The physical characteristics of property, its potential as a sound asset and the relationship between tenants and landlord means that the lease that is generated turns the rental income flow into a type of bond for prime property.
- *Information asymmetries* arise from thin markets; much less is known about secondary markets and there are concerns about non-core regional markets (Henneberry, 1999). Information is typically widest and deepest in the prime investment market, particularly in London.

Even so, the efficient markets literature applied to property is not generally indicative of the efficient use of price information from prime markets – in other words, profitable opportunities remain from the possibility of predicting future prices (Ball et al, 1998).

- *Property cycles* are endemic to property markets (and have generated a massive literature – see Ball et al, 1998). Expectational effects, supply lags and swings in market sentiment affect all of the interrelated markets and can operate in, for example, the office development market, relatively independently of real economic cycles.

- *Tight markets* and planning restrictions can provide super-normal profit opportunities for landowners and developers, leading to actions that can heighten market volatility; at the same time, industrial markets have been in certain places and at specific times undermined by public sector provision. Bramley and Lambert (in this volume) argue that in certain regions, planning policy has oversupplied industrial space relative to new housing.

- *Spatial fixity* means that property is sensitive to a wide range of positive and negative external effects from the local environment or neighbourhood. This is particularly important because of the wide range of interventions and their historical impact on property markets This is most obviously felt through supply-side planning and building control regulations but also through subsidies, spatial competition for inward investment and the displacement and spillover effects these can generate.

Although these multi-sectoral real estate models are equilibrium constructions in a setting where disequilibrium is the norm, their value is that they trace adjustment relationships and interactions between different sectors. It may well be that, empirically, certain markets do not work well, but these models can still provide us with important insights concerning the likely consequences of adjustment lags, regime changes, supply shocks and so on. Indeed, when they are combined with the distinctive features of property, one can start to see why property markets sometimes do experience extended adjustment periods, or why there are market failures and other related problems.

Institutional perspectives

The grouping of papers and research described as 'institutional' refers to a wide spectrum of work that to greater or lesser extent eschews traditional economics analysis (D'Arcy and Keogh, 1999). The range of material could provide a review paper in its own right but suffice it to say that the body of work is diffuse and is not always in agreement. Ball et al (1998) review this literature. They differentiate institutional from non-institutional analyses on the basis of whether they theorise about the institutional role within property markets and whether they complement or compete with existing non-institutional theories. Of course, as the authors point out, 'neo-classical' or mainstream economics makes some use of institutions via transactions cost economics, game theory and information theory perspectives. All three of these perspectives are ripe for use within the property market paradigm. For instance, the property market can be viewed as an institution in an otherwise thin market that allows transactions costs to be minimised (D'Arcy and Keogh, 1999). Game-theoretic ideas could inform, for instance, property development bargains over planning permission and the decision rules of landowners. Asymmetric information issues play an important role in property finance and the pricing of investments and, for instance, options for purchasing land.

Structure-agency (Healey and Barrett, 1990) is probably the best known and most widely used attempt to bring institutions fully into explanations of the property market, particularly the process of property development as a set of relationships between actors with relative powers to influence outcomes, constrained by the structures (rules, institutions and material resources) they face. This is a very flexible, empirical framework for analysing micro-phenomena but Ball et al (1998) are critical of the approach on a number of grounds (including that the model has no adequate explanation of institutional formation – D'Arcy and Keogh, 1999). However, in highlighting the strategic role in property development, they do indicate the weakness of ascribing a competitive market explanation to the development sector. Moreover, it is important to stress that the development market is probably the least like a competitive market of the sectors suggested in the multi-sectoral property economics model. It is reasonable to suggest, therefore, that Krugman's objective of moving urban economic modelling away from the standard competitive model and his interest in strategic theory suggests the possibility of fruitful ways of bringing realism into more conventional models of development (Fujita et al, 1999).

Perhaps the most interesting work in the UK property market in recent years has come from Henneberry (1999) who has explicitly set out to bring together economic and institutional/sociological explanations of property market (investment and development) processes in different regions. Despite the fact that Henneberry's analysis is broad-based in a disciplinary sense, it does suggest that a specific form of market failure arises in the investment market (regional investment and, effectively, development decisions are taken using London market rules and criteria such that profitable opportunities are missed and financial mistakes are made). Essentially, there is too much investment in London and the South East despite the opportunity for higher returns in other (perhaps less dynamic, or at least perceived to be so) British regions and this is attributed to the 'parochialism' of investors and property agents. Aside from institutional irrationality, a number of more mainstream economic reasons could be attributed to this phenomenon: risk-averseness to new or smaller, thinner markets; hierarchical rigidities within organisations with regional offices (that is, a transactions cost economics explanation); simple monopolistic discrimination on the part of institutional investors; or basic informational problems brought on by the integrated nature of the UK property market, which has much more regular information flows within London relative to elsewhere. From the market failure perspective, the key point is whether and to what extent these lessons are not learnt – is there a sustained segmentation going on or is it in fact transitory and perhaps related to cyclical market backwashes. More research is required. However, it is clear that Henneberry's findings challenge economists to debate and understand counterintuitive processes in much the same way that Krugman elsewhere raises the debate with non-economists (see next section).

Urban economic competitiveness and the property market

In this section, we begin by asking how the property sector might relate to urban economic competitiveness. Before looking at two perspectives on this question (from the hard asset view and that of the property sector professionals), the discussion starts by asking basic questions about urban economic competitiveness and urban land and property.

Property and urban economic competitiveness

There are three fundamental levels of analysis that one needs to consider when seeking to understand the role of property in the competitive urban economy:

• What do we mean by the urban economy and how is it conceptualised?
• What exactly do we mean by economic competitiveness and how is it applied to the urban scale?

- In the light of the first two questions, what role do land and property play to enhance or otherwise the impact on the performance of the urban economy?

This chapter is not primarily about the meaning of competitiveness nor is it fundamentally about the underlying model of the urban economy. Nonetheless, it is necessary to comment on these questions, particularly as the property market does not exist in a vacuum and should, ideally, be conceptually integrated with a defensible position on the urban economy and the meaning of competitiveness. Indeed, a longer term aim must be to develop thinking about land and property processes in such a way as to enhance our understanding of the urban economy, particularly when policies are designed with some form, albeit implicit, of urban economy/property market model.

The question of competitiveness seems to have become bedevilled by Krugman's powerful mercantilist criticism (Krugman, 1991) in which he argues that competitiveness espoused on the international economic stage is code for protectionist trade policy and fails to grasp the economic costs of not pursuing policies for international comparative advantage. By extension, urban economic competitiveness may be viewed as equally wrong-headed (although in a different context). The Krugman view could therefore be characterised as promoting urban-level competition through identifying and promoting urban comparative advantage as distinct from zero-sum territorial competition and 'local protectionism'. Begg (1999) recognises that, regardless of whether it is positive or not in the wider sense, cities do compete with each other (although this is likely not to be in the pure sense suggested by Krugman) and that it is therefore appropriate to explore and contrast the determinants of how well they are competing. The Krugman criticism is nonetheless clearly an issue for policy makers, given that individual firms are allowed to get on and compete.

Quite how inter-urban competition can be made to be a positive-sum game probably rests on one's conceptualisation of the urban economy. Krugman (see Fujita et al, 1999) has made a detailed appraisal of conventional urban and regional economics (see Boddy, 1999) and has sought to modernise the urban economics paradigm through a renewed theoretical appraisal of cities. He has sought to develop formal models that can explain agglomeration effects (without circular logic or other black box devices) and, from an economic perspective, the interesting development in his work is the extensive use of models of imperfect competition (as Layard and colleagues have similarly done in applied labour economics, Layard and Nickell, 1986). The work is also a search to formalise the cumulative causation processes (and historic accident) that have been originally associated with Myrdal, Pred and Richardson (Boddy, 1999; Fujita et al, 1999). He attempts to do this through linking scale economies that encourage spatial concentration and market structure/ size with lower spatial transactions costs. Larger markets encourage further concentration and so on. The key is the role of increasing returns, which is effectively ruled by all but special cases of the perfectly competitive model. This of course allows a much richer array of market structures. However, the modelling becomes correspondingly more complex and, as Fujita et al (1999) recognise, more detached from the real world.

Krugman's spatial work has been a source of much debate and criticism, primarily from outside the economics field (Krugman, 1991; Boddy, 1999; Fujita et al, 1999). So far, much of their specific research programme has been theoretical and polemic; it has still to undergo detailed empirical testing and may indeed be quite a long way away from quantifiable simulation analysis that could be used to predict outcomes from changes to initial conditions (Fujita et al, 1999). What it has done, however, when allied to issues such as endogenous growth, is to raise questions and turn the focus back on the theoretical basis of urban economics. The empirical debate particularly as regards specialisation versus urban economic diversity is further examined by Duranton and Puga (2000). Krugman has also revitalised the sub-discipline by explicitly confronting the failures of existing spatial models. Boddy (1999, p 834) alludes to this controversial debate involving the economics profession about the direction and validity of urban economic models and argues that renewed controversy is more useful than the continued ignorance of spatial questions by economists. Interestingly, Krugman (1991) argued that there was no complete model of the urban land and property market, primarily because of its complexity and, moreover, because of the way the property sector interacts with urban economic processes.

Property as a 'hard' asset

In a recent paper, Begg (1999) set out to describe schematically the factors that affect urban economic performance (and hence 'competitiveness') drawing on a format from the work of Michael Porter. Begg argues (p 801) that these forces may be 'mutually reinforcing, [or] contradictory'. The focus is on four key elements: sectoral trends, company characteristics, the business environment, and innovation and learning. Of these elements, the business environment is of primary concern. This set of variables concerns those factors outside the direct control of individual firms but which 'exert a significant influence on the attraction of the locality as a place of business by affecting the ease with which business can be done. Many of the telling influences on urban competitiveness concern the mix of factors that affect the input costs of employers in the urban area' (p 803). Chief among these factors is 'the supply, quality and cost of the various factors of production', that is property (presumably including land). Begg argues that the property market can affect locational attractiveness by, for example, exhibiting supply constraints that can undermine otherwise well-functioning property investment markets. Equally, high rents may deter new occupiers.

Essentially the same 'asset' argument is made by Scottish Enterprise in terms of its 'competitive locations' approach (Scottish Enterprise, 1996; McGilp, 2000). Scottish Enterprise stresses the importance of developing the appropriate supportive economic environment of both 'hard' and 'soft' assets. Necessary conditions for effective *place competition* include a stable macroeconomic environment, a flexible operating environment and a trainable skilled workforce. However, in addition, it argues that a physical and wider business infrastructure is required for successful business. Scottish Enterprise identifies five key elements: telecommunications, transport, the environment, the quality of life, and property and land. McGilp (2000) argues that the availability of low cost property, while still of importance, is no longer the deciding factor in attracting inward investment. The emerging competitive locations strategy is no longer property dominated but instead draws on a range of hard and soft assets – quality of life, skills, the transport and communications infrastructure and so on. Property strategy still plays a role but one which seeks to facilitate or enable the private sector to build rather than to provide. However, land and property can indirectly influence soft assets by their contribution to city centre vitality and through the maintenance of attractive urban living environments. As is discussed in more detail further on, Scottish Enterprise intends to provide property infrastructure only when the market has completely failed, and as a last resort.

The land and property sector (markets, institutions, actors in the different component markets) is thus often conceived of by policy makers as a factor of production or 'shaper' of urban economic performance. In short, it is simplistically reduced to the level of an exogenous driver of the urban economic system – if it is functioning well, then this will improve the flexibility and dynamism of the economy; if it is working badly or is constrained, then it will impede urban economic performance by frustrating locational choices and by leading to the misallocation of economic resources across space. In this world, as an essential factor of production for manufacturing and services (e-commerce matters aside), individual firms are deemed to be essentially price takers of property services and thus one can conceive of the land and property sector as an exogenous driver. The Scottish Enterprise point is, additionally, that an inward investment strategy should not simply focus on one element of the multifaceted package that attracts investors; instead, it has embraced a particular perspective that is a much more restrictive (albeit flexible) attitude to market intervention. It is not surprising, therefore, that D'Arcy and Keogh (1999) suggest that many urbanists looking at economic performance processes view the property sector as essentially unproblematic.

The view from the property sector

This is not the way that the role of the property sector is conceived of by the sector itself. Fundamentally, property market players – developers, investors, managers and agents – see the property sector simply as a series of interconnected markets interacting with and endogenous to wider economic forces. Indeed, the typical view is that property is a derived demand of the firm's product/service demand. In short, the role of the property sector is endogenous to the urban/regional economy rather than exogenous. There are countless examples of this type of derived demand analysis, both from within the property professionals' publications and in studies such as the annual Scottish Property Market Report published by Scottish Enterprise.

Qualitative findings on the Scottish property market

As part of the study for Insignia Richard Ellis research, the authors asked a range of property professionals (property developers, property investors within the institutions, property companies, development agencies, officials of two public agencies – Scottish Enterprise and the Scottish Executive – as well as property occupiers, lawyers and lenders) about what they considered to be the main drivers of the Scottish property market. There was a strong emphasis on the role of the demand-side of the property market, particularly, occupier demand. Also important was the role of economic expectations, both in terms of property market variables but also for the overall performance of the economy. Also mentioned in this context was the role of expectations and lags in fuelling speculative property development opportunities (and cycles). The standard macroeconomic forces: GDP growth, consumption, manufacturing investment, fiscal policy and so on, were all seen as important lead indicators of the respective property sectors. Financial variables were also believed to be key drivers across the industry, in particular the comparison between different asset classes, the price and availability of credit, the increased role of foreign property investment, and also the inclinations (animal spirits) of fund managers. Mention was also made of more specific local factors, be they the business and financial cluster in Edinburgh or the level of infrastructure and the spatial distribution of population in Scotland. The main drivers on the supply side related to the planning system and the preferences of local councils for types of development.

It is of course perfectly possible to reconcile the exogenous versus endogenous role of the wider property sector (the separate markets, institutions and actors) with the urban economy – in contrast to the more traditional partial equilibrium analysis of individual property markets. In fact, the property sector both influences, and is influenced by, urban and wider economic forces. In terms of economics, a general rather than a partial equilibrium framework, with feedback between sectors, is more plausible than a one-way set of relationships in either direction (between the city and the property market). Developing this theme of recursiveness, the key actor interviewees were asked whether they thought the property market constrained the performance of the economy or whether economic problems might in fact hinder property market functioning. Apart from the usual suspects (for example, the planning system), development agencies saw property as an important facilitator for economic prosperity and growth. They did acknowledge, despite a faith in the self-regulation of property markets, that development lags were a problem. It was also felt by some of the interviewees that older, obsolete industrial space constrained the development of new business and frustrated a private market for industrial space as a result of oversupply but also negative externalities – echoing some of the findings of Hill and Nowak, this volume). This negative impact was, however, argued to be lessening as a result of the sale of several public sector property portfolios. In fact, one respondent argued that it was difficult to make the connection between property and economic performance outside the housing sector, where links between bad housing and health, for instance, are well known.

A recurring theme was the constraint imposed by the small size of the Scottish economy (see also Peat and Boyle, 1999) and its weakness on certain fronts (for example, remoteness, peripherality, poor infrastructure and communications). This smallness is concerned with, on the one hand, insufficient size to reap scale economies, and on the other with a lack of demand for Scottish locations. One respondent argued that the Scottish economy did not produce either sufficient new occupiers or building choice for occupiers and that there were significant shortages of quality office space in Scottish cities. Again, the point was made about lot size – international investors are looking for major investment opportunities that do not exist in Scotland and the size of the Scottish economy is a constraint on profits and encourages investors and developers to look elsewhere. There was little evidence, however, that financial constraints were limiting the property sector.

The relationship between property and the economy means that the property sector does not simply passively respond to changes in the drivers mentioned above, but has an intimate relationship with the evolving urban and regional economy. One approach to both conceptualise and to order policy interventions between the property sector and economic development is through analysis based on the principles of market failure. In the next section of the chapter, the market failure approach to property sector policy responses is critically examined, drawing on recent experience in Scotland.

Market failure

Intervention in markets is often justified on the basis of market failure. Before the merits of specific interventions can be assessed, we need to be clear what economists mean by market failure and contrast that with the views held by policy makers. Clearly, property market policies are critically determined by the way the property market is believed to operate. Furthermore, there is a set of beliefs about the impact of intervention; for example, what consequences for the property market follow from changing land use categories, planning restrictions, or a decision by the public sector to produce factory units to meet a perceived shortage? We look at these issues in more detail below.

What is market failure?

Market failure arises when markets cannot produce socially optimal (pareto) outcomes. Thus, situations where markets are not competitive (for example, local monopolies exist), where information is limited or absent about the price or quality of a product (for example, situations of asymmetric information), where the non-rivalrous nature of certain activities means that the private sector cannot produce specific goods or services (for example, public goods) and externalities where spillovers (positive or negative), cannot be internalised by the market and sub-optimal levels of production are achieved. A second class of situations where markets literally do not work is where merit good arguments apply, that is, voter preferences (which can be conceived of as tax donor preferences) support political platforms which override the market to ensure certain social ends, such as free health care for all. This is a different perspective on the social welfare function and raises public choice issues that we do not need to go into.

It is important to stress that none of the elements of this market failure typology relate to inelastic supply. Slow adjustment on the supply side to demand shocks is generally not viewed as a market failure – it is a (relatively inefficient) process of change between equilibria as the market adjusts. However, it does often present examples of market dysfunction such as high prices and shortage which are symptomatic of supply-side constraints or slow adjustment but not market failure. However, this problem, also described as a market gap (Jones, 1996), is often the real basis for property market intervention by public agencies. This is understandable in that supply adjustment operates in a context where the long run is a long time indeed. The problem is a real one and raises a number of important problems, but it is not market failure. This needs to be stressed because the basis for intervention and the appropriate mode are clearly different and we need to separate out the two arguments because they have different consequences and implications for appropriate policy responses.

Fitting the crime?

As an example or case study of the use of a market failure typology in property sector public policy, we can observe Scottish Enterprise and its approach to market intervention. Scottish Enterprise (1996) concludes that property and land constrain place competitiveness. They cite six problems in the sector:

- A market failure in low cost premises without long leases for small, start-up firms. It is not clear whether this assertion takes full account of the existing second-hand stock, nor whether the quality of new supply in this market sector is too high and therefore unaffordable without subsidy.
- Large parts of the existing business sector stock are inflexible both in terms of space and in ICT terms. This is a strong market signal to build out-of-town low-rise developments, with cumulative and wider implications for spatial developments in urban economies.

- Derelict land is a major problem. Vacant and derelict land may emerge as a disequilibrium response to the underlying land market, as a result of poor information about contamination and may be worsened by spatial externalities and risk aversion on the part of investors and developers.
- Inadequate levels of information about the existing Scottish stock of property. This is primarily due to two factors: the price sensitivity and commercial confidentiality of property market information, but also the thinness of these highly segmented markets.
- Businesses, the space-users, have failed to articulate their emerging property demands to the development sector.
- Public sector intervention in property and land markets often leads to worse outcomes than the initial free market symptom of market failure. Information or land assembly policies are mitigated by direct public provision and regional policy, but redistributing economic activity, it is argued, often leads to displacement rather than additional economic activity (although it is not clear on what evidence this is actually based). Scottish Enterprise supports a shift towards demand-side subsidy to occupiers as one possible solution.

There is prima facie (albeit anecdotal) evidence of market failure in the property development 'cluster', that is, developers, construction firms and their suppliers.

There are different things going on in this list of property market problems. First, there is a set of informational problems: business space users failing to articulate their property needs while at the same time insufficient information exists about the existing stock (although much of it is inflexible). This will particularly hinder the small start-up firms and is also presumably what is meant by the market failure in the 'property sector cluster' – who are failing to supply what is demanded, although this may simply be a market gap and slow adjustment.

Second, derelict land reflects classic externality problems of market failure and coordination failure between land owners. In general, spatial externalities are likely to be significant forms of market failure because of the fundamental nature of urban land markets. Planning policy will in part seek to address externalities, although other forms of regulation, tax and subsidy instruments will also be used to combat underprovision caused by spillovers.

Third, Scottish Enterprise argues that previous policies have had damaging consequences for market development by both undermining rentals and displacing economic activity through both regional policy and direct provision. Hence, although Scottish Enterprise does not appear to have resolved what is a market failure and what is simply a gap or adjustment problem (and therefore requiring different types of intervention/solution), it has nonetheless come up with a flexible mechanism with which to tailor responses to land and property problems. A central tenet of market failure economics is that the intervention should fit the problem (regulation, information or support, fiscal/financial packages, or direct provision – depending on the extent or seriousness of the market failure). Equally, policies to promote supply adjustment might involve processes by which land supply is encouraged, certain regulations may be relaxed or, alternatively, demand might be stimulated by subsidy to increase price signals to suppliers in flat markets.

Scottish Enterprise has developed a framework known as RAPID (Resources and Action for Private Industrial Development) which is designed to offer graduated support depending on the level of difficulty:

- *Advice and information*: here the Local Enterprise Company (LEC) is essentially an information broker to assist the space user find premises.
- *Bank mortgage guarantees*: here the LEC helps the space user buy property by underwriting their commercial mortgage.
- *Rental guarantees*: rental income is guaranteed to the developer/investor of space which is deemed too risky given the type of occupier (for example, small start-up businesses)
- *Grants/loans*: in this case, grants or loans are provided to make a development financially feasible for the developer (presumably in a location where alternative supply for that market segment is not forthcoming).
- *Joint ventures*: the LEC shares the risk (and return) with the developer by entering into a partnership with a private sector developer (this is really a modified, intensive version of the grant/loan approach).
- *Rent concessions*: tenants receive rent concessions as an incentive and this may be tied to the rent guarantees mentioned above.
- *Direct provision of premises*: in exceptional circumstances, where the private sector will not provide, the LEC may directly develop industrial space – but this is on a very different basis from the traditional public agency industrial park.

The seven policy responses are graded in terms of the extent of state intervention. Fundamentally, however, there are two approaches involved with different depths of intervention. On the one hand, assistance is being steered toward the property development sector in terms of the efficient creation of new supply (rental guarantees; grants/loans; joint ventures and direct provision). On the other, the support is not for the property sector but for the business space user (advice/information; mortgage guarantees for owner–occupiers and rent concessions). While direct provision is deemed to be a last resort, a more proactive reading of these policies would stress the use of public finance or joint ventures to reduce the risk borne by developers or where public provision stimulates competition within the private sector. There is no evidence of the latter approach being used in Scotland (despite the claims of a market failure in the property development cluster).

This policy approach is based on two arguments – one, that policy responses have to fit the market problem and, second, that direct public provision is likely to displace more efficient and responsive market supply. The implication would seem to be that large-scale public provision of sites is not considered additional (that is, for Scotland as a whole, though by implication, it may be at local level, although this would be against the Scottish Enterprise mission to avoid its programme creating interregional competition for investment within Scotland). It is argued that direct public provision displaces economic activity either directly or indirectly through higher taxes and is less flexible or efficient than a private sector response. The merit good case for localised public provision for job creation reasons is then essentially about redistribution (via economic displacement) rather than economic performance per se, unless one is willing to invoke wider arguments about the promotion of 'soft assets' for cities associated with localised economic growth (but would such alleged positive–sum benefits to a city offset the displacement losses across the wider region?). Is this a coherent approach to advancing the competitiveness of Scottish property market locations? It certainly reflects a strong belief in the market and the role of the public body as an enabler rather than a provider. It belies a belief, also, in the validity of both the market failure framework as a diagnosis of property market constraints and that there exist feasible corrective policies that tackle the problem. Property market professionals interviewed as part of the Insignia Richard Ellis project, universally agreed with the SEN position. Consequently, direct public provision across swathes of Central Scotland is now an anachronism and has no policy role at the margin of new non-residential development.

Returning to the earlier themes of the paper, a market failure framework appears to be a useful way to analyse intervention and policy responses in the property market. It is complementary to the judicious use of the user-investment multi-sectoral model of the property sector outlined earlier, together with economic research on property as a complex commodity. Allied to institutional insights about property market processes (including those from mainstream economics), these different perspectives can actually be used as a menu of approaches to help us understand urban land and property markets processes. This rather pragmatic approach is consistent with Krugman's critique of the property market and his own mix and match approach to modelling the urban economy, drawing on more or less formal techniques and stylised facts (Boddy, 1999).

We have not fully considered the economic problems associated with intervention by the state either in general microeconomic circumstances or, more specifically, in the property sector. The public choice literature (Mueller, 1989) includes a detailed attack on the capacity of non-market organisations to have the incentives or the structures in place to render themselves economically efficient. Thus, intervention can create opportunities for rent-seeking behaviour and produce scope for worse inefficiencies than would be the case in their absence. This literature is controversial, although very influential in terms of contributions to debates about the proper role of the state, privatisation and contracting out (Heald, 1983). The pervasive intervention by the state in the property sector through mechanisms such as planning permissions and building control has been the subject of similar attacks (for example, Evans, 1988). It has not been the purpose of this chapter to assess the validity, either a priori or empirically, of these arguments. But we must acknowledge their presence and the fact that it is not enough to identify market failures per se – they have to be corrected and we must recognise that there are wider economic consequences of intervention.

Conclusion

The primary themes of this paper have concerned how land and property 'fit' into the performance of the urban economy; different approaches to modelling the property sector; and the relationship between policy interventions and the property market (and hence the urban economy's performance). The motivation for the paper stemmed from the fact that the urban property sector has been the subject of extensive intervention and, indeed, that property initiatives were the mainstay of urban policy for much of the last 20 years (for example, Turok, 1992). Planning, financial assistance, direct provision for the market and the public sector operating as an occupier – all impact on the property sector and in the urban built environment. The rationale for intervention has not always been clear or thoroughly argued. This paper has therefore sought to expose these issues to a more critical scrutiny.

The main findings from the paper's review can be summarised in the following points:

- The role of property within the urban economy is contested, but this is largely because of the partial nature of the analysis conducted by urban economists and by property analysts. Within a more general equilibrium framework, it is quite possible to conceive of the relationship as neither wholly exogenous nor endogenous.
- There are useful insights, nonetheless, from using neoclassical or institutional economic perspectives in approaching the interlinkages and nuances of the urban property sector.
- Urban economic competitiveness is also a contested term. Treated narrowly from the economics tradition it tends to be viewed in terms of protectionist zero- or negative-sum games. Analysed empirically, it is clear that urban economic competition takes place and should therefore be analysed. Recent urban economic analysis has been reinvigorated by the work of Krugman and colleagues. Although this has not been explicitly about the land and property sectors, different facets of the work, for example cumulative causation, has significant ramifications for the role and impact of the property sector within urban economies.
- In terms of economic competitiveness, property and land can be analysed as one of a set of 'hard assets', required by city-regions in order to attract and retain investment and to facilitate better economic performance. Equally, identification of the market failure of this asset may lead to corrective market interventions. The market failure framework is a useful for considering the strengths and weaknesses of individual approaches to intervention, although it is not without its limitations, notably, the question of whether the responses by state organisations are themselves beneficial.

Whether property is to be viewed as a factor of production, a driver of urban competitiveness, or as a market sector that interacts with wider economic forces in a more subtle two-way relationship, is not really the pivotal issue for urban economic competitiveness. One can use either perspective depending on the level and the location of the analysis. The perspective is very different for a body such as Scottish Enterprise as compared with a property investment house. Standing back, from the perspective of the ESRC research programme on cities, the key issue must be whether it is in fact correct to state as McGilp (2000) inter alia has, that land and property are no longer the key elements in competitiveness strategies. The broadening of the requirements of a successful contemporary strategy into explicit labour market and other, 'soft' asset, dimensions is undeniable, but it remains the case that a well-functioning land and property sector is at least a necessary condition for a durable competitive urban economy.

Notes

[1] Acknowledgements are due to the helpful comments of participants at the Competitiveness seminar at South Bank University in April 2000, as well for the detailed comments on the chapter by Glen Bramley, Geoff Meen and Benito Giordano. This research was funded by the ESRC (the 'Cities' research programme, specifically; the Central Scotland integrated case study), along with valued contributions from Scottish Homes, Scottish Enterprise and the Scottish Executive.

[2] Research carried out by the Department of Urban Studies, University of Glasgow, with Insignia Richard Ellis entitled 'The Role of Property in the Scottish Economy' by Kenneth Gibb, Daniel Mackay and Michael White.

References

Ball, M., Lizieri, C. and MacGregor, B. (1998) *The economics of commercial property markets*, London: Routledge.

Begg, I. (1999) 'Cities and competitiveness', *Urban Studies*, vol 36, no 5/6, pp 795-810.

Boddy, M. (1999) 'Geographical economics and urban competitiveness: a critique', *Urban Studies*, vol 36, no 5/6, pp 811-42.

D'Arcy, E. and Keogh, G. (1999) 'The property market and urban competitiveness', *Urban Studies*, vol 36, no 5/6, pp 917-28.

DiPasquale, D. and Wheaton, W. (1996) *Urban economics and real estate markets*, Princeton, NJ: Prentice-Hall.

Duranton, G. and Puga, D. (2000) 'Diversity and specialisation in cities: Why, where and when does it matter?', *Urban Studies*, vol 37, no 3, pp 533-55.

Evans, A. (1988) *'No Room! No Room!'*, London: Institute of Economic Affairs.

Fujita, M., Krugman, P. and Venables, A. (1999) *The spatial economy: Cities, regions and international trade*, Cambridge, MA: MIT Press.

Heald, D. (1983) *Public expenditure*, Oxford: Marion Robertson.

Healey, P. and Barrett, S. (1990) 'Structure and agency in land development processes: some ideas for research', *Urban Studies*, vol 27, no 1, pp 89-104.

Henneberry, J. (1999) 'Convergence and divergence in regional office development cycles', *Urban Studies*, vol 36, no 9, pp 1439-65.

Jones C. (1996) 'The theory of property-led land economic development policies', *Regional Studies*, vol 33, no 4, pp 797-801.

Krugman, P. (1991) *Geography and trade*, Cambridge, MA: MIT Press.

Layard, R. and Nickell, S. (1986) 'Unemployment in Britain', *Economica*, vol 53, pp S121-S69.

McDonald, J. (1997) *Fundamentals of urban economics*, Upper Saddle River, NJ: Prentice-Hall.

McGilp, N. (2000) 'Competitive locations: an introduction and overview', Scottish Property Market Report 1999, Glasgow: Scottish Enterprise.

Mueller, D. (1989) *Public choice II*, Cambridge: Cambridge University Press.

Peat, J. and Boyle, S. (1999) *An illustrated guide to the Scottish economy*, London: Duckworth.

Scottish Enterprise (1996) *Competitive locations enquiry report*, Glasgow: Scottish Enterprise.

Turok, I. (1992) 'Property-led urban regeneration: panacea or placebo?', *Environment and Planning A*, vol 24, no 2, pp 361-79.

SIX

Long-run trends in the competitiveness of British cities[1]

Iain Begg, Barry Moore and Yener Altunbas

Introduction

The UK is a heavily urbanised and, compared with most of the other OECD countries, very densely populated country. Moreover, in some parts of the country, large and small cities are clustered close together, notably in the central belt of Scotland, the heartland of England from Liverpool in the west to Hull in the east, and around London. There is a preponderance of 'older' cities that grew rapidly in the 19th century as the country industrialised, many of which owed their expansion to the development of particular industries, such as textiles, coal and steel or heavy engineering. The briefest of looks at the map of urban Britain shows that the spatial pattern of urban Britain does not conform to an obvious central-place pattern. Instead, it can be argued that the geographical locations reflect characteristics that once provided competitive advantages for traditional manufacturing, such as proximity to coal, water or industrial raw materials, or ease of access to imported materials.

These characteristics are not, however, necessarily well suited to a national economy increasingly dominated by modern service industries, with the result that the competitiveness of many cities has diminished. Their history inevitably affects their prospects and the scope for policy to improve their functioning and competitive advantage. Cities cannot easily shed their historically determined institutional, economic, social and physical structures and the performance of a city in maintaining full employment and a high quality of life for its residents is crucially determined by this legacy.

The extent and nature of a city's economic and social problems reflect not only the effective and efficient functioning of it as a place supporting the employment, income and quality of life of its residents, but also its competitiveness and role within the wider urban system. 'Competitiveness' (an abused term, Krugman [1996], argues) is, however, an elusive and slippery notion that is capable of being interpreted in different ways (Kresl, 1995; Begg, 1999). Successful cities can be defined as those that function well and compete effectively with other cities for private and public sector resources (the sources of jobs, income and quality of life). Unsuccessful cities tend to be characterised by a population loss and lack of employment or by an inability to surmount evident social and economic problems.

The aim of this chapter is to chart the long-run trends in the competitiveness of British cities, focusing primarily on their success in generating employment since the 1950s. We recognise at the outset that this only captures one component, albeit a crucial one, of competitiveness. The findings show that there are very wide variations in performance, with some cities registering substantial increases in employment while others have consistently lost jobs. There are some obvious systematic patterns over the long sweep, such as the relative decline of the large conurbations or the growth of smaller cities close to London, but there are also notable exceptions. The stability of rankings also stands out, though the fact that several cities appear to have achieved some sort of renaissance is of interest.

The next section briefly reviews the notions of competitiveness and urban performance. The following section presents the results of empirical work on trends in British cities and discusses the evolution of the British urban system. A concluding section focuses on policy implications.

What makes a city more or less competitive?

Making effective use of urban 'assets' requires the differences as well as the complementarities of cities in the urban system to be recognised. There are gains to be achieved from exploiting the characteristics that distinguish cities and give them their identity. Both specialisation and diversity can, depending on the circumstances, provide the basis for a superior economic performance as Duranton and Puga (2000) show. It is, therefore, worth reflecting on what it is that makes individual cities more or less competitive.

The implications for inter-urban performance of long-term sectoral restructuring, such as the post-war shift towards a more service orientated economy, have been addressed by Suarez-Villa (1988), who argued that sectoral restructuring can be expected to have important implications for the size distribution of cities and the urban system in general. Agglomeration (dis)economies play an important role in determining the spatial tendencies of many industries and, in particular, point to the decentralisation of manufacturing from larger to smaller cities as they start to decline. The reduced importance of increasing returns technologies has run parallel to the relative decline of manufacturing, as customised production, smaller factories and a growing emphasis on informational products have displaced traditional smoke-stack industries (Glaeser, 1998). Declining freight bills have also worked to end the link between cities and increasing returns/high transport costs industries. In 1990 in the US, only two out of the eight largest cities had a larger share of manufacturing than the US average (Glaeser, 1998).

Increases in manufacturing productivity due to organisational and technological advances and the segmentation of production processes also permit some industries to be more footloose. Henderson (1983) suggests that for many newly emerging industries, localisation rather than urbanisation economies may become more important, reflecting greater intra-industry specialisation, labour market economies for industry specific skills and significant collaboration between firms on innovation and operational strategies. At the same time, location in the medium-size cities in the hinterland of the larger cities may become increasingly attractive through lower costs vis-à-vis the metropolis. The vehicles for such change are branch plants (back-office functions in service industries), and mergers and acquisitions (Massey and Allen, 1988).

The shift of many advanced economies from material production to knowledge-intensive activities, which exhibit strong agglomeration economies, also contributes to an explanation of the emergence and long-run growth of, for example, high-technology activities in relatively dynamic cities such as Cambridge and higher order management functions in the financial services in the City of London (Fujita, 1996). Fujita stresses the importance of the transfer of tacit knowledge through face-to-face communications and the competitive advantages that a city can derive from a heterogeneous labour force. He further argues that because variety in people is a crucial factor encouraging human communication, unless a city (economy) is constantly supplied with such people, convergence in knowledge/information will occur and this source of increasing returns will eventually diminish.

Black and Henderson (1997) model the evolution of cities within which there are knowledge spillovers as well as scale externalities. Cities grow with individual human capital accumulation and local knowledge spillovers, which accentuate the scale economies of urbanisation. At the same time cities grow in number if population growth is fast enough such that the rate of city expansion cannot accommodate the expanding national population. Simon and Nardinelli (1996) in their study of the growth of English cities from 1861 to 1961 conclude that human capital (defined as the skills connected with the production and spread of information), exerted a systematic influence on the long-run growth of cities. Cities with greater concentrations of highly educated individuals should become relatively more productive and increase in population. They also argue that, at the level of the nation, it is the growth of real income per capita that indicates economic success. However given the tendency in the long run for real incomes to equalise across cities within a nation one should look at population (quantities), not real incomes, as a measure of city success and performance. In a subsequent paper on US cities Simon (1998) also found a positive relationship between employment growth and the average level of human capital across the US over the period 1940-86.

Specialisation

The mix of activity in any location – city, region or country – will inevitably influence its overall performance. However, because specialisation can work in diverse ways, it does not follow that being relatively specialised in activities that are apparently unattractive is always a problem. There is, first, a purely arithmetic argument. If some areas have a disproportionate share of a particular activity, others will appear to be under-represented. Thus, in financial services – an industry that is widely assumed to be a desirable specialisation – London dominates, but other cities have been able to compete in these industries without attaining the degree of specialisation achieved by the capital. The other side of the calculation is that if a city is under-represented in one industry, it must necessarily be over-represented in others. Some care is needed, therefore, in computing and interpreting specialisation or in relating it to expected values for a type of city.

A second issue is niche markets: specialisation may be very narrow, yet still represent a local strength, as is the case for asset management in Edinburgh or legal services in the Leeds/Bradford area. Specialisations may, moreover, be in segments of industries that are losing ground overall, but in which the niche is a particularly successful one. High value clothing or speciality steels are examples of markets in which a city (or region) may be able to nurture a cluster of activity. Equally a broad but vulnerable specialisation – especially one which has been diminishing – may be symptomatic of a decline in competitiveness and thus a cause for concern. Cities dependent on a few major industries will struggle if those industries start to decline, and the enduring problems of cities in which traditional industries were prominent testifies to this phenomenon.

Consequently, the analysis of specialisation has to be conducted with care to avoid drawing misleading conclusions. Orthodox theory suggests that by specialising in areas of comparative advantage, cities will ultimately achieve the best outcomes. Yet there are grounds for believing that it is better, bearing in mind the caveats raised above, to shift towards the more dynamic and successful industries. A related issue is the degree to which diversity should be sought. A diversified economy is plainly less vulnerable to the vagaries of individual industries, but in a comparatively small urban economy there may be a trade-off between diversity and agglomeration benefits. The latter may only surface if an industry is on a sufficient scale to generate the pools of labour and the subcontracting networks that underpin economies of scale. Alternatively, this may occur if the city is able to offer conditions that encourage clustering and the informal networks that have been associated with innovation in the literature on *milieux innovateurs* (Jacobs, 1969; Glaeser et al, 1992; Duranton and Puga, 2000; Gordon and McCann, 2000).

In an earlier paper, one of the authors (Begg, 1999) suggested that there are four categories of determinants of urban competitiveness, some of which are top down, while others depend on the characteristics of the city, notably those that shape the local business environment. The recent burgeoning literature on urban growth and performance, particularly that which draws its inspiration from endogenous growth theories, supports the above characterisation of sources of urban competitive advantage. There are, thus, disparate ways of appraising urban competitiveness and measuring the performance of a city, and it follows that different empirical approaches will be appropriate depending on the purpose of the exercise. The authors argue that there are at least three conceptual approaches that can be adopted. The first is to measure outcomes on key economic variables; the second is to look at intermediate measures which signal how well the city is competing in the modern economy; while the third is to look at broader measures of well-being or quality of life. An appreciation of the urban system as a whole is also useful.

Indicators that measure outcomes, such as either the rate of growth (of output, income or employment) or success in maintaining employment or unemployment rates better than the national average (or some other benchmark) are the most direct way of assessing performance. These have differing characteristics, but will tend to be correlated with one another. Output measures the performance of the city as a production centre, rather than as a place of residence and it is worth noting that larger cities, of which London is the leading example in the UK, draw in labour from outside the city, which adds to the resident workforce. This, combined with the diversity of their economies, means that they are less vulnerable to external shocks. Although population growth and employment growth are not necessarily closely correlated, successful cities tend to attract a growing share of the national population. Unemployment, as the balance between two much larger numbers (labour demand and supply), will be influenced by trends in both magnitudes, although it is not unreasonable to equate high unemployment with 'poor' performance.

A richer interpretation of performance might draw on the notions of equilibrium, polarisation and quality of life. A balanced city is one in which demand and supply are reasonably matched and even where there has been a fall in employment, a contrast can be drawn between cities for which the loss of jobs is matched by a fall in the economically active population and those where it leads to unemployment. A very congested city – Cambridge is, arguably, an example – is one in which the average quality of life may well be diminished in spite of highly favourable economic indicators. Polarisation within many large cities is evident in the conjunction of affluence and deprivation, and is often associated with increased costs of personal security or fear of crime. However, this is beyond the scope of the present chapter.

Empirical work

Approach and methodology

Bearing in mind the various possible meanings of 'performance' and 'competitiveness', there are a variety of ways to measure how well a city is doing. Here, the authors predominantly focus on population, and employment and unemployment trends, largely using descriptive material.

Data and classifications

Because of changes in industrial classifications and local authority boundaries, it is difficult to obtain consistently defined data over the long term. Two main data sources were used in the present study: the Population Census, which provides figures on demography and various household indicators for 1951 to 1991 at ten-year intervals; and the Employment Census (later Annual Employment Survey). The last Population Census was conducted in 1991, and various data were therefore used to obtain estimates for 1997, in order to bring the research more up to date. The first year for which employment data were obtained is 1959, and this has been complemented by data for 1971, 1981, 1991 and later years up to 1997.

In order to define cities, all settlements with a population in excess of 65,000 (an arbitrary cut-off point) were included. The urban areas in question were as shown in *Key Statistics for Urban Areas* publications for different parts of the country from the 1991 Census of Population.[2] These urban areas were then matched as closely as possible to local authority districts (LAD) on the boundaries in force in 1991. The result was a list of 109 cities, most of which coincide with recognised city boundaries. For some areas, however, the resulting cities bring together more disparate urban settlements. An extreme case is the West Yorkshire conurbation which combines Leeds and Bradford, two cities with separate traditions. Similarly, the Brighton urban area is made up of contiguous settlements of Brighton, Hove, Littlehampton and Worthing, and the advice given to us by the Bristol ICS team was to amalgamate all the settlements around the Avon into a composite 'Bristol urban area'. In London, the built-up area stretches marginally beyond the usual definition of the city in terms of the GLC area to encompass certain adjacent districts in Surrey and Hertfordshire.

For some cities, and especially those that have seen substantial expansion, the effect of this approach is to include some rural hinterland in the definition, an outcome which is unavoidable unless much finer spatial disaggregations are used. Thus, the Cambridge urban area comprises the districts of Cambridge and South Cambridgeshire. The latter was largely rural in the 1950s, but the growth of the Cambridge economy has seen considerable expansion of the villages surrounding the city and much of the green space between villages has disappeared. Much the same is true of our constructed 'North Hampshire urban area'.

For later years, Employment Census data are readily available on the 1991 LAD boundaries, but for earlier years the boundaries are based on (more numerous) employment exchange areas. These had to be matched as closely as possible to cities based on LADs. In a small number of cases, the matching may not be entirely perfect. For the Population Census, the project has benefited from the careful work of Dorling (see, for example, Dorling, 1995) who established longitudinal data based on the local authority areas (LAA) in force in 1951.[3] These are over three times more numerous than LADs, but the great advantage is that Dorling has generated consistent data on these boundaries for 1971, 1981 and 1991. For present purposes the 1951 data have been added. Once again, an exercise to match these boundaries as closely as possible to the 1991 LAD boundaries was carried out. For some cities, the matching is imperfect with the result that boundaries used for the employment and population statistics differ slightly. Since the focus of the research is on change rather than levels this is not a major problem.

For industrial classifications, change over a 40-year period is considerable, with not only the emergence of new industries but also the evolution of existing ones. Both factors give rise to revisions of the classifications with areas of industries sometimes being shifted from one part of the classification to another. The approach adopted to deal with this was to look for the maximum disaggregation consistent with having the same activities in a group across time spanning the four changes in classifications that have occurred since the 1950s. It is a measure of the fluidity in these classifications that just 32 industries could be unambiguously identified in this way and some of the industries that have had to be merged together are somewhat eccentric bedfellows. In addition a separate series – which is shown simply as a 33rd industry – has been estimated for self-employment. While the disaggregation over time is limited, a much more detailed breakdown of activity can be achieved either for a single year of the data or for years close together.

Various other indicators have also been assembled to provide clues to the determinants of competitiveness. These include geographical attributes, information on the breakdown of industry by city, VAT registrations and deregistrations, policy variables, and variables such as airport access or presence of universities.

Analyses

Most of the findings presented in this paper are confined to simple descriptions of trends, using tabulations of variables, aggregations into relevant geographical groupings and measures of statistical association. The results of shift-share analyses are also presented for different periods to give some insight into the explanations for trends in performance.

Results

Because population and employment tend to be correlated, there is inevitably a similar story to be told whichever is examined. Examination of trends in the working-age population or the economically active also paints much the same picture. Unemployment, however, depends on the interaction between the labour force and the demand for labour and can, therefore, elucidate different facets of competitiveness.

Population

Over the full period from 1951 to 1997, there have been big shifts in population. Urban Britain (the 109 cities as we have defined them, with some rural hinterland included for certain cities for reasons explained above) as a whole has seen its total population increase marginally as total population grew, but has seen its share of the national total decline from 73 per cent to 67 per cent. This shift in favour of smaller towns and rural areas is principally attributable to the exodus of population from the seven major conurbations.[4] Between them, these cities actually lost some two million residents between 1951 and 1997, just over 10 per cent of the 1951 total. All the other classes of cities gained in population, though as Table 6.1 shows, there are significant disparities between the groupings. Both the larger 'free-standing' cities and the smaller cities in the 'North' lost some residents in the 1980s, whereas the smaller cities in the 'South' and the new towns gained substantial numbers of residents in each sub-period from 1951 to 1997.

Since the whole point of new towns was to absorb part of the population, there is little to be said about their expansion, but the difference between the northern and southern smaller cities is one of the most striking findings. These aggregates, inevitably, mask disparities in population trends and, as the tables for individual cities make clear, there is a wide discrepancy in performance. Thus, among the conurbations, Merseyside and Glasgow have lost population consistently, but three others (London, West Yorkshire and Greater Manchester) seem to have turned a corner in the 1990s.

Unemployment

Data on trends in unemployment (Table 6.2) show that it tends to be most heavily concentrated in urban areas. Table 6.3 presents summary indicators of the unemployment to population ratio.[5] From the table it can be seen that unemployment is most acute in the large conurbations and has, moreover, become relatively more prevalent in these cities. This is especially true of Merseyside and Glasgow, both of which have concentrations of unemployment nearly double the national average in 1997. There has also been a relative rise in unemployment in the free-

Table 6.1: Trends in population by city type

	Population			Change (%)				Share (% of GB total)	
	1951	1991	1997 (est)	1951-97	1951-81	1981-91	1991-97	1951	1997
Conurbations	19,395,461	17,185,453	17,417,605	-10.2	-9.8	-1.7	1.4	39.7	31.1
Free-standing	7,760,636	8,511,023	8,656,146	11.5	9.2	0.5	1.7	15.9	15.5
'Northern' smaller	2,419,420	2,422,063	2,428,509	0.4	1.1	-1.0	0.3	5.0	4.3
'Southern' smaller	3,350,227	4,818,482	4,954,307	47.9	37.5	4.6	2.8	6.9	8.8
Expanded	1,202,404	1,723,429	1,759,635	46.3	37.1	4.5	2.1	2.5	3.1
New towns	700,521	1,489,023	1,537,040	119.4	88.9	12.5	3.2	1.4	2.7
Coastal	903,342	1,145,405	1,173,182	29.9	19.4	6.2	2.4	1.8	2.1
Great Britain	48,840,704	54,855,760	56,022,436	14.7	9.7	2.4	2.1	100.0	100.0

Table 6.2: Trends in unemployment by city type

	Unemployment			Change (%)				Share (% of GB total)	
Total	1951	1991	1997	1951-97	1951-81	1981-91	1991-97	1951	1997
Conurbations	199,904	973,818	781,354	290.9	375.5	2.4	-19.8	42.1	40.7
Free-standing	72,988	400,928	309,123	323.5	471.1	-3.8	-22.9	15.4	16.1
'Northern' smaller	25,651	108,745	78,642	206.6	398.6	-15.0	-27.7	5.4	4.1
'Southern' smaller	24,078	192,272	145,890	505.9	613.2	12.0	-24.1	5.1	7.6
Expanded	13,001	74,875	50,694	289.9	499.2	-3.9	-32.3	2.7	2.6
New towns	3,636	65,020	44,408	1121.3	1586.1	6.1	-31.7	0.8	2.3
Coastal	14,293	44,502	39,914	179.3	211.5	0.0	-10.3	3.0	2.1
Great Britain	475,353	2,482,071	1,920,098	303.9	425.0	-0.5	-22.6	100.0	100.0

standing cities since 1971, whereas both groups of smaller cities have improved relatively. The coastal towns have, however, seen a relative worsening of their position in the 1990s, with areas such as Thanet, the East Anglian ports and Blackpool standing out.

Employment

The shifts in population that have occurred in the post-war period are, on the whole, mirrored in employment trends. Indeed, the rate of decline in total employment in the conurbations between 1959 and 1997 was more rapid than the population loss (Table 6.4). There has been a modest recovery in the 1990s, although this is accounted for principally by an apparent turnaround in London's fortunes: in aggregate the growth in employment in conurbations between 1991 and 1997 was marginally below the national rate. Glasgow and Merseyside are again shown to be the worst performers, with further job losses of 1.4 per cent and 4.9 per cent respectively, in spite of the national upturn. The performance of the West Yorkshire and Greater Manchester conurbations in the 1990s is more encouraging, but the stabilisation of employment in the West Midlands may be precarious given the problems at Rover. Similar fears can be expressed about Tyneside.

The main winners in the employment stakes are the smaller cities in the South and both groups of new towns. The group of smaller southern cities increased its employment by 51 per cent between 1959 and 1997, and it is striking that this has not only been a consistent trend over time, but is also true for most of the cities within a group that is defined purely

Table 6.3: Trends in unemployment ratio by city type (unemployed as % of total population)

	1951	1971	1981	1991	1997 (est)
Conurbations	1.033	2.721	5.447	5.681	4.495
Free-standing	0.962	2.466	5.028	4.836	3.666
'Northern' smaller	1.108	2.792	5.620	4.843	3.500
'Southern' smaller	0.672	1.852	3.463	3.733	2.750
Expanded	1.081	2.450	4.725	4.345	2.881
New towns	0.509	1.777	4.556	4.228	2.831
Coastal	1.623	2.808	4.268	4.022	3.528
Great Britain	0.973	2.421	4.660	4.525	3.427

Table 6.4: Trends in employment by city type

	Employment, including self-employment					Change (%)				Share (% of GB total)	
	1959	1971	1981	1991	1997	59-97	59-81	81-91	91-97	1959	1997
Conurbations	10,165,144	9,517,476	8,495,363	8,445,313	8,767,343	-13.8	-16.4	-0.6	3.8	44.9	34.0
Free-standing	3,598,231	3,868,482	3,698,042	3,931,766	4,037,918	12.2	2.8	6.3	2.7	15.9	15.7
'Northern'	1,211,010	1,238,410	1,140,142	1,181,878	1,202,948	-0.7	-5.9	3.7	1.8	5.4	4.7
'Southern'	1,612,210	1,961,268	1,979,610	2,301,181	2,430,347	50.7	22.8	16.2	5.6	7.1	9.4
Expanded	561,670	637,671	668,507	749,267	818,450	45.7	19.0	12.1	9.2	2.5	3.2
New towns	389,464	544,573	592,606	765,296	881,313	126.3	52.2	29.1	15.2	1.7	3.4
Coastal	372,513	416,814	396,281	464,241	457,253	22.7	6.4	17.1	-1.5	1.6	1.8
Great Britain	22,628,300	23,476,254	23,208,468	24,646,884	25,775,164	13.9	2.6	6.2	4.6	100.0	100.0

in terms of geography. The contrast with the smaller northern cities is evident, as the latter group underperforms in each of the sub-periods. What is also striking is how many of the smaller cities in the North conform to this pattern and, by the same token, how few in the South do not.

What is also striking about the results is the consistency of the performance patterns across periods (see also Turok and Edge, 1999). The stability of rankings has been assessed using a simple Spearman rank correlation test for pairs of periods and in all cases the outcome is a correlation coefficient that is statistically highly significant, implying that the rate of change in one period is a good predictor of growth in other periods.

To obtain an overview of growth trends, the 109 cities were grouped (Box 6.1) according to their performance relative to the urban average in successive periods (1959-71, 1971-81, 1981-91 and 1991-97). The rationale for constructing these groupings relative to the urban average rather than taking either absolute change or change relative to GB is that this approach provides a means of identifying which cities have performed relatively well or poorly compared with a null hypothesis that all should perform identically. The groups are:

- *Steady growth*: cities that have exceeded the urban GB average in each of the four periods distinguished.
- *Steady decline*: cities that have been below the urban GB average.
- *Recovering*: cities that have improved latterly by exceeding the average in the later periods.
- *Backsliding*: cities that have lost ground in later sub-periods.
- *Unstable*: cities that have been above average in some periods and below in other, without displaying a consistent pattern.

Although these groupings are based on a fairly crude benchmarking exercise, the results are, nevertheless, revealing. 'Steady growers' are predominantly new towns and smaller cities in the South of Britain, whereas 'steady decliners' are the familiar conurbations in the North, together with a number of cities that have obvious connections with declining industries, such as Mansfield (coal) or Dundee (textiles). That there is only a small number of 'recovering' cities is also revealing, although as two of them are London and the West Yorkshire conurbation (both of which are relatively specialised in key business services), they represent a sizeable proportion of aggregate 'urban Britain'. The 'backsliders' are a much more mixed bunch, comprising cities of different sizes and from all

Box 6.1: Cities according to growth classes (based on changes in total employment)

Steadily growing	Steadily declining	Recovering	Backsliding	Unstable
Brighton Urban Area	West Midlands	Greater London	Edinburgh	Nottingham
Leicester	Greater Manchester	West Yorkshire	Blackpool	Bristol Urban Area
Reading/ Wokingham	Merseyside	Halifax	Plymouth	Teesside
Bournemouth	Glasgow	Accrington	The Medway Towns	Southend
Preston	Tyneside		Derby	Wigan
Southampton	Sheffield		Aberdeen	Portsmouth
Slough	Coventry		Grimsby/ Cleethorpes	Doncaster
Cambridge Urban Area	The Potteries		Kirkcaldy	Luton/ Dunstable
Warrington	Sunderland		Maidstone	Cardiff
Northampton	Swansea		Bedford	Dearne Valley
Milton Keynes	Kingston upon Hull		Norwich	Gravesend/ Grays
Swindon	Motherwell/ Hamilton		Ipswich/ Martlesham Heath	Gosport/ Fareham
North Hampshire Urban Area	Burnley/ Nelson		Oxford	Chesterfield/ Staveley/ Wingerworth
High Wycombe	Dundee		Lowestoft	Hastings/ Bexhill
Peterborough	Falkirk		Crewe	Basildon

Box 6.1: contd.../

Steadily growing	Steadily declining	Recovering	Backsliding	Unstable
Harrogate	Coatbridge/ Airdrie Urban Area		Chelmsford	Blackburn
Colchester	Mansfield		Shrewsbury	Newport (Gwent)
Livingston/ Bathgate	Hartlepool		Cannock	Dunfermline
Telford	Inverclyde		Great Yarmouth	Morecambe/ Lancaster
St Albans			East Kilbride	Thanet
Runcorn			Eastbourne	Guildford
Torbay/ Paignton			Cumbernauld New Town	Cheltenham
Warwick/ Leamington				Carlisle
Chester				Darlington
Gloucester				York
Exeter				Hatfield
Pontypool/ Cwmbran				Worcester
Gatwick Urban Area				Rhondda
Lincoln				Islwyn
Redditch				Scunthorpe
Stevenage				
Harlow				
Brentwood				
Tamworth				

regions, although it is perhaps significant that some new towns are included in the group. 'Unstable cities' is also a diverse grouping and there is no immediately obvious pattern within it.

The authors also examined the spread of growth rates in successive sub-periods. Although the mean and median growth rates differed between periods, the variances were only higher in the first of our sub-periods, 1959-81. Moreover, this higher variance was largely attributable to the very rapid growth of new towns: excluding them from the calculation meant that there was not a statistically significant difference in the variances between periods. The inference to draw from this finding is that although there are fluctuations in the performances of individual cities from one period to another, there is no evidence of a convergence in growth rates. Indeed, the persistently better performance of the group of steady growers testifies to a substantial long-term shift in the British urban system.

Explaining change

Although, as indicated above, geography seems to have been an important factor in explaining urban performance, many other reasons for trends can be adduced. The broad trends in urban performance are broken down in shift-share analyses (Tables 6.5-6.9) into the usual 'structural' and 'differential' components. The latter is often presumed to be a crude measure of competitiveness in that it indicates that a city has exceeded expectations of how it ought to perform given its industrial structure. Looking at the long-run shift share analysis 1959-97 (Table 6.5), all the cities with the most rapid growth of employment have strongly positive differential components, and vice versa. Structure, too, plays an important role for many cities, explaining a substantial part of the decline of many. Variations between classes of cities have been calculated using a number of different geographical criteria. In each of these groupings, employment has been aggregated across the cities that form each class to give a measure of change in the urban areas in the particular geographical grouping. Thus, Table 6.6 shows shift-share results by region, although it should be noted that this measures only urban areas in that region, not the whole of the region. Over the long term (1959-97), urban areas in the South East and the South West have benefited from a favourable industrial structure and, together with cities in the eastern region, exhibit the most positive differential components. The usual suspects (North East, North West, Scotland and Wales) have negative differential and structural components, while London's favourable structure is more than offset by a very highly negative differential component. These regional patterns are broadly

Table 6.5: Shift-share analysis by city (1959-97 – total employment including the self-employed %)

City name	National	Industry mix	Differential	Total
North Hampshire Urban Area	13.9	27.7	78.4	120.0
Cambridge Urban Area	13.9	18.4	67.1	99.4
Swindon	13.9	-19.1	103.6	98.4
St Albans	13.9	19.3	53.2	86.5
Maidstone	13.9	10.6	60.0	84.5
Inverness	13.9	26.6	40.5	81.0
Cheltenham	13.9	8.8	57.9	80.7
Exeter	13.9	26.7	39.3	79.9
Brentwood	13.9	28.3	37.3	79.6
Harrogate	13.9	29.3	34.7	77.9
Warwick/Leamington	13.9	8.7	54.8	77.4
Colchester	13.9	14.7	42.4	71.0
Guildford	13.9	14.8	39.2	67.9
Bedford	13.9	5.8	47.4	67.1
Aberdeen	13.9	5.3	46.4	65.6
Chelmsford	13.9	7.2	43.9	65.0
Southampton	13.9	1.2	47.7	62.8
Ipswich/Martlesham Heath	13.9	-0.2	46.4	60.1
High Wycombe	13.9	1.4	43.2	58.6
Slough	13.9	0.3	39.6	53.8
Torbay/Paignton	13.9	41.9	-4.4	51.4
Southend	13.9	24.9	9.7	48.5
Lincoln	13.9	-1.0	35.6	48.5
Brighton Urban Area	13.9	25.6	7.5	47.0
Gosport/Fareham	13.9	5.6	27.5	47.0
Bournemouth	13.9	26.2	4.5	44.5
Portsmouth	13.9	8.9	20.3	43.1
Bristol Urban Area	13.9	5.0	21.6	40.5
Norwich	13.9	-2.3	25.8	37.4
Chester	13.9	18.4	4.8	37.1
Gloucester	13.9	-9.7	32.3	36.4
Shrewsbury	13.9	25.6	-5.0	34.5
York	13.9	4.9	15.2	34.0

Table 6.5: contd.../

City name	National	Industry mix	Differential	Total
Lowestoft	13.9	-9.1	27.1	31.8
Cardiff	13.9	15.2	-2.2	26.9
Hastings/Bexhill	13.9	34.6	-22.5	26.0
Great Yarmouth	13.9	9.0	2.6	25.5
Eastbourne	13.9	49.8	-39.6	24.1
The Medway Towns	13.9	-4.2	13.3	23.1
Plymouth	13.9	7.3	1.4	22.6
Blackpool	13.9	27.9	-20.2	21.6
Oxford	13.9	6.2	1.0	21.1
Leicester	13.9	-19.3	26.4	21.0
Worcester	13.9	11.1	-4.6	20.5
Nottingham	13.9	-11.7	15.8	18.0
Cannock	13.9	-46.9	50.8	17.8
Luton/Dunstable	13.9	-33.2	37.0	17.7
Edinburgh	13.9	11.7	-9.9	15.6
Grimsby/Cleethorpes	13.9	-5.4	6.7	15.2
Thanet	13.9	34.3	-34.1	14.2
Dearne Valley	13.9	-34.1	30.4	10.3
Gravesend/Grays	13.9	-9.6	3.6	8.0
Blackburn	13.9	-14.0	7.9	7.9
Mansfield	13.9	-37.8	28.7	4.9
Crewe	13.9	-24.8	14.9	4.0
Carlisle	13.9	11.3	-22.3	3.0
West Yorkshire	13.9	-18.4	7.2	2.6
Islwyn	13.9	-50.9	39.0	1.9
Teesside	13.9	-16.7	3.0	0.3
Derby	13.9	-23.4	8.6	-0.9
Scunthorpe	13.9	-30.4	15.0	-1.5
Morecambe/Lancaster	13.9	12.1	-27.6	-1.6
Newport (Gwent)	13.9	8.4	-24.1	-1.8
Coventry	13.9	-33.5	17.4	-2.2
Dunfermline	13.9	-30.9	12.1	-4.9
Darlington	13.9	-13.5	-7.1	-6.7
Kingston upon Hull	13.9	-2.8	-20.2	-9.0
Falkirk	13.9	-19.3	-4.3	-9.7

Table 6.5: contd.../

City name	National	Industry mix	Differential	Total
Chesterfield/Staveley/Wingerworth	13.9	-31.0	7.2	-9.9
Doncaster	13.9	-36.0	11.4	-10.8
West Midlands	13.9	-16.6	-8.4	-11.1
Halifax	13.9	-31.0	4.9	-12.2
The Potteries	13.9	-22.5	-3.8	-12.3
Greater Manchester	13.9	-11.8	-14.7	-12.6
Greater London	13.9	21.4	-48.0	-12.7
Tyneside	13.9	-12.1	-15.7	-13.9
Motherwell / Hamilton	13.9	-11.5	-16.3	-13.9
Coatbridge/Airdrie Urban Area	13.9	-22.0	-6.3	-14.4
Hartlepool	13.9	-11.9	-16.5	-14.5
Accrington	13.9	-28.6	-2.4	-17.1
Dundee	13.9	-9.6	-22.6	-18.3
Swansea	13.9	-19.8	-14.9	-20.8
Sheffield	13.9	-19.3	-16.4	-21.8
Burnley/Nelson	13.9	-32.7	-6.8	-25.6
Inverclyde	13.9	-17.5	-22.5	-26.1
Glasgow	13.9	-4.3	-38.7	-29.0
Merseyside	13.9	1.9	-46.0	-30.2
Rhondda	13.9	-29.8	-39.1	-55.0
New and Enlarged Towns				
Milton Keynes	13.9	-20.9	361.0	354.0
Basildon	13.9	-7.2	206.4	213.1
Cumbernauld New Town	13.9	-34.0	208.7	188.6
Tamworth	13.9	-12.5	143.3	144.8
Gatwick Urban Area	13.9	-1.6	127.5	139.9
Telford	13.9	-16.5	139.2	136.6
Stevenage	13.9	-28.0	143.7	129.7
Reading/Wokingham	13.9	21.8	91.8	127.6
Redditch	13.9	-27.2	127.4	114.1
East Kilbride	13.9	-20.0	120.0	113.9
Harlow	13.9	-11.5	104.8	107.2
Peterborough	13.9	-19.9	108.3	102.3
Livingston/Bathgate	13.9	-18.6	100.8	96.1

Table 6.5: contd.../

City name	National	Industry mix	Differential	Total
Northampton	13.9	-6.5	82.8	90.3
Warrington	13.9	-11.0	67.1	70.0
Hatfield	13.9	-23.5	79.0	69.4
Runcorn	13.9	-20.1	65.4	59.2
Pontypool/Cwmbran	13.9	-43.5	48.7	19.1
Preston	13.9	-14.5	11.2	10.6
Kirkcaldy	13.9	-23.6	18.8	9.1
Wigan	13.9	-31.6	13.2	-4.5
Sunderland	13.9	-21.8	1.8	-6.1

replicated in the shift–share results for 1981–87, but some notable changes occur in the 1991–97 period. The signs of the differential components switch for London (which appears to have recovered competitiveness on this measure) and the West Midlands cities (which become negative).[6]

Using the same geographical breakdown as shown in Tables 6.1 to 6.4, Table 6.7 highlights the extent of the difference between cities of different sizes. The strongly negative differential component for the conurbations is striking evidence of a decline in competitiveness over the long term, as the structure of employment in the conurbations has consistently been favourable. However, the recovery of London and West Yorkshire is reflected in the positive differential component for the 1991–97 shift share. Strong disparities are evident between the small northern cities and their southern counterparts. The former suffer from an adverse industrial structure, while for the latter the structure has been broadly neutral. But the southern smaller cities have exhibited a very strong competitiveness that has clearly underpinned their comparative growth in successive sub-periods.

In Table 6.8, the cities are divided into growth classes and it is striking how strong the differential component is for the steady growers. By contrast, the steady decliners have been affected both by a 'wrong' structure and by adverse competitiveness. It is also noteworthy that the small towns and rural areas (that is the residual of GB employment) have shown themselves to be competitive without having a favourable structure.

Table 6.9 shows how proximity to London is a strong feature of competitiveness, as revealed by the contrast between the differential components. To some extent, this finding corresponds to the regional results shown in Table 6.5, but it suggests more emphatically that cities

Table 6.6a: Shift-share analysis by regions (1959-97)

Regions	Level of employment					Change (%) 1959-97	Shift-share	
	1959	1971	1981	1991	1997		Industry mix	Differential
North East	160,875	160,593	143,632	147,462	146,325	-9.0	-14.8	-8.2
Yorkshire and Humberside	186,240	184,722	169,445	175,221	182,174	-2.2	-18.1	2.0
East Midlands	111,255	121,991	120,130	126,807	132,871	19.4	-17.7	23.2
East of England	43,633	56,833	57,648	68,825	73,056	67.4	-3.9	57.4
South East	68,968	84,895	88,212	104,080	112,682	63.4	11.6	37.8
South West	92,656	112,887	110,387	128,280	137,416	48.3	8.9	25.5
West Midlands	182,188	192,269	171,879	178,089	182,126	0.0	-17.2	3.3
North West	202,708	198,508	176,278	179,832	182,020	-10.2	-7.6	-16.5
Wales	76,052	79,428	70,026	74,684	75,362	-0.9	-7.8	-7.0
Scotland	121,269	119,573	113,916	114,725	113,709	-6.2	-5.4	-14.8
Greater London	5,003241	4,497,762	4,115,173	4,082,190	4,368,471	-12.7	21.4	-48.0
Small towns and rural	4,737143	5,316,120	6,270,535	6,807,942	7,179,592	51.6	-0.4	38.0
Great Britain	22,628,300	23,476,254	23,208,468	24,646,884	25,775,164	13.9		
Urban area	17,891,156	18,160,134	16,937,932	17,838,942	1,859,5572	3.9		

Table 6.6b: Shift-share analysis by regions (1959-97 by sub periods)

Regions	1959-81 Industry	1959-81 Differential	1959-81 Total	1981-97 Industry	1981-97 Differential	1981-97 Total	1991-97 Industry	1991-97 Differential	1991-97 Total
North East	-8.8	-4.5	-10.7	-2.9	-6.3	1.9	1.7	-7.1	-0.8
Yorkshire and Humberside	-11.0	-0.6	-9.0	-7.4	3.8	7.5	-0.6	0.0	4.0
East Midlands	-10.1	15.6	8.0	-8.3	7.9	10.6	-1.3	1.5	4.8
East of England	-0.9	30.5	32.1	-1.1	16.8	26.7	-0.1	1.6	6.1
South East	5.7	19.6	27.9	1.6	15.1	27.7	1.2	2.5	8.3
South West	5.0	11.6	19.1	1.2	12.2	24.5	1.1	1.5	7.1
West Midlands	-8.7	0.5	-5.7	-6.8	1.7	6.0	0.3	-2.6	2.3
North West	-4.7	-11.0	-13.0	-2.3	-5.5	3.3	0.5	-3.8	1.2
Wales	-4.5	-6.0	-7.9	0.9	-4.4	7.6	2.7	-6.4	0.9
Scotland	-3.3	-5.3	-6.1	-0.8	-10.5	-0.2	0.8	-6.2	-0.9
Greater London	13.9	-34.2	-17.7	6.9	-11.8	6.2	2.5	0.0	7.0
Small towns and rural	-1.8	31.6	32.4	1.4	2.1	14.5	-2.5	3.3	5.5
National	2.6			11.1			4.6		

Table 6.7a: Shift-share analysis by city types (1959-97)

City types	Level of employment						Change (%) 1959-97	Industry mix 1959-97	Differential 1959-97
	1959	1971	1981	1991	1997				
Conurbations	1,452,163	1,359,639	1,213,623	1,206,473	1,252,478		-13.8	5.0	-32.6
Free-standing	171,344	184,213	176,097	187,227	192,282		12.2	-7.8	6.2
Northern	54,178	55,175	50,342	51,386	52,302		-3.5	-15.5	-1.9
Southern	53,740	65,376	65,987	76,706	81,012		50.7	1.0	35.9
Expanded	70,209	79,709	83,563	93,658	102,306		45.7	-12.2	44.0
New towns	29,959	41,890	45,585	58,869	67,793		126.3	-15.8	128.2
Coastal	46,564	52,102	49,535	58,030	57,157		22.7	25.3	-16.5
Small towns and rural	4,737,143	5,316,120	6,270,535	6,807,942	7,179,592		51.6	-0.4	38.0
Great Britain	22,628,300	23,476,254	23,208,468	24,646,884	2,577,5164		13.9		
Urban area	17,891,156	18,160,134	16,937,932	17,838,942	18,595,572		3.9		

Table 6.7b: Shift-share analysis by city types (1959-97 by sub periods)

City types	1959-81 Industry	1959-81 Differential	1959-81 Total	1959-87 Industry	1981-97 Differential	1981-97 Total	1981-97 National	1981-97 Differential	1991-97 Total
Conurbations	3.6	-22.6	-16.4	1.9	-9.7	3.2	1.7	-2.5	3.8
Free-standing	-4.3	4.5	2.8	-3.2	1.3	9.2	0.2	-2.1	2.7
Northern	-9.7	0.1	-7.1	-7.5	0.3	3.9	-0.5	-2.3	1.8
Southern	0.9	19.3	22.8	-0.4	12.1	22.8	0.4	0.6	5.6
Expanded	-7.6	24.0	19.0	-3.1	14.4	22.4	0.4	4.3	9.2
New towns	-7.9	57.5	52.2	-5.0	42.6	48.7	-0.2	10.7	15.2
Coastal	12.2	-8.4	6.4	3.9	0.4	15.4	0.8	-6.9	-1.5
Small towns and rural	-1.8	31.6	32.4	1.4	2.1	14.5	-2.5	3.3	5.5
National	2.6			11.1			4.6		

Table 6.8a: Shift-share analysis by growth classes (1959-97)

Growth classes	Level of employment					Change 1959-97	Shift-share Industry mix	Differential
	1959	1971	1981	1991	1997			
Steadily growing	58,978	71,089	75,735	907,80	100,775	70.9	2.2	54.8
Steadily declining	315,878	307,397	267,707	261,914	261,463	-17.2	-12.5	-18.6
Recovering	1,499,384	1,365,560	1,247,416	1,255,907	1,341,391	-10.5	14.5	-39.0
Backsliding	64,411	74,357	76,983	85,421	83,671	29.9	2.0	14.0
Unstable	82,322	93,482	86,440	94,553	98,686	19.9	-7.0	13.0
Small towns & rural	4,737,143	5,316,120	6,270,535	6,807,942	7,179,592	51.6	-0.4	38.0
Great Britain	22,628,300	23,476,254	23,208,468	24,646,884	25,775,164	13.9		
Urban area	17,891,156	18,160,134	16,937,932	17,838,942	18,595,572	3.9		

Table 6.8b: Shift-share analysis by growth classes (1959-97 by sub periods)

Growth classes	1959-81 Industry	1959-81 Differential	1959-81 Total	1981-97 Industry	1981-97 Differential	1981-97 Total	1991-97 Industry	1991-97 Differential	1991-97 Total
Steadily growing	0.9	24.9	28.4	-0.4	22.4	33.1	0.3	6.2	11.0
Steadily declining	-6.8	-11.0	-15.2	-3.3	-10.1	-2.3	1.1	-5.8	-0.2
Recovering	9.4	-28.8	-16.8	4.5	-8.0	7.5	1.8	0.4	6.8
Backsliding	0.9	16.1	19.5	-1.0	-1.4	8.7	0.5	-7.1	-2.0
Unstable	-4.1	6.6	5.0	-4.2	7.4	14.2	0.2	-0.4	4.4
Small towns and rural	-1.8	31.6	32.4	1.4	2.1	14.5	-2.5	3.3	5.5
National	2.6			11.1			4.6		

Table 6.9a: Shift-share analysis by the proximity to London (1959-97)

Proximity to London	Level of employment					Change (%)	Industry mix	Differential
	1959	1971	1981	1991	1997			
More than 75 mins	11,126,437	11,438,920	10,539,752	11,010,156	11,263,047	1.2	-10.7	-2.0
Less than 75 mins	1,761,479	2,223,452	2,283,008	2,710,037	2,929,515	66.3	7.7	44.7
London	5,003,241	4,497,762	4,115,173	4,082,190	4,368,471	-12.7	21.4	-48.0
Small towns and rural	4,737,143	5,316,120	6,270,535	6,844,501	7,214,131	52.3	-0.4	38.8
Great Britain	22,628,300	23,476,254	23,208,468	24,646,884	25,775,164	13.9	0.0	0.0
Urban area	17,891,156	18,160,134	16,937,932	17,802,384	18,561,032	3.7		

Table 6.9b: Shift-share analysis by the proximity to London (1959-97 by sub periods)

Proximity to London	1959-81 Industry	1959-81 Differential	1959-81 Total	1981-97 Industry	1981-97 Differential	1981-97 Total	1991-97 Industry	1991-97 Differential	1991-97 Total
More than 75 mins	-6.1	-1.7	-5.3	-3.7	-0.5	6.9	0.4	-2.7	2.3
Less than 75 mins	4.1	23.0	29.6	0.9	16.3	28.3	0.8	2.7	8.1
London	13.9	-34.2	-17.7	6.9	-11.8	6.2	2.5	0.0	7.0
Small towns and rural	-1.8	31.6	32.4	1.4	2.6	15.0	-2.4	3.2	5.4
Great Britain	0.0	0.0	2.6	0.0	0.0	11.1	0.0	0.0	4.6
National	2.6			11.1			4.6		

close to London, rather than the 'South' as a whole have gained most and can thus be regarded as the most competitive in each of the sub-periods examined. A possible explanation for this is access to airports: cities within easy striking distance of Heathrow (the UK's one 'global hub' airport) do significantly better after 1981 than those with access only to smaller airports, despite London being aggregated with the group.

Industry structure and employment growth

Further insights into the impact of specialisations can be gleaned by comparing the structural and differential components of shift-share analyses. It might be expected that once allowance has been made for the effects of structure, the performance of the city will depend on its underlying competitiveness, but if there are dynamic benefits from a favourable specialisation, then the structural and differential components would be positively correlated. A visual inspection of the shift-share tables suggests that the two might be positively correlated and various tests have been conducted to explore this relationship. A scatterplot for the period 1981-97 is inconclusive, although it suggests a positive relationship, while a rank correlation for the same period and for 1959-97 does not suggest a significant association. However, for the period 1991-97, a rank correlation suggests that there may indeed be a relationship. When each of the shift-share components is compared with overall employment growth a test for association is positive. This means that a 'good' industrial structure is linked to growth, while a bad one presages poor performance. Similarly, a positive differential component is associated with higher employment growth.[7]

Scatterplots relating the growth of total employment to particular types of activity also suggest some explanations for trends in employment change. A high concentration of 'traditional' industry (mining, textiles and basic metals) seems to be a disadvantage, whereas being relatively specialised in some of the modern service industries is favourable. Thus Figures 6.1 and 6.2 show that there is a statistically significant negative relationship between the concentrations of traditional industry and the rate of growth of employment. Other industry groupings we have examined do not seem to have the same predictive power, although the slope of relationships is generally as expected.

Figure 6.1: Total employment growth versus initial share of industries (1959-97)

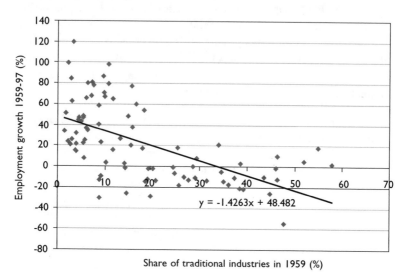

Share of traditional industries in 1959 (%)

Figure 6.2: Total employment growth versus initial share of industries (1981-97)

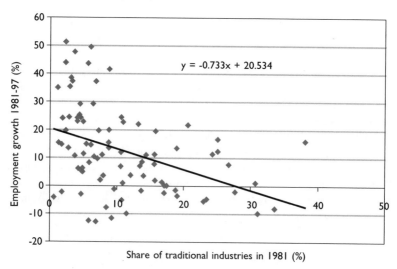

Share of traditional industries in 1981 (%)

Conclusions and policy implications

The long-term analyses presented in this chapter have shown that the topography of urban Britain has changed substantially since the 1950s. To give just one example: employment in the five mid-Anglian cities of Bedford, Cambridge, Milton Keynes, Northampton and Peterborough now exceeds that in the Merseyside conurbation, yet in 1959 it was less than a third of Merseyside's. Although the data reveal that smaller cities have gained relatively at the expense of larger ones, especially the conurbations, there are many exceptions. Large cities such as Bristol have gained substantially and the West Yorkshire conurbation had 2.7 per cent more jobs in 1997 than it had in 1959. At the same time, cities that were important centres of industrial activity in the 19th century, such as Burnley/Nelson or Dundee, now have fewer jobs than new towns such as Telford or Basildon.

The very diverse trends in urban Britain are the result of complex and varied processes of change that have uneven spatial impacts. Import penetration, the decline of traditional industries and the emergence of new staple activities are just some of the influences behind the shift-share analyses presented in this chapter. Overall, the drift over much of the post-war period has been away from larger cities and towards smaller towns and rural areas, and from North to South. This is true both of population, suggesting a residential preference for smaller southern settlements, and (despite the growth of commuting) of employment. But there are also systematic patterns among cities. Thus proximity to London has been an advantage, while relative specialisation in traditional industries has been a drawback.

In the face of this diversity, a one-size-fits-all policy is unlikely to be either desirable or viable in addressing urban issues. Moreover, there are important national goals to bear in mind when formulating urban policy. The ultimate target of public policy is the standard of living, adjusted to allow for non-pecuniary influences on the quality of life. This will encompass a range of variables and be open to subjective weighting criteria, and tensions between different objectives will arise. Higher incomes plainly raise the standard of living, but could be offset by environmental degradation or threats to personal security. Some thought consequently needs to be given to how to weight targets in order to appraise the relative merits of progress on some fronts but not others. In the same way, it is likely that progress towards one target may impede advances towards another, and such a trade-off has to be looked at with care.

Urban policy has to steer a course between efforts to boost the competitiveness of cities and dealing with the consequences of economic change. Improved economic performance by cities can be achieved in a number of ways. The most obvious and enduring is to raise productivity, enabling an economy to generate more output from a given supply of inputs. Regeneration can, however, also be attained by activating otherwise unemployed resources. This suggests that the focus of attention should be both on capacity building *and* on capacity utilisation.

The many economic changes that have occurred in the UK – growth of services, increasingly intensive use of technology, the expansion of commuting to work and so on – have fundamentally changed what makes a city 'competitive'. As these processes have developed, the competitiveness of some cities has been reinforced, while others have lost ground. Policy, too, has had an impact: new towns have expanded precisely because this is what was intended in the policy decision, with the corollary that the older cities from which the populations of new towns are drawn must, *ceteris paribus*, be expected to contract. This shift manifests itself in the way new towns in the South East and Scotland have attracted population and economic activity away from larger neighbouring cities, notably London and Glasgow. Competition is also increasingly felt from other European cities (Jensen-Butler et al, 1997).

Various characteristics of different cities have, in the past, worked to their advantage or disadvantage. Many of these features will have gone or moderated in their importance. However, in developing a framework for urban policy, it is important to recognise that today's cities have different starting points and that these starting points will in part shape the future trajectory of the city and influence the role and effectiveness of urban policies. In other words urban policy must be both sensitive to its context and recognise that the context differs from city to city. At the same time, policy must take due cognisance of the city as competing with other cities and being embedded within an evolving urban system.

Policy measures have, at times, pulled in opposing directions, pointing to one of the main issues that needs to be confronted in trying to influence the long-term performance of cities. This is that a coherent overview of the aims of policy is needed. Coherence implies, first, ensuring that the different policies targeted at a city by the many agencies involved (quangos, government departments, local bodies) do not conflict. In the past, policy measures aimed at boosting some cities or neighbourhoods within them have tried to pull jobs in, while others have tended to disperse economic activity.

Coherence also, however, has to be assured at the level of the urban system as a whole. The long-run trends identified in this chapter show the extent of relative gains and losses in different classes of cities. These in turn have led to problems of congestion in the most favoured cities, and under use of social capital and dysfunctional property markets in declining areas. These outcomes are partly the result of market forces that attract some forms of economic activity to certain cities, but not to others. There may be some scope for seeking to foster the conditions that appear to have worked in successful cities elsewhere. However, in an urban system, the opportunities for replication may be modest because of limits to the aggregate demand for some of the growth industries. For declining cities, one of the key market failures that has to be addressed is the slow pace of adjustment and the social problems to which this gives rise.

Notes

[1] The authors are grateful to the ESRC for financial support under research grant L130251005. Helpful comments were received from other researchers in the ESRC Cities: Competitiveness and Cohesion programme. The conventional disclaimer applies.

[2] Other approaches that might have been taken include the use of functional urban regions (as was done, for example, by Cheshire and Hay, 1989); or travel-to-work areas, but there is no ideal solution.

[3] We are grateful to Daniel Dorling for providing us with re-aggregated census data.

[4] Greater London, West Midlands, Merseyside, Greater Manchester, West Yorkshire, Tyneside and Clydeside.

[5] This ratio, because it takes total population as the denominator, is lower than alternative definitions such as the unemployed as a proportion of the economically active. However, most such indicators will exhibit similar patterns.

[6] Because the shift-share analyses start from the base year in each exercise, comparisons across periods have to be treated with caution, as the starting industry mix may be very different.

[7] There is, inevitably, a degree of tautology in these last observations, since the shift-share is a decomposition of actual growth.

References

Begg I. (1999) 'Cities and competitiveness', *Urban Studies*, vol 36, no 5/6, pp 795-809.

Black, D. and Henderson, V. (1997) 'Urban growth', Working Paper 6008, Cambridge, MA: National Bureau of Economic Research.

Cheshire, P.C. and Hay, D.G. (1989) *Urban problems in Western Europe: An economic analysis*, London: Unwin Hyman.

Dorling, D. (1995) *A new social atlas of Britain*, Chichester: John Wiley & Sons.

Duranton, G. and Puga, D. (2000) 'Diversity and specialisation in cities: why, where and when does it matter?', *Urban Studies*, vol 37, no 3, pp 533-55.

Fujita, M. (1996) 'On the self organisation and evolution of economic geography', *The Japanese Economic Review*, vol 47, no 1, March.

Glaeser, E.L. (1998) 'Are cities dying?', *Journal of Economic Perspectives*, vol 12, no 2, pp 139-60.

Glaeser, E.L., Kallal, H.D., Scheinkman, J.A. and Shleifer, A. (1992) 'Growth in cities', *Journal of Political Economy*, vol 100, no 6.

Gordon, I.R. and McCann, P. (2000) 'Industrial clusters: complexes, agglomeration and/or social networks?', *Urban Studies*, vol 37, no 3, pp 513-32.

Henderson, V. (1983) 'Industrial bases and city size', *American Economic Review*, vol 73, pp 164-68.

Jacobs, J. (1969) *The economy of cities*, New York, NY: Vintage.

Jensen-Butler, C., Schacher, A. and van Weesep, J. (eds) (1997) *European cities in competition*, Aldershot: Avebury.

Kresl, P. (1995) 'The determinants of urban competitiveness', in P. Kresl and G. Gappert (eds) *North American cities and the global economy: Challenges and opportunities*, Urban Affairs Annual Review, no 44, London: Sage Publications.

Krugman, P. (1996) *Pop internationalism*, Cambridge, MA: MIT Press.

Lever, W. (1993) 'Competition within the European urban system', *Urban Studies*, vol 30, no 6, pp 935-48.

Massey, D. and Allen, J. (1988) *Uneven redevelopment: Cities and regions in transition*, London: Hodder & Stoughton.

Suarez-Villa, L. (1988) 'Metropolitan evolution, sectoral economic change, and the city size distribution', *Urban Studies*, vol 25, no 1, pp 1-20.

Simon, C.J. and Nardinelli, C. (1996) 'The talk of the town: human capital, information and the growth of English Cities, 1861 to 1961', *Explorations in Economic History*, vol 33, pp 384-413.

Simon, C.J. (1998) 'Human capital and metropolitan employment growth', *Journal of Urban Economics*, vol 43, pp 223-43, March.

Turok, I. and Edge, N. (1999) *The jobs gap in Britain's cities: Employment loss and labour market consequences*, Bristol/York: The Policy Press/Joseph Rowntree Foundation.

SEVEN

Dimensions of city competitiveness: Edinburgh and Glasgow in a UK context

Nick Bailey, Iain Docherty and Ivan Turok

Introduction

For a private firm, competitiveness is a relatively simple concept concerned with commercial performance or the ability to provide sufficient returns on capital to attract investment. For a city, competitiveness is more complex and multidimensional, not least because the various tiers and agencies of government responsible for promoting economic growth cannot neglect the implications for social welfare and the environment. The value of a firm to a city is determined not only by its current profitability and future growth prospects but also by factors such as the income it generates for residents through returns to labour, the quality of employment opportunities it offers, its impact on the physical environment and image of the city, and its contribution to the overall quality of life. A competitive city can be considered as one that can attract and retain suitable sorts of activity, defined in these economic, social and environmental terms, to meet the needs of its residents. Thus 'competitiveness' is not a simple technical concept, but involves trade-offs between a variety of interests.

This chapter examines the relative competitiveness of the two major Scottish cities, Edinburgh and Glasgow, focusing on economic and social dimensions and setting them within a UK context through comparisons with the major English conurbations. With a similar geographical setting on the periphery of an increasingly integrated Europe but very different histories, the Scottish cities have enjoyed contrasting economic fortunes over the past three decades. Edinburgh has been one of the most successful British cities, enjoying slow but steady growth and an international profile through its tourism, cultural and government activities. Glasgow has been an archetypal city of industrial decline. Part of the challenge is to get beyond the historic divergence to examine in more detail how they have performed in recent years. Glasgow has gained an international reputation as a city that has 'remade' itself into a post-industrial success story. Growth in service sector employment, a revitalised city centre and a series of one-off events have done much to change external (and internal) perceptions (Mooney and Johnstone, 1998; Pacione, 1995). As others have noted, however, reputations in regeneration are not always supported by evidence of a change in performance (Wolman et al, 1994). In addition, the aim of this chapter is to analyse the performance of each city on different dimensions.

In recent years much has been written about theories of city competitiveness (Begg, 1999; Jensen-Butler, 1997) but little empirical assessment has been undertaken. Competitiveness is difficult to measure directly, not least because it is a forward-looking concept, concerned with the attributes or assets required for future success. There is no guarantee that having what is thought to be the 'right' asset set at one point in time will lead to positive outcomes subsequently. Unforeseen changes in the environment in which cities operate – new technological developments, or changes in government regulation of economic activity, for example – may affect outcomes substantially. There is also circularity or feedback in the process of competition with both virtuous and vicious circles. This makes determining the direction of causality between the attributes of a place and its subsequent performance difficult, if not impossible. Finally, there are geographical issues to consider. Some indicators of competitiveness are affected by the boundaries that are drawn around cities (problems of over- or under-bounding) and by the open nature of these boundaries (notably the flows of commuters into and out of major cities). This chapter attempts to illustrate some of these difficulties and to urge a more cautious and critical approach to the use of competitiveness indicators. We draw upon some sources of data that have only recently become available for cities, and examine their relevance or value as competitiveness indicators.

Output, productivity and labour utilisation

The best single measure of the economic performance of a region is frequently taken to be economic output or gross domestic product (GDP) per capita. GDP measures the capacity of the local economy to create wealth and, notwithstanding a number of qualifications, GDP per capita has a positive relationship with average levels of income earned by residents, and therefore to living standards. GDP per capita is used by the Department of Trade and Industry as one of its key indicators of regional competitiveness (DTI, 2000). It is also used by the European Union as the main indicator of relative affluence in determining the allocation of structural funds for regional assistance. As a measure of economic performance, GDP per capita has the drawback that it reflects historic outcomes and is relatively slow to change. A more sensitive indicator would be change in GDP per capita. Both indicators can be disaggregated in various ways to reflect different dimensions of competitiveness. Most simply, GDP per capita can be broken down into a measure of the productivity of economic activity (GDP per employed resident) and a measure of labour utilisation (the employment rate, defined here as employed residents per head of population). The latter provides some indication of the level of income inequality since, for a given level of economic output, the lower the employment rate, the smaller the proportion of the population that benefits directly from the income generated.

The government has recently begun producing data on GDP for sub-regional 'local areas' with the series now covering the period 1993 to 1998 (ONS, 2001). Great care needs to be exercised in using these figures to judge relative performance of cities as the GDP figures are produced on a workplace basis. For small areas with large net commuting flows, GDP per capita (resident) becomes meaningless as an indicator of economic performance or welfare. The figures for core cities, in particular, are inflated while those for commuter suburbs are depressed. For example, the ONS cites Edinburgh as having the third highest GDP per capita in Britain (47 per cent above the national average), while neighbouring East Lothian/Midlothian is second from bottom (40 per cent below average). Similarly, Glasgow City is 26 per cent above the national average while surrounding areas such as Dunbartonshire or Lanarkshire are over 20 per cent below average.

For larger and more self-contained areas (for example city-regions), the figures can be used as performance indicators provided they are adjusted to a residence basis as is the case here. Workplace GDP figures need to be scaled up or down to provide an estimate of the GDP produced by the resident population. The adjustment factor is the ratio of the number of residents in employment (regardless of where they work) to the number of people employed in the area (regardless of where they live). There is an assumption that the average GDP per worker is the same for 'in' and 'out' commuters. This is reasonable provided self-containment is relatively high and the adjustment factor is close to one, as is the case for the city-regions considered here. For smaller and more open areas such as core cities, this assumption becomes much less valid. Figures on employed residents and workforce are drawn from the Labour Force Survey (first and third quarter of each year) and smoothed over a two-year period to reduce sampling errors. For Edinburgh, this is not possible so data from the 1991 Census Special Workplace Statistics are used instead. Comparisons between LFS and Census data for the other city-regions show strong agreement on the overall level of net commuting while the LFS figures show very little variation over time (one or two per cent at most). The GDP figures have also been adjusted for inflation using the national GDP deflator, so that changes over time reflect real change. It should be noted that the ONS at present classes the local area GDP figures as provisional, due to forthcoming changes in the methods of calculating public accounts and revisions to data series such as the Annual Business Inquiry which have yet to be incorporated.

Using the static measure of average GDP per capita for the period 1993-8, Edinburgh performed far better than Glasgow. Greater Edinburgh's GDP per capita was 16 per cent higher than the British average, and second only to Greater London among the cities examined here. Greater Glasgow's GDP per capita was five per cent below average (Figure 7.1). This suggests a significantly higher level of wealth and income generation in the east than the west of Central Scotland. This performance gap is partly explained by the difference in firm productivity between the cities (a six per cent gap) but the more important reason is the difference in labour utilisation (a 14 per cent gap). In Greater Edinburgh there were 47 people in employment for every 100 residents, while in Greater Glasgow there were just 40. These figures suggest that the challenge of raising economic performance is quite different in the two cities. There is comparatively little scope to increase labour participation rates in Edinburgh further so the emphasis will need to be on raising productivity by attracting higher value added activities to the city, upgrading skills and so on. In Glasgow, the main challenge is getting a larger proportion of the population into productive employment. Raising productivity should be a secondary concern, although the two are not exclusive since boosting productivity may well assist future economic and employment growth.

Both Scottish cities performed well on GDP per capita in comparison to the English conurbations outside London, although it is not clear whether this is reflected in higher personal incomes north of the border. Greater London is in a different league from the other conurbations due

Figure 7.1: Output, productivity and employment rates: average (1993-98)

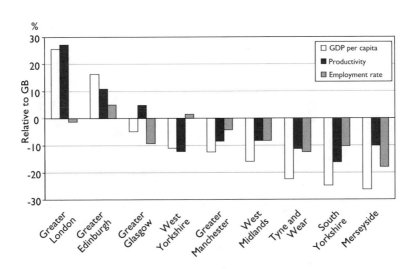

Note: GDP figures are provisional figures (ONS, 2001). Residents in employment from LFS LADB. Population from ONS/GROS mid-year estimates.

Sources: GDP from ONS local area GDP figures adjusted to residence basis using net commuting flows from QLFS

to the high productivity of its firms, reflecting its position as a 'world city' and a major centre for financial services as well as national government functions. West Yorkshire and Greater Manchester had a level of performance a little below that of Glasgow but this was the result of higher employment rates, particularly in West Yorkshire, offset by lower productivity. This suggests rather different strategic challenges for these conurbations compared with Glasgow. Tyne and Wear, South Yorkshire and Merseyside fared notably worse with GDP per capita 22-26 per cent below the national average. These three conurbations all suffered from the double disadvantage of low productivity and low employment rates.

Glasgow's performance appears stronger if the more sensitive change indicator is used (Figure 7.2). Over the period 1993-98, it outperformed all other conurbations. According to this source, GDP per capita fell by four per cent in Edinburgh so the gap between the two Scottish cities narrowed (from 23 per cent to 16 per cent). Glasgow's positive performance was driven entirely by an increase in productivity greater than that for any other conurbation. Its employment rate, low in 1993,

Figure 7.2: Output, productivity and employment rates: change (1993-98)

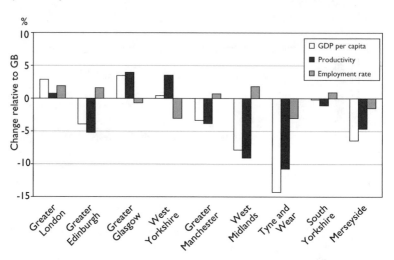

Note: GDP figures are provisional figures (ONS, 2001). Residents in employment from LFS LADB. Population from ONS/GROS mid-year estimates.

Sources: GDP from ONS local area GDP figures adjusted to residence basis using net commuting flows from QLFS

fell further behind the average. Edinburgh's weaker performance stemmed from a sharp fall in productivity, but employment rates rose further above the national average. In this respect, the gap between the cities widened. Glasgow's performance on employment rates can be contrasted with that for South Yorkshire or the West Midlands. Both of these conurbations had below average employment rates in 1993 but saw increases by 1998. West Yorkshire was the only conurbation other than Glasgow and London to show growth in GDP per capita relative to the national average over 1993-98. This growth occurred in a similar manner to Glasgow's, as above average rises in productivity were offset by lower than average employment rate growth. This pattern appears more appropriate to West Yorkshire's situation, however, given that it started from a base of relatively low productivity and above average employment rates.

These indicators can be portrayed slightly differently by resolving them into independent dimensions, one representing 'output' or income per head, and the other representing the degree of labour intensity (Figure 7.3). All figures are shown relative to the national average for the relevant year, to allow for cyclical growth from 1993 to 1998. Total output or income per capita is the product of the employment and the productivity rates, shown by movement up the leading diagonal. This represents growth without any relative change in labour intensity; that is, it is growth achieved by raising productivity and employment rates at the same rate relative to the national average. This might be termed 'balanced' or 'all-round' growth. The other diagonal shows an independent dimension, labelled 'labour intensity'. Cities closer to the top-left corner have comparatively high employment rates and low productivity for any given level of output or income. Cities may move down this axis when a firm uses capital investment to achieve the same level of output using less labour. As employment rates are an (admittedly crude) indicator of income equity, movement down this axis shows a less equitable situation for any given level of output or income. Overall income remains the same but productivity rises and the employment rate falls. Greater Glasgow and West Yorkshire have similar levels of income on the figure but West Yorkshire achieves this in a far more equitable manner.

The arrows for each city-region in Figure 7.3 indicate components of change on the two dimensions ('labour intensity' and 'output or income per capita') between 1993 and 1998. In five cases (Greater Edinburgh, West Midlands, Greater Manchester, Tyne and Wear and Merseyside), the pattern of change can be described as 'equitable decline'. Income appeared to fall relative to the national average between 1993 and 1998 but the

Figure 7.3: Productivity and employment rates (1993 and 1998)

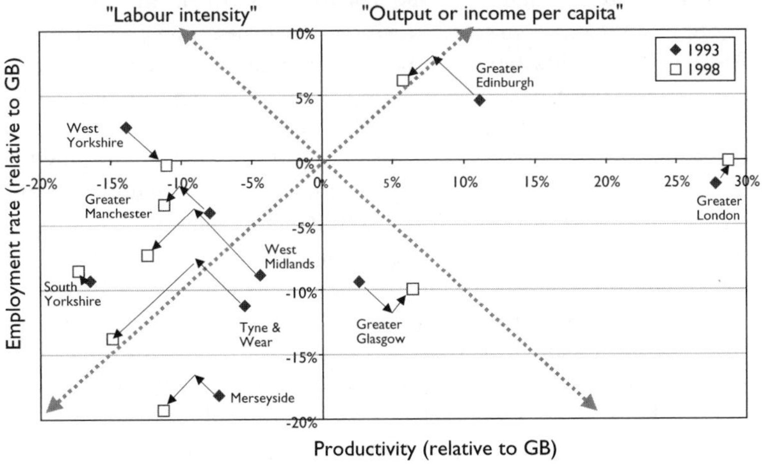

Source: GDP from ONS local area GDP figures; residents in employment – LFS LADB; population – ONS/GROS mid-year estimates

conurbations also increased their employment rates at the expense of productivity. One conurbation (Greater London) achieved broad or 'job-rich' growth, with productivity and the employment rate increasing at the same rate. Arguably London should have done more to raise employment rates given its comparatively poor starting point in this regard. Changes in Greater Glasgow might be labelled 'narrow' or 'jobless' growth as a rise in income occurred but the city's already poor employment rate worsened. The only other conurbation with a similar pattern of change was West Yorkshire but this was from a very different starting point. South Yorkshire performed well in comparison with other conurbations at a similar starting position, keeping pace with rising national productivity and employment rates.

Restructuring employment

The difference in levels of GDP per capita between Edinburgh and Glasgow is the result of a long period of deindustrialisation and economic restructuring. Greater Glasgow has been more adversely affected by the shift from manufacturing to services than Greater Edinburgh, partly because a higher proportion of its jobs were in manufacturing to begin with, and partly because the rate of decline has been higher in the west than the east. Greater Glasgow lost 70 per cent of its manufacturing jobs between 1971 and 1998, compared with 44 per cent for Greater Edinburgh. For services, Greater Glasgow gained 39 per cent compared with 59 per cent in Greater Edinburgh. Labour market adjustment in Glasgow has not been sufficient to maintain the balance between supply and demand. Although there has been substantial out-migration from the city, a significant number of people were unable or unwilling to move (Bailey et al, 1999; Bailey and Turok, 2000). The result can be seen in the rising employment rate gap between the cities. In 1971, Greater Glasgow had an employment rate just 3.6 per cent below Greater Edinburgh's but this had widened to 9.6 per cent by 1991 (Census figures). The gap has remained more or less constant throughout the 1990s. The GDP per capita figures are greatly affected by these historic processes and tell us much less about current performance.

If absolute employment is used as a performance indicator (making no distinction between full- and part-time jobs), Greater Glasgow appeared to turn the corner around 1986. It lost a fifth of all jobs between 1971 and 1986. Since then, employment has remained more or less stable overall. Looking at change relative to the national average, however, the break in the late 1980s appears less decisive (Figure 7.4). Both Edinburgh and Glasgow city-regions outperformed the British average for a brief spell in the late 1980s and early 1990s, a time when recession in the South East depressed national growth rates. Both cities subsequently fell back as the national economy grew during the 1990s. The most positive sign for Glasgow appears in the figures for the last year or two, which show it outperforming the national average. If this trend continues, we might tentatively put a date on Glasgow's turnaround at about 1996. The most recent employment figures for Edinburgh appear unreliable so comparisons between the two cities are not useful on this indicator.

In addition to east-west comparisons, these employment data shed light on the relative performance of the core and outer rings of cities. There has been only a modest shift in employment from the city cores to surrounding areas. Glasgow City accounted for 56 per cent of the city-region's employment in 1971 and this had fallen only marginally to 54 per cent in 1998. For Edinburgh City, the share fell from 75 to 72 per cent. For Glasgow at least, decentralisation has slowed enormously compared with the 1950s and 1960s, when employment was declining in the core but growing in the outer ring (Lever and Mather, 1986). In addition, employment decentralisation has not been as rapid as population decentralisation so the core cities are acting increasingly as employment centres for a population spread across a wider area. The outer areas of both city-regions have included areas of significant decline (such as Motherwell, Paisley, Coatbridge and Midlothian) as well as areas of growth. The areas of strongest growth have been the new towns of Livingston,

Figure 7.4: Employment change in Edinburgh and Glasgow (1971-98)

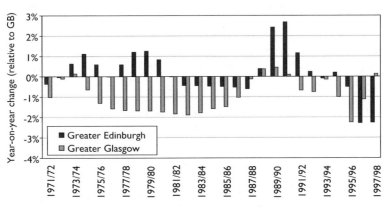

Source: Census of Employment/Annual Employment Survey via NOMIS. Data smoothed.

Cumbernauld and East Kilbride, which have all experienced growth in manufacturing as well as services employment. Their success indicates the important role of the public sector in facilitating net decentralisation of employment from the core, through major investment in physical infrastructure, land, buildings and housing.

Industrial specialisation

These changes have had important effects on the industrial structure of the two cities. Looking at this structure tells us something about the competitive advantages of different locations and their roles in the wider urban system. As with GDP and employment data, however, indicators of specialisation such as location quotients reflect historical strengths as well as current trends. Figure 7.5 compares the employment structure in the two core cities and their surrounding areas with the national structure, using average figures for 1996 to 1998 to smooth out irregularities. Employment figures have been converted to full-time equivalents. The figures represent the number of jobs in each sector, minus the number of jobs one would have expected if each area had the same employment structure as Britain as a whole. They therefore reflect not just the degree of specialisation but also the absolute scale of each sector. The two outer rings are combined for simplicity as they have similar structures.

The two broad sectors in which Edinburgh and Glasgow core cities are over-represented are public services (36,000 more jobs than expected) and financial services (11,000). The high levels of public service employment are due to concentrations in health services (17,000), public administration (10,000), higher education (8,000), social work (3,000) and social security (3,000). These reflect the roles that the core cities play in the provision of high-level services to their city-regions and to Scotland as a whole (that is, metropolitan, regional and capital city functions), and the higher levels of poverty and social need in the west. The importance of public sector employment as a driver of local economic growth is often ignored or underplayed (Lovering, 1997). The concentration of employment in financial services reflects the general agglomeration economies for this sector and the prestige that many of the major Scottish financial institutions attach to a location in Edinburgh.

Manufacturing is the most under-represented activity in the two city-regions with 35,000 fewer jobs than expected. Levels are above average in the outer rings (14,000 more jobs than expected). This is almost entirely due to the presence of electronics manufacturing in the 'Silicon Glen' of West Lothian, Lanarkshire and Renfrewshire (13,000 more jobs

Figure 7.5: Industrial specialisation in Edinburgh and Glasgow (1996-98)

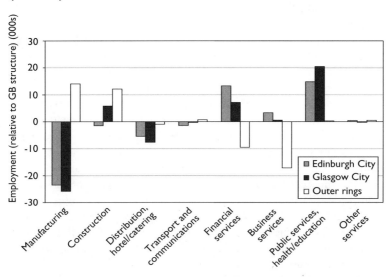

Source: Annual Employment Survey via NOMIS. Average full-time equivalent employment for 1996-98

than expected). These concentrations reflect the success of inward investment strategies in attracting foreign plants to greenfield locations outside the core cities. The closures and cutbacks in electronics jobs in 2001 (the loss of 3,000 jobs at Motorola in Bathgate, 1,000 at Compaq in Erskine, and 600 at NEC in Livingston, most notably) highlight the fragility of some of this 'high-tech' employment. The core cities have 49,000 fewer manufacturing jobs than expected, although Glasgow City remains the largest manufacturing district in Scotland in absolute terms with 35,000 jobs. Only 13 per cent of these are in foreign-owned plants, compared with 45 per cent in Renfrewshire, 40 per cent in South Lanarkshire, and 30 per cent in North Lanarkshire. This reflects the lack of inward investment in the city.

Edinburgh and Glasgow city-regions have much less employment in business services than the national average (13,000 fewer jobs than expected) but this largely reflects the dominance of London in this sector. Within the city-regions, business services are concentrated in the core cities. Two low value-added sectors within business services are strongly over-represented – industrial cleaning and security services – with 6,000 extra jobs. Architecture and engineering provide a further 2,000 extra jobs. For other business services, there is a deficit of 21,000 jobs. One striking finding is the low level of employment in computer and related sectors (6,000 below average for the two cities). Nationally, these have been among the fastest growing sectors over the 1990s, but concentrated in London and the South East.

Neither core city appears to have a particularly strong leisure sector, compared with the average. Retail employment in the two core cities is 4,000 below the national level. Although employment in comparison shopping (that is, specialised outlets often in major shopping centres) is 1,000 above average, employment in non-specialised shops is 4,000 down. Wholesale employment is 12,000 below national levels. Hotel, restaurant and catering employment is just 1,000 above the national average due to Edinburgh City's strength as a tourist destination; it has 2,000 more jobs than expected. There are 4,000 extra jobs in sports and recreation activities but the other sectors which fall under the heading of 'cultural industries' (film, video, TV, radio, entertainment, news, libraries and museums) are under-represented by 1,000 jobs (Edinburgh City is again above average in this regard). This is surprising considering the policy effort that has been devoted to these sectors and the presence of radio, television and newspaper publishers in the region. London's dominance is part of the explanation. The recent opening of two large call centres by the satellite television company BSkyB (in Livingston and Dunfermline) has raised employment in film and TV in Scotland considerably but these are administrative rather than creative activities.

Comparisons with other conurbations in Britain show both similarities and differences. Greater London has exceptionally high concentrations of financial services, transport and communications, and other service jobs, and it has correspondingly low levels of manufacturing and construction employment. This pattern skews the picture so it is more helpful to compare Glasgow and Edinburgh to the other English conurbations (Figure 7.6). The English conurbations other than London have much higher levels of manufacturing than the two Scottish cities; this is their strongest specialisation, reflecting concentrations of such employment in the outer rings of these cities (42 per cent above average). This may suggest that manufacturing companies move out of core cities but seek to remain close to them because of the specialist business services which they can offer, or in order to retain access to their original workforce. It may also show the impact of extensive public sector initiatives to attract employment to locations close to the major cities through new towns or Enterprise Zones (Lever and Mather, 1986; Potter and Moore, 2000).

The figure also highlights the strengths of the Scottish cities in services when compared with the English conurbations other than Greater London.

Figure 7.6: Industrial specialisation for British conurbations (1996-98)

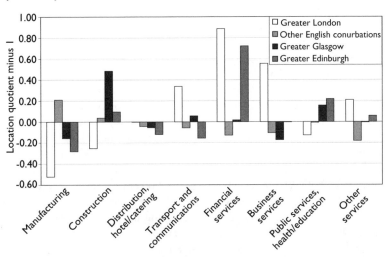

Source: Annual Employment Survey via NOMIS. Average full-time equivalent employment for 1996-98

Edinburgh's strength in financial services is particularly clear but it also does well in business services. Glasgow also does better than the English conurbations in financial services but worse in business services. On the basis of their current industrial structures, and the poor performance of manufacturing in Britain in recent decades, both Scottish cities appear better placed for economic growth than their English counterparts. On the other hand, the loss of manufacturing in Glasgow is the principal explanation for its particularly severe problems of unemployment and poverty.

New firm formation

The rate of new firm formation is often seen as a direct measure of competitiveness (for example DTI, 2000). It is believed to indicate a capacity for innovation and a culture of entrepreneurship, and is therefore a guide to future prospects. New firm formation rates can also be seen as an indicator of performance or outcomes, however, as the number of firms in an area grows as the economy expands, and falls as it contracts. Firm formation rates may also be influenced by factors other than competitiveness, including the 'push' factors of high unemployment or the efforts of policy makers. Raising the rate of business start-ups has become an important policy objective in many areas, including Scotland (Scottish Enterprise, 1993). New firm formation rates are of little value unless considered alongside firm failure rates. What matters is the ability to start up and sustain businesses so that the stock of firms expands. Firm formation rates may also reflect historic performance in other ways. An important constraint on firm formation in more depressed locations is access to finance. Lack of home ownership, low housing values and low earnings make it more difficult for people to raise capital (Ashcroft et al, 1991). Finally it should be noted that boundary effects are also important as people do not necessarily set up their business in the area in which they live. One should be particularly cautious about how differences in firm formation rates between core and outer areas of cities are interpreted.

The stock of business is higher in Greater Edinburgh than in Greater Glasgow (208 VAT registered firms per 10,000 population compared with 168 in 1998) but both city-regions lagged behind the average for Scotland (229) and even further behind that for England and Wales (274). Edinburgh and Glasgow city-regions had very similar rates of new firm formation over the period 1994-98 but Edinburgh had a much lower rate of business failure (Figure 7.7). Glasgow actually had more deaths than start-ups so the stock of business declined. While the core of the city had a higher rate of start-ups than the surrounding areas, it also saw a higher rate of net loss. Of the English conurbations, only Greater London had a stock of businesses higher than the national average and all except Greater

Figure 7.7: New business births and deaths (1994-98)

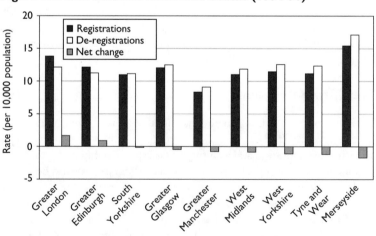

Source: DTI VAT registrations, via NOMIS

London showed a net loss of firms in the period 1994–98. Glasgow was not unique in this respect and, indeed, its rate of net loss was lower than that for most other conurbations. Merseyside showed relatively high rates of firm formation but even higher rates of closure, and had the largest rate of net loss. This high level of 'churn' warrants further investigation.

The figures do not support the idea that Glasgow's relatively poor performance can be blamed on the lack of entrepreneurial drive among its residents. What they do suggest is that 'push' and 'pull' factors have an impact on both formation and failure rates. Push factors (for example high unemployment or policy intervention) may drive up formation rates in more depressed locations but local demand factors may make firm survival more difficult. This might explain high formation and high failure rates in cities such as Glasgow and Liverpool, but high formation and lower failure rates in places such as Edinburgh or London. A focus simply on creating new businesses in a generally weak environment may be less helpful than a focus on improving the survival rate for those businesses that do get off the ground. More generally it could be argued that strategies to promote small business development are likely to be held back in the absence of a wider improvement in the local business environment.

Labour markets

A plentiful supply of high quality labour is clearly a competitive asset for a city, but the relationship between competitiveness and indicators such as official unemployment rates is less clear. A high unemployment rate could be seen as a positive measure of competitiveness as it indicates a labour surplus, which may in turn be associated with lower wage levels or a more flexible or motivated workforce. The competitive value of this labour, however, will depend upon skills and other attributes not reflected in crude rates. A high unemployment rate can be seen as a negative indicator of past performance, reflecting economic decline and a lack of labour market adjustment in former industrial and mining areas (Begg et al, 1986; Beatty et al, 1997). It is also an indicator of higher levels of inequality and lower levels of income. It is, of course, important to use resident rather than workforce unemployment rates in all instances. Commuting effects mean that the workforce unemployment rates produced by ONS are meaningless at the scale of local authority areas. They systematically understate the scale of the unemployment problem in core cities and overstate it in neighbouring commuter suburbs.

Residence-based rates are preferable, although they still suffer from the drawback that they fail to capture a large proportion of the unemployed workforce, particularly in areas of high unemployment. These areas have higher levels of 'discouraged workers' who have given up looking for work and are therefore recorded as inactive; many have taken early retirement or claim long-term sickness benefits. A variety of alternative indicators have been advocated to measure the scale of labour market surpluses more accurately: 'real' unemployment rates (Beatty et al, 1997), 'want work' rates (TUC, 2001) or employment rates (the proportion of the working age population in employment), for example. It is worth noting, however, that there are strong correlations between all these measures and official unemployment rates (Webster, 2000). Official rates may fail to measure the absolute scale of the problem but they are useful as indicators of the relative situation across areas and they have the advantage that data are readily available.

Resident unemployment rates for the larger local authorities are available from the LFS 'local area database' from the third quarter of 1993. Four-quarter moving averages are used here to reduce the impact of sampling errors and remove seasonal variations, making the second quarter of 1994 the earliest period for which data can be presented. Unemployment rates in Greater Glasgow in 1994 were 2.2 per cent above the national average (10.1 per cent), while those in Greater Edinburgh were 0.8 per cent below. The gap between the core cities was even wider, with Glasgow 3.9 per cent above average and Edinburgh 1.6 per cent below. Looking at change over the period 1994 to 2000, the gap between the two cities has actually widened at both city-region and core city scales (from 3.0 to 4.1 per cent and from 5.5 to 6.4 per cent respectively). Looked at in more detail, Glasgow showed a deterioration relative to the national average until 1997, followed by a slow but steady improvement. The core city also narrowed the gap with Edinburgh during this period. Employment rates show a very similar picture.

Over the period 1994-2000, Glasgow's performance looks poor in comparison to most other conurbations (Figures 7.8 and 7.9). The conurbations of Greater Manchester, Greater London, South Yorkshire and Merseyside all show unemployment falling relative to the national average, and a corresponding rise in employment rates. In every case, the core cities in these areas also performed well. In Greater Glasgow and Glasgow City, unemployment rose relative to the national average although employment rates also rose slightly. The West Midlands and Birmingham showed the opposite tendency with relative improvement in unemployment rates but a deterioration in employment rates. West

Figure 7.8: Employment and unemployment rates, city regions (1994 and 2000)

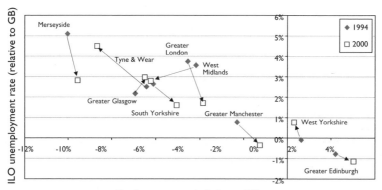

Source: Labour Force Survey LADB (re-weighted). Four quarter moving average used to reduce sampling errors

Figure 7.9: Employment and unemployment rates, core cities (1994 and 2000)

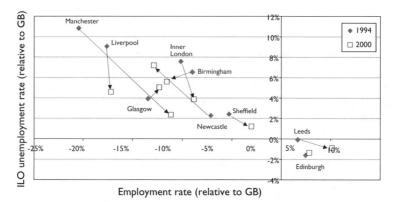

Source: Labour Force Survey LADB (re-weighted). Four quarter moving average used to reduce sampling errors

Yorkshire performed poorly, with rising unemployment and falling employment rates but it started from a much higher position. The worst performance by far was recorded by Tyne and Wear conurbation, and Newcastle, which saw its poor position worsen significantly in relative terms.

Table 7.1: Working age population on non-work benefits (2000) (% of total working age population)

	Unemployed	Sick or disabled	Lone parents	Other	Total
Great Britain	3	8	2	1	14
Liverpool	8	18	5	1	32
Glasgow	6	19	5	1	30
Manchester	5	15	6	1	27
Birmingham	6	10	4	1	21
Newcastle upon Tyne	5	12	3	1	21
Inner London	5	8	4	1	19
Sheffield	6	9	2	1	18
Leeds	3	7	3	1	14
Edinburgh	3	8	2	1	13

Source: DSS (2001). Figures are for August 2000. Key benefits are: Jobseeker's Allowance (JSA) for unemployed; Incapacity Benefit (IB), Severe Disablement Allowance (SDA) or Disability Living Allowance (DLA) for sick or disabled; Income Support (IS) for lone parents; and National Insurance Credits Only (through JSA or IB) for others.

Some insight into the scale of 'hidden unemployment' not revealed by official unemployment rates can be found in recently released DSS statistics on the number of people of working age not in employment and claiming benefits (Table 7.1). These show the extent to which groups such as the sick/disabled or lone parents are concentrated in the areas with highest unemployment. In Glasgow, there were three times as many people on Incapacity Benefit or related benefits as there were on Jobseekers' Allowance; in absolute terms, 72,000 people compared with 22,400 (in 2000). In total, 30 per cent of the working age population claimed a non-work benefit compared with just 13 per cent in Edinburgh. Only Liverpool fared worse. These differences mean that national labour market policies are likely to have quite different impacts locally. While the various New Deal initiatives to increase labour supply may bring benefits in a tight labour market such as Edinburgh, they are not addressing the nature of the problem in places such as Glasgow where there is already a large surplus of labour.

Vacant and derelict land

The relationship between land supply and city competitiveness is also complex. The availability of cheap readily developable land (like surplus labour) is obviously an asset for a city; a tight land market is one of the most important feedback mechanisms checking the growth of 'successful' cities (Fothergill et al, 1987; Adams, 1994). A measure of the total amount of land vacant or derelict, however, is much less useful as a guide to future competitiveness. It does not reflect important characteristics of the land: the size and distribution of sites; location in relation to other uses; extent of fragmentation of ownership; quality of access; costs of upgrading infrastructure or services; or the extent and risk of contamination (Adams et al, 2001; Urban Task Force, 1999). A large supply of such sites can also be a negative factor, worsening the quality of the urban environment in general. Vacant sites undermine land and property values in adjoining areas and create significant gaps in the physical structure, reducing the efficiency of the urban system. As with unemployment figures, the availability of vacant or derelict land indicates past performance as much as future competitiveness. Indicators of change or uptake of land may be a better guide to recent performance.

Both stock and change figures may also reflect the impact of public policies as well as market processes, given the importance of planning and public investment in activities such as site consolidation, decontamination and infrastructure provision. Assumptions about the types of site which private investment will favour guide public actions, but there is no certainty that these are correct. Land uptake by private actors can therefore be significantly influenced by public strategies. Finally, a lack of currently available sites may not be a barrier to competitiveness. Cities with little vacant or derelict land may secure a supply for high value uses by the direct displacement of lower value users (most commonly manufacturing or distribution) to fringe or ex-urban locations, and by redeveloping at higher densities. In the residential market, there is the analogous process of gentrification. Greenbelt release is another option, albeit often politically sensitive. The scale of this potential supply is not picked up in vacant and derelict land statistics.

Almost one third of vacant and derelict land in Scotland is concentrated in two local authority areas in the Glasgow city-region – North Lanarkshire and Glasgow City. The proportion of land vacant and derelict in Glasgow is 8.6 per cent, and over half of this has been disused for more than ten years. In North Lanarkshire, 4.4 per cent of land is vacant or derelict although the absolute total is greater than in Glasgow because the council covers a much larger territory. In the east, West Lothian contains the third largest amount of vacant or derelict land of any authority in Scotland but this represents just 2.9 per cent of its total. In Edinburgh City, the figure is just 0.6 per cent. Between 1993 and 2000, very little progress was made in clearing the backlog of land in Glasgow compared with Lanarkshire, once allowance is made for the effects of boundary changes between 1996 and 1997 (Figure 7.10).

In Edinburgh City, the low supply of land from vacant and derelict stocks appears to have been boosted by the displacement of existing, lower value users to other areas. In this sense there have been mutual benefits for Edinburgh City and West Lothian from policies designed to encourage the location of industrial development into the depressed areas of West Lothian, notably through Livingston New Town. This process presumably benefits the individual firms as well but it should be noted that it may bring disbenefits to certain groups of city residents (manual workers) who would previously have sought work with these companies. Edinburgh has also added to its land supply through significant Greenbelt release, and through major regeneration schemes launched for Leith and the North Edinburgh Waterfront, which are more easily financed given the overall high demand for land in the city.

Industrial development policies pursued in areas surrounding Glasgow have arguably had more detrimental effects for the core of the city. The slack land market in parts of the city was undermined for many years by programmes that subsidised development opportunities in the two adjoining new towns and the two Enterprise Zones in Clydebank and Lanarkshire. City authorities also failed to intervene in the land market to promote industrial uses on any scale for many years – or lacked the resources to do so. Since 1995, however, a programme of developing and

Figure 7.10: Vacant and derelict land (1993-2000)

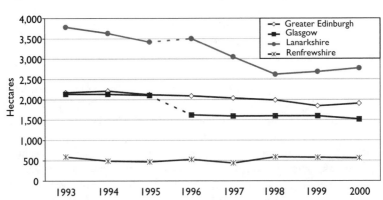

Note: Discontinuities in series for Glasgow and Lanarkshire. Local government reorganisation meant that one area moved from the former to the latter.

Source: Scottish Executive Statistical Bulletin ENV/2001/1

marketing sites in Glasgow City (the Strategic Sites Initiative) has been implemented with some success. City agencies believe there is a case for much greater public investment in these sites because many are well located in relation to the roads network and are close to areas of particularly high unemployment.

Conclusions

Many of the indicators highlight the gulf that exists between Edinburgh and Glasgow in economic and social terms, as a result of the differential impacts of several decades of deindustrialisation and economic reorganisation. In the west of Central Scotland, these processes have led to the accumulation of labour surpluses, which depress average incomes. In the east, employment growth has created high levels of labour utilisation and high average incomes. Land is in relatively short supply in the east but in Glasgow there are major areas of vacant or derelict urban land. Measures of GDP per capita, unemployment or employment rates, or stocks of vacant or derelict land are all affected by these long-term processes. They probably tell us little about current performance or future competitiveness.

The change indicators provide more useful insights into recent performance and can be used to reflect both economic and social dimensions of competitiveness. The picture that emerges for Edinburgh and Glasgow is mixed. In economic terms, Glasgow city-region performed strongly in the period 1993 to 1998, narrowing the output or income gap with Edinburgh (GDP per capita) though concerns about the figures for Edinburgh have been noted. Glasgow performed worse than Edinburgh in terms of employment to 1996 but experienced a significant improvement thereafter, so that employment growth in Glasgow between 1993 and 1998 was greater than in Edinburgh at both city-regional and core city scales. In this sense, the rhetoric of Glasgow's regeneration has a real foundation, although it will take another year or two before the evidence can be considered robust. Dating Glasgow's turnaround any earlier than 1996, however, would seem premature.

In terms of social equity, Glasgow's performance appears weaker than Edinburgh's. Between 1994 and 1998, the gap between Edinburgh and Glasgow widened on unemployment and employment rate indicators at both city-regional and core city scales. Growth in income in Glasgow seems to have stemmed from increasing productivity but at the expense of lower employment rates. This was unusual among British conurbations in this period, particularly as Glasgow already had relatively high productivity and a relatively low employment rate. The city's failure (until recently) to ensure that vacant and derelict land was reused for industrial uses seems to be at least one contributory factor here. A more positive picture is emerging for the most recent period. Labour market data show a narrowing of the gap between Glasgow and Edinburgh on unemployment and employment rates for the period 1998-2000. It may be that Glasgow's improved economic position is bringing in its trail broader social benefits.

In comparison with English conurbations outside London, Edinburgh and Glasgow both appear in a relatively positive light. They have higher levels of output per resident than any English conurbation other than London. They have employment structures that are more heavily weighted towards the growth areas of financial and business services and public services, with less manufacturing employment than their English counterparts. Among the English conurbations, London is clearly in a different league with output or income levels far above the national average. Relatively low employment rates do not appear to hamper its competitive position. With its concentration of financial and business services, as well as transport and communications employment, it appears relatively well placed for the future. West Yorkshire also comes out as performing strongly on both economic and social dimensions while Tyne and Wear and Merseyside appear weak on both.

This assessment raises at least four implications for policy. First, the study exposes some of the weaknesses in official data for Britain's cities and the need for closer interrogation of the reliability and validity of some of the measures used as indicators of economic performance or competitiveness. Second, there is a need to recognise that the goal of economic development is not simply to raise output or incomes, or to improve the productivity of private firms. Competitiveness has social and environmental dimensions, as well as economic ones. Growth can be achieved in different ways and, as such, there are choices involved with trade-offs between different interest groups. There is scope for much greater debate about these strategic issues in local and regional economic development policies. Third, cities face very different challenges or starting points so different strategies are relevant to each. In particular, the balance between the need to promote growth and the need to ensure a better distribution of economic resources will vary. Glasgow appears to have a more narrowly based economy than other conurbations, so might aim to widen its base. The relatively poor performance of the northern English cities suggests the need for an enhanced regional as well as urban economic policy. Fourth, it follows from this that national economic and social programmes will vary in their relevance to different cities. Active labour market policies such as the New Deal aim to increase labour supply by increasing skills, motivation and flexibility. This may help to boost competitiveness in relatively tight labour markets such as London or Edinburgh but the benefits are likely to be more modest in cities such as Glasgow, Liverpool or Newcastle which already have such large labour surpluses. There should be greater scope for local policy makers to use national resource flows and programmes flexibly, to reflect local needs and circumstances.

Acknowledgements

The research was funded by the Economic and Social Research Council (award number L130251040) as part of the Glasgow and Edinburgh Integrative Case Study under the Cities: Competitiveness and Cohesion programme. Co-funding was also received from the Scottish Executive, Scottish Enterprise and Scottish Homes. We are grateful for their support.

Notes

[1] These figures would appear to underestimate the scale of growth in Edinburgh during this period. This could well be due to known problems in the employment data for the city, feeding through into estimates for GDP.

[2] Provisional data for 1999 are available but are known to contain major errors for Glasgow, where the toral unemployment recorded is at least four per cent too low.

[3] According to Scottish Executive definitions, derelict land is "land which has been so damaged by development or use that it is incapable of being developed ... without rehabilitiation". This includes urban and rural areas, and all sites where contamination is known or suspected. Vacant land is "land in urban settlements ... which is unused or unsightly, or which would benefit from development or improvement etc".

References

Adams, D. (1994) *Urban planning and the development process*, London: UCL Press.

Adams, D., Disberry, A., Hutchison, N. and Munjoma, T. (2001) 'Managing urban land: the case for urban partnership zones', *Regional Studies*, vol 35, no 2, pp 153-62.

Ashcroft, B., Love, J.H. and Malloy, E. (1991) 'New firm formation in the British counties with special reference to Scotland', *Regional Studies*, vol 25, no 5, pp 395-409.

Bailey, N. and Turok, I. (2000) 'Adjustment to job loss in Britain's cities', *Regional Studies*, vol 34, no 7, pp 631-53.

Bailey, N., Turok, I. and Docherty, I. (1999) *Edinburgh and Glasgow: Contrasts in competitiveness and cohesion*, Glasgow: Department of Urban Studies, University of Glasgow.

Beatty, C., Fothergill, S. and Lawless, P. (1997) 'Geographical variation in the labour market adjustment process: the UK coalfields 1981-91', *Environment and Planning A*, vol 29, pp 2041-60.

Begg, I. (1999) 'Cities and competitiveness', *Urban Studies*, vol 36, no 5-6, pp 795-810.

Begg, I., Moore, B. and Rhodes, J. (1986) 'Economic and social change in urban Britain and the inner cities', in V.I. Hausner (ed) *Critical issues in urban economic development* (vol 1), Oxford: Clarendon Press, pp 10-49.

DSS (Department of Social Security) (2001) *Client group analysis: Quarterly bulletin on the population of working age on key benefits, August 2000*, London: DSS Analytical Services Division.

DTI (Department of Trade and Industry) (2000) *Regional competitiveness indicators, February 2000*, London: DTI.

Fothergill, S., Monk, S. and Perry, M. (1987) *Property and industrial development*, London: Hutchinson.

Jensen-Butler, C. (1997) 'Competition between cities, urban performance and the role of urban policy: a theoretical framework', in C. Jensen-Butler, A. Shachar and J. Van Weesep (eds) *European cities in competition*, Aldershot: Avebury, pp 3-42.

Lever, W. and Mather, F. (1986) 'The changing structure of business and employment in the conurbation', in W.F. Lever and C. Moore (eds) *The city in transition: Policies and agencies for the economic regeneration of Clydeside*, Oxford: Clarendon Press, pp 1-21.

Lovering, J. (1997) 'Global restructuring and local impact', in M. Pacione (ed) *Britain's cities: Geographies of division in urban Britain*, London: Routledge, pp 63-87.

Mooney, G. and Johnstone, C. (1998) 'Imagining and reimagining Glasgow: Glasgow's role in urban discourse in twentieth century Britain', a paper presented at the 'Cities and the Millennium' conference, RIBA, London, December.

ONS (Office for National Statistics) (2001) *Local area and sub-regional gross domestic product*, London: ONS.

Pacione, M. (1995) *Glasgow: the socio-spatial development of the city*, Chichester: John Wiley & Sons.

Potter, J. and Moore, B. (2000) 'UK Enterprise Zones and the attraction of inward investment', *Urban Studies*, vol 37, no 8, pp 1279-312.

Scottish Enterprise (1993) *Business birth-rate strategy*, Glasgow: Scottish Enterprise.

TUC (Trades Union Congress) (2001) *Labour Market Briefing*, London: TUC Economic and Social Affairs Department.

Urban Task Force (1999) *Towards an urban renaissance*, London: E & F.N. Spon.

Webster, D. (2000) 'The geographical concentration of labour market disadvantage', *Oxford Review of Economic Policy*, vol 16, no 1, pp 114-28.

Wolman, H.L., Ford, C.C.I. and Hill, E. (1994) 'Evaluating the success of urban success stories', *Urban Studies*, vol 31, no 6, pp 835-50.

EIGHT

Innovation and clustering in the London metropolitan region

James Simmie, James Sennett and Peter Wood

Introduction

This chapter addresses the question of why the London Metropolitan Region (LMR) is home to more innovation than any other single region in the United Kingdom (UK). While functional definitions of the LMR indicate that it extends out from Greater London and incorporates most of the Outer Metropolitan Area (OMA), it is difficult to construct data sets for this precise area. Using only Greater London seriously underbounds any study of the area that functions as a whole. Therefore, for the purposes of this study, we have chosen to use the whole of the Greater South East as the LMR. This probably over-bounds London's functional daily urban system but has the merit of clearly including the whole of the London regional economy.

We have adopted a widely used European definition of innovation. This is that 'Innovation is the commercially successful exploitation of new technologies, ideas or methods through the introduction of new products or processes, or through the improvement of existing ones. Innovation is a result of an interactive learning process that involves often several actors from inside and outside the companies' (European Commission DGs XIII and XVI, 1996, p 54).

The outstanding significance of the LMR with respect to innovation in the UK has been identified by a number of previous studies. These include, among others, Hilpert (1992) who showed that London is one of only ten major 'islands of innovation' in Europe. These are defined according to the following criteria:

- islands which are specialised in more than one of the three studied techno-scientific fields;
- islands which are covering more than 20 per cent of public R&D expenditures in the country;
- strong presence in the islands of both research institutions and enterprises;
- islands which are European 'knots' in the web of cooperation links (Hilpert, 1992, p iv).

The rate of innovation in the South East (SE) has been considerably higher than that for any other region in the UK since at least the 1940s. Harris (1988), for example, using a database of significant innovations held at the Science Policy Research Unit (SPRU), University of Sussex, calculated that the level of innovation in the SE was one third higher than the UK average between 1945 and 1983. This database was developed from consultations with 400 industry experts who identified major technological developments. These were located in their respective workplaces.

In addition to the introduction and a concluding section, this chapter is divided into two main substantive sections. The first of these examines some of the secondary evidence on innovation in the region. This shows both the most innovative sectors and their level of concentration in the LMR counties, providing an empirical background to a discussion of whether or not clustering makes a major contribution to the innovative performance of these sectors in the LMR.

Following a recent Department of the Environment, Transport and the Regions (DETR) study of clusters (renamed after the 2001 general election as the Department of Local Government, Transport and the Regions) we define them as geographic concentrations of interconnected companies, specialised suppliers, services providers, firms in related industries and associated institutions, in particular, that compete but also cooperate' (DETR, 2000, p 8). Their defining characteristics are considered to be geographic concentration, and, within that concentration, supplier, collaborator and customer linkages and networks. We therefore focus on the nature of this geographic concentration and connections in the second substantive section, which provides some evidence drawn from the project's survey of innovative firms that have acquired awards for Basic Research for Industrial Technologies for Europe (BRITE).

The Brite-EuRam III programme provided support to industry, academia and research organisations for pre-competitive collaborative research in materials, design and manufacturing technologies. The main aims of the programme were to:

- stimulate technological innovation;
- encourage traditional sectors of industry to incorporate new technologies and processes;
- promote multi-sectoral and multidisciplinary technologies; and
- develop scientific and technological collaboration.

In principle, using this sample frame should influence the research findings in favour of higher than 'usual' levels of inter-firm and university collaboration, and higher than 'usual' levels of European collaboration. On the other hand, it also identifies innovations that were 'owned' and developed by firms located in the LMR that had received the awards in the UK.

The survey suggested that a distinction should be drawn between two types of connections between firms. These are mainly traded linkages and untraded networks. The former characterise supply-chain, producer and customer connections. The latter form a set of more intangible interrelationships concerned with knowledge transfers and urbanisation economies.

The evidence from our survey of firms suggests that strong local or regional linkages and networks is not a major feature of innovation in the LMR. Instead, international connections with clients and customers play a much more significant role in the development of innovations. Regional infrastructure such as Heathrow airport plays a significant role in facilitating the multiple personal contacts that are required to develop innovations.

A further highly important feature of the LMR that makes high rates of innovation possible is the presence of highly qualified pools of technical and professional labour. This is shown to be the most significant prerequisite for innovation. Because of the higher incomes and therefore higher degrees of residential locational choice of this type of labour, innovation needs to be examined not just from the point of view of firms and the economy but also in terms of quality of life choices by high quality labour.

Further work has also been conducted to compare these findings for the LMR with data gathered in a similar way by local teams in Amsterdam, Milan, Paris and Stuttgart (Simmie, 2001).

Innovation in the London economy

Innovative sectors in the LMR

The rate of innovation in the South East has been considerably higher than that for any other region in the UK. Some of this may be accounted for by the above average levels of key inputs to innovation in the region. These include professional staff such as scientists, engineers and designers in higher proportions than the UK average (Llewelyn-Davies et al, 1996a, p 51), and business enterprise R&D at around twice the UK average (Foy et al 1999, p 59).

The effort devoted to innovation in the LMR is reflected in the levels of outputs of innovations. Table 8.1 shows a comparison of the most innovative sectors in the UK as identified in the 1999 Community Innovation Survey (CIS), and the proportions of those firms located in the LMR. The CIS is a European-wide survey of a representative sample of all businesses with ten or more employees. The Office for National Statistics conducted the UK survey in 1997. This produced a total sample of 1,596 manufacturing and 744 services firms. For the purposes of the analysis in this chapter the most innovative sectors are defined as those in which more than half of the firms interviewed reported the introduction of an innovation during the survey period.

Table 8.1 shows two sets of figures derived from the CIS. Column 1 shows the percentage of firms in each sector in the UK that reported the introduction of a new technological product or process between 1994 and 1996. Column 2 shows the percentage of those innovative firms that were located in the LMR. It also shows the total percentage of innovative firms in the defined sectors that were located in the LMR.

Column 1 shows that top of the list of innovative sectors is chemicals and chemical products. This is the sector, which includes pharmaceuticals. Some 83 per cent of firms in this sector reported introducing innovations between 1994-96. This was followed by insurance and pensions (78 per cent); radio, TV and communications equipment (77 per cent); office, accounting and computing equipment (76 per cent); medical, precision and optical instruments (75 per cent); and electrical machinery (72 per cent).

Column 2 shows that 27 per cent of all innovative firms in the UK's most innovative sectors were located in the LMR. Part of the explanation of this large proportion is the sheer size of the LMR. But what is particularly significant in column 2 is the concentration of the six most innovative UK sectors in the LMR. Thus, whereas the average

Table 8.1: Innovative sectors in the London metropolitan region

Sectors	NACE code	Firms innovating England and Wales (%)[1]	Proportion of innovating firms in LMR (%)[2]
Chemicals and chemical products	24	83	**34**
Insurance and pensions	66	78	na
Radio, TV and communications equipment	32	77	**32**
Office, accounting and computing	30	76	**49**
Medical, precision and optical instrsuments	33	75	**51**
Electrical machinery	31	72	**29**
Leather products and footwear	19	68	17
Machinery	29	64	24
Rubber and plastic products	25	64	25
Computer and related activities	72	63	na
Other transport equipment	35	63	21
Motor vehicles	34	61	9
Post and telecommunications	64	60	na
Financial intermediation	65-67	58	na
Food products and beverages	15	58	21
Non-metallic mineral products	26	54	10
Basic metals	27	54	12
Textiles	17	54	7
Research and development	73	51	na
Proportion of all innovative forms in these sectors located in the LMR			27

Notes: [1]Sectors in which > 50% of firms introduced new technological product or processes between 1994-1996; [2]Proportion of firms in >50% innovating sectors located in the LMR; Na = Sample numbers of firms too small for analysis.

Source: CIS 1999

concentration for all innovative sectors in the LMR is 27 per cent, the concentration of chemicals and chemical products is 34 per cent; insurance and pensions are high – but the CIS sample numbers are too small to place a figure on how high – radio, TV and communications equipment is 32 per cent; office, accounting and computing equipment is 49 per cent, medical, precision and optical instruments is 51 per cent, and electrical machinery is 29 per cent.

Thus, a key feature of innovation in the LMR is the relatively high concentrations of some of the most innovative sectors in the UK. In this respect its historical industrial structure is highly favourable to innovation.

Not only is innovation in certain key sectors heavily concentrated in the LMR as a whole, but also it tends to be concentrated still more in some parts of the region rather than others. Table 8.2 shows that innovation in manufacturing is especially concentrated in an arc of eight of the home counties and the Rest of the South East (ROSE) stretching from Cambridgeshire, Bedfordshire and Hertfordshire in the north, through Buckinghamshire, Oxfordshire and Berkshire in the west, to Hampshire and Surrey in the south. In all these counties some 60 to 80 per cent of all manufacturing firms reported introducing innovations in the mid-1990s. These eight counties may be ranked from 1 (Berkshire) to 13 (Hertfordshire) among all UK counties. Thus only a small minority of the remaining counties in Britain can match them for rates of innovation output. There is also no other such concentration of innovative counties in the UK.

Table 8.2 also shows that Greater London appears rather like the hole in a doughnut as far as manufacturing innovation is concerned. Only around half the firms there reported the introduction of innovation during 1994-96. Table 8.3, however, suggests that there may be some compensation for Greater London's relatively poor performance in manufacturing innovation as a result of the concentration of innovative service sectors such as financial intermediation (with a location quotient – LQ, a measure of relative specialisation – of 2.27) and auxiliary financial intermediation (LQ 2.73). The LQs show that employment in these two sectors is more than twice the national average in Greater London.

Table 8.3 shows location quotients for employment in the most innovative service sectors identified by the CIS. Table 8.4 shows a similar analysis for manufacturing employment. In terms of employment, both tables show the high degrees of sectoral specialisation within LMR counties in different types of innovation. This indicates the co-location of different types of innovative firms in particular counties. Frequently these counties turn out to be located in the western arc.

Table 8.2: Proportion of manufacturing firms in LMR counties introducing new technological products and processes (1994-96)

County	Sample size number	Introducing innovations (%)	UK county ranking
Berkshire	32	81	1
Buckinghamshire	25	76	2
Bedfordshire	15	73	4
Cambridgeshire	22	73	5
Oxfordshire	17	71	6
Surrey	16	68	8
Hampshire	49	64	12
Hertfordshire	27	63	13
Essex	40	58	21
Kent	42	55	23
Greater London	100	51	27

Source: CIS 1999

Table 8.3 shows that, in addition to the concentration of innovative services in Greater London, employment in research and development services is concentrated in the western arc with particularly high LQs in Berkshire (5.79), Hertfordshire (4.13), Oxfordshire (3.61) and Cambridgeshire (4.96). The western arc features again with respect to computer and related activities with the highest LQ (4.06) in Berkshire.

Table 8.4 shows that there are also some noteworthy concentrations of innovative manufacturing sectors in the western arc counties. These include office machinery and computers in Berkshire (3.06), Buckinghamshire (2.02), Hampshire (2.37), Hertfordshire (2.83), and Cambridgeshire (2.40). Medical precision instruments is another important innovative sector in the LMR. This is particularly concentrated in Bedfordshire (2.32), Buckinghamshire (2.05), Hampshire (2.38) and West Sussex (2.65).

Despite these geographic concentrations of employment in innovative sectors, it should be noted that the western arc covers a very large area. The total area of the OMA and ROSE taken together is around 25,000 sq. km. The western arc probably includes at least half of this total. Many of the specialised employment concentrations are not even located in contiguous counties. This raises questions about the time proximity barriers that follow spatial separation and militate against the maintenance of strong regular linkages between them. This issue will be raised again below.

Table 8.3: Location quotients for most innovative service sectors in the London metropolitan region (1996)

Service sectors	NACE code	Bedfordshire	Berkshire	Buckingham-shire	East Sussex	Essex	Counties Hampshire	Hertfordshire	Kent	Oxfordshire	Surrey	West Sussex	Cambridge-shire	Greater London
Water transport	61	0.04	0.43	0.10	1.10	0.81	3.3	0.18	10.35	0.12	0.58	0.10	0.03	1.26
Post and telecommuni-cations	64	0.94	1.72	1.04	1.07	0.86	0.93	1.31	0.98	0.92	1.09	0.85	1.16	1.43
Financial intermediation	65	0.54	0.79	1.08	1.40	0.95	0.87	0.66	0.72	0.61	0.77	1.12	0.64	2.27
Insurance and pensions	66	0.30	1.42	1.09	1.13	1.02	1.29	1.05	1.37	0.30	2.16	1.94	1.98	1.41
Financial intermediation auxiliary	67	0.64	0.76	0.47	0.83	0.79	0.80	0.91	0.95	0.38	1.60	1.10	1.44	2.73
Computer and related activities	72	1.58	4.06	2.68	1.01	1.23	1.96	2.06	0.59	1.30	2.82	1.00	1.49	1.46
Research and Development	73	2.96	5.79	1.31	0.27	2.62	0.63	4.13	1.03	3.61	3.03	0.39	4.96	0.94

Notes: Location quotients: a value of 1.00 would occur if the county had the same proportion of employees for each sector out of total employment to that of Great Britain as a whole, ie LQ = (county employment sector X / total county employment) / (GB employment sector X / total employment). Most innovative sectors = 50% or more of firms in the UK introducing technological product and process innovations between 1994 and 1996 from the CIS survey combined with Butchart's (1987) definition of high-tech industries.

Source: Annual Employment Survey

Table 8.4: Location quotients for most innovative manufacturing sectors in the London metropolitan region (1996)

Manufacturing sectors	NACe code	Bedfordshire	Berkshire	Buckingham-shire	East Sussex	Essex	Hampshire	Hertfordshire	Kent	Oxfordshire	Surrey	West Sussex	Cambridge-shire	Greater London
Food products and beverages	15	0.53	1.18	0.77	0.51	0.60	0.38	0.37	0.51	0.68	0.18	0.42	1.22	0.37
Tobacco products	16	0	0	3.12	0	0	3.82	0	0	0	3.90	0	0	0
Leather products and footwear	19	0.16	0.05	0.39	0.09	0.46	0.07	0.17	0.58	0.11	0.09	0.42	0.67	0.48
Chemicals and chemical products	24	0.84	0.95	0.70	0.52	0.67	0.88	1.37	1.06	0.53	0.58	1.73	0.90	0.53
Rubber and plastic products	25	1.38	0.46	1.05	0.79	0.90	0.77	0.97	0.96	1.04	0.63	0.60	1.16	0.30
Other non-metallic products	26	0.95	0.46	0.28	0.67	0.80	0.41	0.35	0.92	0.35	0.40	0.60	0.96	0.21
Fabricated metal products	28	1.28	0.65	0.89	0.52	0.88	0.78	0.84	0.66	0.51	0.56	0.78	0.60	0.31
Machinery and equipment	29	1.96	0.81	1.23	0.62	1.04	1.36	0.97	0.67	0.70	0.57	1.00	1.97	0.21
Office machinery and computers	30	1.10	3.06	2.02	1.08	1.93	2.37	2.83	0.41	1.23	1.37	0.69	2.40	0.52
Electrical machinery/ apparatus	31	1.70	0.61	1.02	1.25	1.26	1.31	1.15	0.84	1.11	0.64	1.05	0.63	0.40

Table 8.4: contd.../

	NACe code	Bedfordshire	Berkshire	Buckingham-shire	East Sussex	Essex	Hampshire	Herefordshire	Kent	Oxfordshire	Surrey	West Sussex	Cambridge-shire	Greater London
								Counties						
Radio/TV communications equipment	32	0.76	1.70	1.94	0.88	1.93	1.68	1.28	0.64	0.23	1.25	1.21	1.55	0.31
Medical precision instruments	33	2.32	1.10	2.05	1.28	1.71	2.38	1.65	1.90	1.53	1.27	2.65	1.67	0.44
Motor vehicles, trailers	34	4.18	0.51	0.33	0.06	0.90	0.85	0.25	0.30	2.31	0.46	0.13	1.08	0.36
Other transport equipment	35	0.48	0.33	0.68	0.26	0.36	2.58	0.45	0.19	0.35	0.75	1.06	0.85	0.11

Notes: Location quotients: a value of 1.00 would occur if the county had the same proportion of employees for each sector out of total employment to that of Great Britain as a whole, ie LQ = (county employment sector X / total county employment) / (GB employment sector X / total employment). Most innovative sectors = 50% or more of firms in the UK introducing technological product and process innovations between 1994 and 1996 from the CIS survey combined with Butchart's (1987) definition of high-tech industries.

Source: Annual Employment Survey

Innovation and clustering in the LMR

Interest in the identification of spatial concentrations of co-located innovative firms has been inspired by the work of Michael Porter (1990, 1998). It has been taken up by the new RDAs in their innovation strategies particularly by the East of England Development Agency (1999) and the Government Office for the South East (1998). Porter has argued that 'Nations succeed not in isolated industries … but in clusters of industries connected through vertical and horizontal relationships' (1990).

One of the key issues raised by this assertion is the importance and significance of intra-cluster linkages and networks. As the concept of clusters has been developed these connections have received increasing emphasis. Waits (1997), for example, argues that 'regional economic performance (quality jobs, wealth creation) is the product of a 'portfolio' of competitive, export-oriented, technology driven industry clusters and is dependent on collaborative actions between industries and public institutions to lay the foundations that support industry competitiveness'. In his view clusters may be initiated either by market actions such as in the most famous of them all in Silicon Valley, or by public intervention such as in the software clusters of Austin, Texas. They are also dynamic in that any given cluster may be emerging where inter-firm linkages are being established; expanding where linkages have achieved critical mass and represent a region's current specialisations; or transforming, in which case mature segments may be in decline and the seeds of new clusters may be forming.

Cooke (1999) also argues that fully functioning clusters have formal sector support infrastructure. Accordingly he defines clusters as 'Geographically proximate firms in vertical and horizontal relationships, involving a localised enterprise support infrastructure with a shared developmental vision for business growth, based on competition and cooperation in a specific market field' (see also Cook, Davies and Wilson in this volume).

While the evidence presented in Tables 8.3 and 8.4 shows that there are spatial concentrations of co-located innovative firms in certain sectors in some counties, there is little empirical evidence on how far these may constitute functioning local clusters. Despite the general enthusiasm shown particularly by both GOSE (1998) and EEDA (1999) for encouraging cluster development as a basis of their new regional innovation strategies, there is also a lack of evidence on precisely what their contributions to innovation might be. These are some of the key issues addressed by the research analysed here.

We argue that the defining characteristics of an established cluster are its geographically concentrated and mainly traded horizontal and vertical linkages. These include supply-chain relationships, collaborations and relationships with customers and clients. In addition, a further defining characteristic is the existence of mainly untraded networks. These include informal knowledge transfers along with other urbanisation economies. Together these represent both supply- and demand-side relationships.

The current policy interest in the identification and encouragement of local clusters has, not surprisingly, discovered some at least 'emerging' clusters with sufficient internal linkages to have formed formal associations and therefore to meet Cookes' (1999) requirement of having a formal local representative organisation. Cooke himself has used existing literature sources to identify clusters of marine construction in Southampton, biotechnology and motor sport in Oxfordshire, biotechnology and ICT in Cambridge, motor sport in Guildford, and financial services and new media in London. GOSE has identified representative sector support associations such as Southern Bioscience, Wired Sussex, Farnborough Aerospace Consortium, Electronics Action Group, Oxfordshire Motorsport Forum and Southern Medical. Interestingly, however, GOSE also comments that 'all these organisations are relatively new (1998, p 9). They are also all market driven and self-organising clusters. In the Eastern region, EEDA has identified clusters of life sciences, information and communications technology, electronics and research centres (1999, p 2). No evidence is offered on whether or not these groupings are formally associated in any way.

While it is possible to identify spatial concentrations of innovative sectors in the LMR, some of which are formally associated clusters, it is not yet clear whether most of the concentrations are moving in this direction or, if they are, whether this will contribute significantly to the innovative performance of individual firms. Furthermore, even where fully functioning local clusters do exist, it is not known what contributions, if any, they make to innovation. Much of the debate on these issues focuses on the relative importance of intra-cluster linkages and networks compared with other regional agglomeration economies on the one hand and international trade on the other (see, for example, Hart and Simmie, 1997; Simmie 1998a, 1998b).

The main question addressed here, however, is: how significant these local traded linkages are for innovation? Second, over and above these types of linkages and networks, what other types of linkages and urban assets make major contributions to stimulating and enabling firms to become successful and competitive innovators? These questions are addressed in the following analysis of a survey of innovative firms in the LMR.

Survey results

Characteristics of the sample

In order to investigate the questions outlined within the resources available it was necessary to identify a sample frame of innovative firms. Because the survey was being conducted in four other innovative cities in Europe, it was also necessary to use a sample frame that was identified on the same criteria throughout Europe. This was achieved by adopting the lists of firms that had won the common European award for Basic Research for Industrial Technologies for Europe (BRITE). This award provided support to industry for pre-competitive collaborative research in materials, design and manufacturing technologies. The aims of the programme were to stimulate technological innovation through the incorporation of new technologies and scientific and technological collaboration.

During the course of the programme up to 1999, the time of interviews, firms located in the South East region had won around 56 awards. Most were located in the LMR. Some firms had won more than one award but were only interviewed with respect to their most recent. Telephone interviews were conducted with all the surviving individual award winning firms. This yielded a total sample of 33 firms. This is a relatively small number and so the results reported should be regarded as suggestive rather than definitive. They were added to similar surveys in our four other European cities to yield a much larger total European sample. They were also used as the basis of a second, more detailed survey of innovative firms in the LMR.

Table 8.5 shows the nature and composition of the sample. From it, it may be seen that a majority (51 per cent) of the firms were private, national, UK firms. A significant proportion (39 per cent) were multinational companies. Small proportions were either public enterprises or other types of organisation. Most of the firms were micro (30 per cent) or small (37 per cent) in terms of their total numbers of employees. There were smaller proportions of medium-sized firms (18 per cent) and a small, but significant element of large companies (12 per cent).

Significance of local clusters, linkages and networks

The firms came from a select collection of manufacturing and service sectors. Prominent among the manufacturing sectors were medical and surgical equipment, and instruments and appliances for measuring and checking, with four firms apiece. Services were represented by software consultancy and supply (four), and R&D on natural sciences and

Table 8.5: Sample structure

Type of organisation (%)	Private national firm	52
	Private multinational firm	39
	Public enterprise	6
	Other	3
	Total N = 100%	33
Size of firm (%)	Micro, < 20 employees	30
	Small, 21 to 250	37
	Medium, 251 to 1000	18
	Large, > 1000 employees	12
	No information	3
	Total N = 100%	33
Industrial sector, numbers	Chemical products less pharmaceuticals	1
	Rubber and plastic products	1
	Non-metallic mineral products	1
	Machinery not elsewhere classified	2
	Electrical machinery	2
	Medical, precision and optical instruments, watches and clocks	1
	Motor vehicles	2
	Pharmaceuticals	1
	Basic metals ferrous	1
	Insulated wire and cable	1
	Electronic components including semiconductors	2
	Medical and surgical equipment	4
	Instruments and appliances for measuring, checking	4
	Aerospace	1
	Software consultancy and supply	4
	R&D on natural sciences and engineering	2
	No information	3
	Total N = 100%	33

Source: BRITE firms survey

engineering with two firms. Taken together they form a reasonably representative set of examples of the most innovative sectors in the UK as identified by the CIS.

Turning first to the question of the relative importance of local clusters for innovation in the LMR, all the definitions cited above are agreed that the first defining characteristics of an established cluster are its horizontal and vertical linkages. These include intra-cluster organisation and production linkages along with external linkages to other firms and customers. The geographic extent of these linkages must also be reasonably local and significant over and above the normal run-of-the-mill connections that all firms have simply by virtue of being in business.

As mentioned above, we distinguished in this study between mainly traded supply and demand linkages, and untraded networks. The survey of BRITE award winning firms shows that they do indeed use external linkages and networks to assist them in the development of specific innovation projects. Firms were asked to rate the importance of different types of linkages and networks on a scale ranging from one (not important) to five (very important) with respect to their specific innovation projects.

Table 8.6 shows that mainly traded business linkages and external collaborations played the most important parts in their innovations. The mean score for traded business linkages, which included customers, suppliers, competitors and business services, was 3.56. Similarly for collaborators which include, predominantly, both public and private research and development organisations, such as government research establishments or research associations, the mean score was 3.61.

Suppliers and customers were also used as mainly untraded sources of knowledge and information. Suppliers were scored 2.38, while customers were rated as slightly more important at 2.94.

Mainly untraded learning and social networks were scored lowest of all. Thus, characteristically, local networks such as those including local universities, training organisations (1.81), friends or ex-colleagues (1.9) were given much lower scores for their contributions to innovation.

While these figures support one of the basic tenets of functioning clusters, namely the significance of external networks and linkages, the data on the geography of these connections tell a somewhat different story. Respondents were asked to specify the locations of their vertical linkages in terms of their suppliers and customers. They were also asked to identify the locations of potential horizontal linkages in terms of where their main competitors were located. In order to simplify these responses they were divided into quartiles and scored 0 for no linkages to a particular location, up to 4 for more than 76 per cent links to the identified area.

Table 8.6: Contact linkages and networks

Type of contact		Importance for innovation Mean score I (not important) to 5 (very important)
Mainly traded linkages	Business (customers, suppliers, competitors or business services)	3.56
	Collaborators (external organisations)	3.61
Mainly untraded sources of knowledge and information	Suppliers	2.38
	Customers	2.94
Mainly untraded networks	Learning (education, training or information)	1.81
	Friends (friends or ex-colleagues)	1.9

Source: BRITE firms survey

Mean scores were then calculated for a range of different locations. The higher the resulting scores, the greater were the linkages with the area identified. Lower total scores signify fewer linkages with the location specified. The results of this analysis are shown in Table 8.7.

In respect of traded vertical linkages between the firms and either their suppliers or their customers, the strongest links are shown to be national and European rather than local or regional. National suppliers and customers located more than 101 km from the innovating firms scored 1.75 and 1.67 respectively. European suppliers scored 1.25 and customers 1.45. These figures compare with 1 or less for suppliers and customers located less than 100 km for the innovating firm.

An element of these results springs from the selection of European BRITE award firms as our sample frame. There is an inbuilt requirement in the award that firms must have other European partners in their innovative projects. While this helps to account for the levels of European linkages, it does not account for the lower levels of local linkages or the fairly high importance attached to linkages with firms in the US.

The potential for horizontal linkages with firms in the same sector as the BRITE award winners was limited by their international dispersion. Assuming that firms working in the same fields are also likely to be competitors, Table 8.7 shows that there is a greater tendency for them to be located in the US (1.84) Europe (1.65) or Japan (1.06) than in the same region (0.74). Thus potential horizontal linkages with competitors are limited by their generally smaller numbers within the LMR than in other advanced national economies.

Table 8.7: Geography of traded linkages and competition

Locations		Suppliers Mean scores	Customers Mean scores	Competitors Mean scores
International	Europe	1.25	1.45	1.65
	USA	0.78	1.09	1.84
	Japan	0.72	0.91	1.06
	Other Pacific Rim	0.56	0.61	0.61
	World-wide	0.66	0.91	1
National	101 km to UK	1.75	1.67	1.1
Regional/local	Regional 51 to 100 kms	1	0.91	0.74
	Local < 50kms	1	0.76	0.74

Note: Mean scores by quartile where 0 = no links to the specified location to 4 = 76 - 100% links to the location.

Source: BRITE firms survey

Reasons for the innovative success of the LMR

Given the above doubts about the significance of clustering as a basis for the undoubted innovative success of the LMR, what other factors that characterise the region are responsible for this success? In order to investigate this issue firms were asked to rank the importance to innovation in the LMR of a wide range of possible contributing factors. A factor analysis was used to simplify their responses into seven groups of closely related variables. Mean scores for the importance of these groups of variables to innovation projects were then calculated. The results of this analysis are shown in Table 8.8.

The relative importance attached by firms to the wide range of variables revealed that they regarded a number of traditional agglomeration economies as significant. These could be classified into Hoover's (1937, 1948) classic distinction between urbanisation and localisation economies. To these may be added both internal and globalisation economies (Simmie and Sennett, 1999).

Urbanisation economies consist in the main of economic effects, which arise outside the firm but within the urban region. Four such groups were identified by the BRITE firms as contributing in different degrees to their innovations. These were transportation infrastructure; general and specialised business knowledge and information; finance, training, knowledge and information; factors of production, and technical and professional labour. The more detailed factors making up these main components were rated by the firms for their importance to innovation. This was done on a scale ranging from one (not important) to five (very important).

It may be seen from Table 8.8 that the factor rated most important by the firms was the availability of professional experts for recruitment (3.77). High quality, usually highly qualified labour, is a crucial requirement for innovation. Without the knowledge and experience possessed by such workers, innovation, particularly high-technology innovation, simply cannot take place. So one of the key reasons why the LMR is the most innovative region in the UK is the interrelationship between the concentration of highly competent professional and technical workers in its local labour markets combined with the concentration of the types of firms shown in Table 8.1. Much of the region's innovative success hangs on the availability of such workers and this issue will be taken up again later in the chapter.

Table 8.8 also shows that firms rated good transportation infrastructure as quite important in their choice of location. In particular, good access to a major airport (3.27) was rated as an important locational consideration by innovative firms. This is a significant finding in the context of the international networks and linkages used by firms, as Heathrow airport is renowned for the number of business destinations served and is a critical piece of infrastructure enabling firms to maintain linkages with their important international suppliers and customers, and to monitor what their main competitors are doing. The scale and numbers of destinations served by Heathrow is unique in the UK. It provides the South East with a major trading advantage over all other regions.

Access to Heathrow is geographically skewed to the west of London for both road and public transport. Road access within one hour extends well beyond Newbury to the west and barely reaches the centre of London in the east (Llewlyn-Davies, 1996a, map 17, p 79). This again favours location in the western arc for firms that are dependent on regular international networks and linkages.

Other factors of production that were of some importance to firms included land and labour in the form of skilled manual labour (2.33) and suitable premises (3.29) at reasonable cost (3.35). Premises and their cost may be regarded as important by firms more because of the difficulties associated with acquiring them than because of their direct contribution to innovation. Planning policy severely restricts the availability of land and buildings in the South East. It contributes to increasing their price and therefore adds to the costs of production in the region. It may well be an important factor in the decentralisation of innovative firms to the outer parts of the western ROSE.

No other factors were rated as important as professional labour, the availability and cost of premises, and good access to a major airport. These represent the major urbanisation effects for the innovative firms surveyed. In addition to urbanisation economies, three groups of variables associated with localisation economies emerged from the factor analysis of all locational considerations. Localisation economies are generally *external* to the firm but *internal* to the industry. If strong industrial clustering was an important requirement for innovative firms, it might be expected

Table 8.8: Importance of reasons for the location of innovative firms in the London metropolitan region (mean scores)

Urbanisation effects, external to the firm but internal to the urban region	Group 1: Transportation infrastructure	Low levels of traffic congestion	2.27
		Good access to London	2.61
		Good rail connections	2.39
		Good access to national road network	2.9
		Good access to major airport	3.27
	Group 2: General and specialised business knowledge and information	Access to private general business services	1.57
		Access to private specialised business services	1.6
		Proximity of collaborators	2.1
		Proximity of business services	1.5
		Proximity of sources of information	1.7
	Group 3: Finance, training, knowledge and information	Access to financial capital	1.97
		Local public business support services	1.62
		Contributions from TECs	1.27
		Contributions from Business LINKS	1.43
		Contributions from Universities	2.42
	Group 4: Factors of production	Availability of skilled manual labour	2.33
		Availability of suitable premises	3.29
		Cost of premises	3.35
		Availability of professional experts to recruit	3.77
Localisation reasons, external to the firm but internal to the industry	Group 5: Local industrial knowledge and experience	Presence of ex-colleagues	1.65
		Presence of friends	1.4
	Group 6: Supply factors	Cost of labour	2.39
		Proximity of suppliers	1.93
	Group 7: Demand factors	Proximity of customers	1.6
		Proximity of competitors	1.23

Note: Mean scores of importance to innovation: 1 = not important to 5 = very important.

Source: BRITE firms survey

that individual variables associated with such arrangements would be rated highly. This is not the case.

The localisation groups of variables that emerged from the factor analysis included supply and demand factors that would be expected to be important if strong local vertical linkages were significant contributors to innovation. They also included local industrial knowledge and experience which could be expected to form the basis of a cluster or new industrial district atmosphere where such a phenomenon existed and was perceived by firms to make important contributions to innovation.

In fact Table 8.8 shows that proximity to both customers (1.6) and suppliers (1.93) is not rated as important by the BRITE firms. The same may be said about the presence of friends (1.4) and ex-colleagues (1.65). This would seem to reinforce the findings shown in Table 8.7 that suggested the greater importance of national and international networks and linkages as compared to those within the LMR.

Given the importance attached by firms to the availability of professional and technical labour in the development of innovations, a closer analysis was conducted of their use, qualifications and recruitment. Firms were asked to say what proportions of different kinds of people were employed in the development of their innovations. Their responses were divided into quartiles and scored from 0 (= none) to 4 (= 76-100 per cent). The higher the mean scores, the higher the proportions of particular types of labour were employed, possessed higher qualifications or were recruited locally. Table 8.9 shows the results of these analyses.

The two types of labour most frequently employed on the development of innovations were technologists (3.0) and those involved in production processes (1.59). The technologists were the most likely to hold higher formal qualifications such as degrees or higher diplomas (3.12). Where recruitment was required to work on the new innovation projects, technologists were also the most likely to have been recruited from within 50 km (2.23).

Local recruitment was not a strong feature of firm behaviour for two main reasons. The first was their already significant internal resources of graduates and R&D employees. The second was their ability to recruit the necessary highly qualified staff over a wide area. This recruitment area extended over much of the South and into international labour markets. It was marked by highly qualified individuals spiraling up their chosen career paths. In order to achieve their career goals they often had to move over significant distances.

Where career advancement is frequently accompanied by residential mobility, the ability to attract and recruit professional and technical labour

Table 8.9: Use and recruitment of professional and technical expertise

	Worked directly on innovation	Staff holding higher qualification	Recruited within 50 km
	Mean scores	Mean scores	Mean scores
Professional expertise			
Technology	3	3.12	2.23
Finance	0.81	1.35	1.93
Marketing	1.25	1.45	1.63
Management	1.09	1.48	1.67
Training or recruitment	0.72	1.19	1.62
Production processes	1.59	1.55	1.66

Note: Mean scores where 0 = 0, to 4 = 76% to 100%.

Source: BRITE firms survey

to innovation projects is partly dependent on their personal quality of life requirements. This was reflected in the survey findings by the high scores recorded for the local requirements of such highly paid workers. These factors are important to insure the presence, retention or recruitment of these crucial human resources. Table 8.10 shows that relatively high scores were recorded for all the major quality of life requirements investigated. These included the availability of good housing (3.58), the proximity of good schools (3.53), the proximity of good leisure facilities (3.06), the proximity of good public services (3.03), and a generally favourable environment (3.85). Residential mobility is an important way of satisfying these requirements. Highly paid professional and technical workers in constantly changing labour markets are likely to have several chances to achieve them in the context of longer distance movements for career reasons. The ROSE, in particular, provides multiple opportunities for the achievement of these quality of life requirements.

A final reason for the relative success of the LMR, in terms of the high rates of innovation found there, is its major function as an international hub or gateway city. Table 8.7 has already shown the importance of international linkages to innovative firms and Table 8.8 the significance of good access to a major airport in facilitating these networks and linkages. There is also the predominance of London Heathrow among other major international hub airports, which contributes to the region's status as the most significant international gateway to the UK. The flows of people, experience, ideas and international best practice through the LMR on a

Table 8.10: Importance of local requirements for human capital

	Mean score for importance 1 (not important) to 5 (very important)
Local requirements	
Availability of good housing	3.58
Proximity of good schools	3.53
Proximity of good liesure facilities	3.06
Proximity of good public services e.g. hospitals	3.03
Good environment	3.85

Source: BRITE firms survey

daily basis provide critical leading edge inputs to innovation there. They also provide the networks and linkages to international clients and customers who are also such an important part of the demand pulls for innovation.

Exports of innovations new to the world are an important manifestation of the outward-looking and international trading role of the LMR. BRITE awards are given to develop inventions, which have already been the subject of some R&D and are regarded as promising commercial innovations. The awards are given before the inventions are brought to market. At the time of interviewing, therefore, some of the projects had not quite arrived in their respective markets. Table 8.11 shows that this amounted to 50 per cent of the total sample. Despite this, all projects were catagorised according to their degree of novelty. This ranged from 'new to the world' through 'new to the UK, sector, or firm'. Those firms producing innovations new to the world are regarded as 'leaders in their fields'. Those developing innovations in the UK, their sector or their firm for the first time are regarded as 'followers'.

Table 8.11 shows that leaders (26 per cent) were twice as likely as followers (12 per cent) to be exporting more than 81 per cent of their innovation. Overall, among those innovations that had been brought to market, 50 per cent of firms were exporting more than a fifth of their total output. The exporting potential and requirements of leaders of innovation in the LMR is considerable. The dual characteristics of leading edge innovation, new to the world, and consequential competitiveness in advanced international markets are a special feature of innovative activity in the LMR. The region's accessibility to new people and ideas from around the world plays an important role in both the inputs to these innovations and their export outputs.

Lessons and conclusions

Looked at from the point of view of the space economy of the LMR, the key components of innovation are the internal characteristics of the firms, the local sectoral linkages and support systems within particular industries, the nature and scale of the region's urban assets, and its connections with and competitiveness in advanced international markets. First, as far as internal characteristics of firms is concerned, research in the Cambridge region has shown that 90 per cent of firms rated sources of innovation within the firm as dominant within their innovative activities (Keeble et al, 1999). In particular the individual entrepreneur's inclination to innovate and the ways in which key internal human resources are organised are very significant factors driving innovation (Vaessen and Wever, 1993; Vaessen and Keeble, 1995).

The survey reported in this chapter suggests the significance of both the inclination of different types of firms to innovate and the importance of their internal organisation and resources in determining their capability to innovate. The strong combinations of these characteristics among the award-winning firms contributed to the high proportion of firms who appeared to be producing highly novel and world beating innovations. Leading firms with innovations new to the world made up 74 per cent of those interviewed.

Second, localisation economies, as first identified by Hoover (1937, 1948), consist of economies that are external to the firm but internal to the industry or sector. Marshall (1952) argued that one of the main

Table 8.11: Innovation and exports

	Innovation novelty		
	New to the world	New to UK, sector or firm	
Exports	Leaders (%)	Followers (%)	Total (%)
Not on market as yet	44	62	50
1 to 20%	0	0	0
21 to 40%	4	0	3
41 to 60%	17	13	16
61 to 80%	9	13	9
More than 81%	26	12	22
Total N = 100%	23	8	31

Source: BRITE firms survey

reasons for the spatial concentration of industries is the fact that market success depends on specialisation and the development of effective industrial organisation. The benefits of localised specialisation include increases in the quality and specialisation of the labour force and the increased use of highly specialised machinery. Taken together the 'concentration of firms in close geographical proximity allows all to enjoy the benefits of large scale production and of technical and organisational innovations which are beyond the scope of (most) individual firms' (Keeble and Wilkinson, 1999). The empirical evidence gathered so far indicates that such intra-sectoral relationships are in the minority in the LMR.

There is no doubt that a number of highly specialised and innovative industrial sectors have many firms co-located in various parts of the LMR. Despite this, there is not much evidence that this leads to these sectors developing functioning sectoral organisation on a local or regional basis. Where such evidence exists, it is often a phenomenon that develops after individual firms have made their innovation and locational decisions on an individual and independent basis. The sample size of this pilot study is not large enough to establish whether there are any particular sectoral exceptions to this general rule.

Third, urbanisation economies consist of external economies available to all firms irrespective of sector. They are therefore external to both the firm and industry but largely confined or internal to the urban region. The main dynamic characteristics of urbanisation economies are that:

> Firms and other actors will change who and what they buy from and sell to, simply in response to current advantage and their very specific requirements. The system is without any particular observable organisation or inter-agent loyalty, and simply functions as an ecology of activities benefiting from proximity, and developing emergent forms of specialisation – possibly including distinct forms of economic culture. (Gordon and McCann, 1998)

This may be defined as a 'pick and mix' space economy. The pick and mix space economy of the LMR benefits from a number of advantages accruing from the sheer numbers and variety of firms located there. During the course of the development of a particular innovation, leading firms will need different types of expertise and inputs to the project. Over the time taken to develop and market the innovation, different combinations may be picked and mixed in different ways to produce the final result. This reflects the continuously changing needs of any given innovation project. The variety of possible inputs located in the LMR makes it easier to satisfy these needs within this region than in others less well endowed.

The possibilities for discontinuity and breakdown of static frameworks required by product innovation are greatest in core metropolitan regions such as London. The sheer numbers and densities of other relevant firms provide endless opportunities for discontinuities and new recombinations of factor inputs to innovation on an irregular 'pick and mix' basis. Some 15 per cent of all UK businesses are located in Greater London alone. Around a third of all the most innovative firms in the UK are located in the LMR. The most innovative sectors are also over-represented in the LMR. Somewhere between one fifth to one third of all the firms in the most innovative sectors are concentrated in the urban region. Many of them are to be found in the 'golden arc' running from Cambridgeshire around the west of Greater London as far as Surrey.

The main urbanisation economies that firms rated as important to their innovations were the availability of professional and technical expertise, skilled labour and premises, and access to a major international hub airport. Professional and technical labour provides the major key to innovation in the LMR. For the firms interviewed, this was particularly true with respect to technologists and production workers. Without these two groups innovation could not take place. Although the concentration of such highly qualified and skilled groups is an important feature of the LMR in general, their recruitment to particular innovation projects often took place over quite long distances. Such recruitment patterns seem to reflect moves made by career spiralists as they improve their employment with each successive geographic move.

The attraction and retention of such key labour is an important reason why firms tended to rate quality of life features as making significant contributions to their innovative capabilities. The ability to offer highly paid key staff the kinds of homes, schools, public services, leisure facilities and environments that they like is an important external advantage to firms located to the arc west of London.

Finally, since Hoover's original work (1937, 1948) major economic changes have taken place. One of the most important, particularly since the 1970s and accelerating during the 1990s (Veltz, 1993; Gordon, 1996), is the globalisation of the world economy. This has involved, among other phenomena, internationalisation, growing instability in product markets, more intense competition, and greater emphasis on competition based on quality and variety rather than price. These changes place a competitive premium on economies which may accrue locally but which may be gathered from around the advanced economies.

At first sight, globalisation would appear to reduce the incentives for firms to invest time and resources in purely local clusters. Instead they clearly need to be competitive in international markets. This requires capabilities for fast changing business strategies, flexibility and constant re-combinations of specialised suppliers and other business partners. Globalisation and changing products has also reduced the importance of traditional localised factors of production. All these factors seem to emphasise the importance of 'weak ties' (Granovetter, 1973) which are multiple, open ended, changing, and link both national producers and international customers.

In the context of globalisation, inputs to innovation are unlikely to be locally confined. In studies of innovation in SMEs in the Cambridge region (Keeble et al, 1999), and in our survey, firms used both national and international inputs to their innovations. These included research collaborations and professional staff recruitment. Both of these key inputs to innovation were more often sought at the UK national and even international level than within the local urban region.

The markets for innovation are mostly found among the more advanced G7 economies or those rich in natural resources such as oil. Demand pulls are one of the most significant elements of the whole process. Without the possibility of selling innovations the main incentive for engaging in the activity at all would be missing. A key feature of globalisation is the growing significance of international markets. Innovative and competitive firms sell much, and sometimes all, of their outputs in to other national markets. In the BRITE survey this was particularly true of the innovations that were described by firms as being new to the world. Linkages with clients and customers in these foreign markets are therefore crucial to the commercial success of innovative new products and services.

The LMR, with its long history of international trade, functions as a major gateway and frontier with international customers and suppliers. Heathrow airport, serving multiple business destinations, is a key infrastructural asset facilitating such contacts. Streams of people flow through it carrying with them ideas and knowledge of international best practice. The communication of this experience is best accomplished with face-to-face meetings. These are especially important during the initial stages of the development of innovations.

It is the ability of innovative firms in the LMR to sell large proportions of their new products into international markets that is the key indicator of the competitiveness of the region. Although these firms are a minority of all firms in the region, they make up a majority of the 30 per cent or so of firms that export beyond UK national markets. This minority makes up the important export base of the LMR. It is argued here, therefore, that the competitiveness of London is indicated by the proportion of firms that export from the region. Innovation, particularly product innovation, is the key underlying factor of this success.

References

Butchart, R. (1987) 'A new UK definition of the high-tech industries', *Economic Trends*, no 400, pp 82-8.

Cooke, P. (1999) 'The networked economy', presentation delivered at ESRC workshop on networks and clusters, Bristol: School for Policy Studies, University of Bristol, December.

DETR (Department of the Environment, Transport and the Regions) (2000) *Planning for clusters*, London: DETR.

East of England Development Agency (1999) *Innovation and technology strategy*, Cambridge: EEDA.

European Commission (1996) *DGs XIII and XVI RITTS and RIS Guidebook, Regional Actions for Innovation*, Brussels: EC.

Foy, S., Walton, F. and Campbell, M. (1999) *The State of the UK regions: A regional profile*, Leeds: Policy Research Institute, Leeds Metropolitan University.

Gordon, I.R. (1996) 'Territorial competition and locational advantage in the London region', paper presented to the American Association of Geographers annual conference, Charlotte, NC.

Gordon, I.R. and McCann, P. (1998) 'Industrial clusters, agglomeration and/or social networks?', paper presented at the Regional Science Association British and Irish Section conference, York.

GOSE (Government Office for the South East) (1998) *Developing a regional innovation strategy for the South East: A report on the conclusions of the Ashdown Park workshop*, Guildford: GOSE, 1-2 July.

Granovetter, M. (1973) 'The strength of weak ties', *American Journal of Sociology*, no 78, pp 1360-80.

Harris, L. (1988) 'SPRU', *SE Economy*, p 51.

Hart, D. and Simmie, J.M. (1997) 'Innovation, competition and the structure of local production networks: initial findings from the Hertfordshire project', *Local Economy*, pp 235-46, November.

Hilpert, U. (1992) *Archipelago Europe – Islands of innovation, synthesis report, vol 18*, Prospective Dossier No 1, Science, Technology and Social and Economic Cohesion in the Community, Fast Programme, Brussels: DG XII, European Commission.

Hoover, E.M. (1937) *Location theory and the shoe and leather industries*, Cambridge, MA: Harvard University Press.

Hoover, E. M. (1948) *The location of economic activity*, New York, NY: McGraw-Hill.

Keeble, D., Lawson, C., Moore, B. and Wilkinson, F. (1999) 'Collective learning processes, networking and "institutional thickness" in the Cambridge region', *Regional Studies*, special issue, Regional networking, collective learning and innovation in high technology SMEs in Europe, vol 33, no 4, pp 319-32.

Keeble, D. and Wilkinson, F. (1999) 'Collective learning and knowledge development in the evolution of regional clusters of high technology SMEs in Europe', *Regional Studies*, special issue, Regional networking, collective learning and innovation in high technology SMEs in Europe, vol 33, no 4, pp 295-303.

King, A.D. (1991) *Global cities: Post-imperialism and the internationalization of London*, London: Routledge.

Llewelyn-Davies, UCL Bartlett School of Planning & Comedia (1996a) *South East economy research study: Summary report*, Guildford: GOSE.

Llewelyn-Davies, UCL Bartlett School of Planning & Comedia (1996b) *Four world cities: A comparative study of London, Paris, New York, and Tokyo*, London: Llewelyn-Davies.

Marshall, A. (1952) *Principles of economics*, London: Macmillan.

Porter, M. E. (1990) *The competitive advantage of nations*, London: Macmillan.

Porter, M.E. (1998) *On competition*, Cambridge, MA:Harvard Business School Press.

Simmie, J.M. (1998a) 'Innovate or stagnate: economic planning choices for local production nodes in the global economy', *Planning Practice and Research*, vol 13, no 1, pp 35-51.

Simmie, J.M. (1998b) 'Reasons for the development of "islands of innovation": evidence from Hertfordshire', *Urban Studies*, vol 35, no 8, pp 1261-89.

Simmie, J.M. (ed) (2001) *Innovative cities*, London: E&FN Spon.

Simmie, J.M. and Sennett, J. (1999) 'Innovative clusters: global or local linkages?', *National Institute Economic Review*, 4/99, no 170, pp 87-98, October.

Vaessen, P.M.M. and Wever, E. (1993) 'Spatial responsiveness of small firms', *Tijdschrift voor Economische en Sociale Geographie*, vol 84, pp 119-31.

Vaessen, P.M.M. and Keeble, D. (1995) 'Growth-oriented SMEs in unfavourable regional environments', *Regional Studies*, vol 29, pp 489-505.

Veltz, P. (1993) 'L'economie des villes, entre la montee du global et le retour du local', Territoires et Societes (mimeo)

Waits, M. J. (1997) 'The state of cluster-based economic development in Arizona', paper presented to the International Society of Optical Engineering, Arizona: Arizona State University.

NINE

Locating the competitive city in England

Iain Deas and Benito Giordano

Introduction

The creation of a 'competitive' city is a goal that has proved consistently alluring to local economic development policy makers. Yet the notion of 'urban competitiveness' remains a somewhat nebulous one, its conceptual turbidity rendering its measurement notably problematic. The purpose of this chapter is to begin to address this by exploring both the means by which competitiveness might be conceptualised in a rather firmer way, and the ways in which it might be measured. Our aim in doing so is to suggest a prototype approach, which can help detect, and make sense of, variations in urban competitiveness across a range of cities.

Academic comment on the concept of urban competitiveness has been notably extensive, in part reflecting disagreements about its meaning (or, at a deeper level, its value). Its popular usage has tended to be as an equivalent of economic performance in the broadest sense of the term, but it is a concept that remains highly contested. Much of the debate has been fractured between two near-antithetic conceptions. At one extreme is the view – prominent, for example, in the wide-ranging economic geography literature on the subject – that an array of contextual components dictates the competitiveness of particular geographical areas. 'Networking', 'innovation', and 'agglomeration', for example, are all frequently cited as essential underpinnings to (and consequences of) a place's competitiveness. 'New industrial districts', 'neo-Marshallian nodes', 'learning regions', 'Porterian clusters' or (sundry) other variants are all examples of the sorts of places in which these competitive circumstances are held to apply most graphically (Boddy, 1999). Porter (1990), for example, contends that the competitiveness of nation-states is the result of a variety of forms of intervention, from broad macroeconomic policy at one level, to business management practices and procedures on the other. And, at the same time, sub-national policy intervention – for instance, in skills and education – also has an important role in creating competitive advantage for certain localised clusters of industries, according to Porter.

By contrast, more equivocal readings challenge the degree to which places (as opposed to firms) can ever be said to be 'competitive'. The crux of this critique centres on the degree to which, in the context of a global economy dominated by transnational firms and flows of capital, national economic performance (or competitiveness) can have any real meaning (Buckley et al, 1988; Rapkin and Strand, 1995). This is a criticism that has been levelled at attempts (notably those by Michael Porter) to conceptualise competitiveness at the level of nation states, but it is also one perhaps with even greater validity in the context of urban competitiveness. For any one city, the strength of competitiveness, it could be argued, is determined to at least some significant extent by the contribution of large transnational firms, whose competitiveness might be as much a reflection of circumstances in the parent country as the host city. By the same token, government sponsored injections of investment (for example, to support research efforts, or to buttress skills development) in a particular city might eventually yield benefits to firms located elsewhere. The ineluctable conclusion of this critique is that competitiveness can only make sense (either conceptually or in terms of measurement) at the scale of the individual firm (Georghiou and Metcalfe, 1993).

Developing a model of urban competitiveness

In this chapter we attempt to chart a middle way through these often polarised debates. We do so by acknowledging, on the one hand, that ultimately it makes sense to measure competitiveness by looking at indicators of firm performance (thereby accommodating the rudiments of the 'geosceptic' critique). But, on the other hand, we attempt to embody arguments regarding the critical role played by a variety of contextual factors in creating the conditions within which firms prosper or wither. We have sought to accommodate these ostensibly conflicting perspectives by attempting to delineate the stock of urban 'assets' which jointly set the context within which firms operate, but measure competitiveness 'outcomes' by focusing upon indicators of economic performance which ultimately reflect the aggregate experience of businesses. In other words, our initial presupposition, in crude terms, is that the stock of assets in a city condition the aggregate competitiveness of firms therein (following Rapkin and Strand, 1995, p 3; Buckley et al, 1988, p 177). As a result, we have attempted to identify and enumerate the asset bases of a sample of English cities and conurbations, and to explore parallel measures of competitive outcome.

A schematic indication of the way in which competitiveness might be visualised is provided in Figure 9.1. For a given city, the asset base can plausibly be conceived as comprising a mix of contextual factors. One set of assets relates to a city's economic context, which includes, inter alia, the skills and qualifications of its residents, the sectoral breakdown of its economy, and the size profile of its constituent firms. Another asset category relates to a city's policy context: the mix of agencies, institutions and policy initiatives in operation, or the level of resources vested in them. Its environmental context relates to underlying physical factors such as the quality and quantity of sites, premises, infrastructure and other physical assets on which firms can draw. Its social context encompasses the cohesiveness of its social relations – seen by some as an essential ingredient underlying competitive performance among firms.

The degree to which firms are able to capitalise upon these various assets (or to obviate any liabilities) is influenced in part by the effectiveness of their own management practices, but is also conditioned by the differential aptitude of local policy actors to initiate, harness, augment or replenish the different sorts of asset (for which in Figure 9.1 we use the less than satisfactory shorthand term, 'governance'). Here, it is important to distinguish, in conceptual terms, between assets (under the policy context heading in Figure 9.1) in the way of public monies or initiatives directed towards a city, and the proficiency with which these assets are marshalled and exploited. This is not an insignificant distinction. For example, different cities might be seen as possessing not dissimilar mixes of publicly funded institutions and agencies, but the adeptness with which local policy actors utilise the resources flowing through these channels could, it is not unreasonable to assert, vary considerably between those cities.

The proficiency with which these different categories of assets are harnessed is, under our model of the competitiveness process, expressed through a number of outcomes, which reflect the collective experience of firms within a given area. In turn, these outcomes themselves may eventually come to represent assets, which sustain the competitiveness of the future urban economy (hence the 'durability' feedback loop in Figure

Figure 9.1: The competitive process: the assets–outcomes model

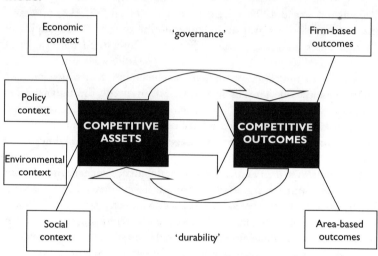

Source: authors

9.1). There are, however, a number of conceptual nuances that underlie this ostensibly straightforward asset-outcome relationship.

The first centres on the potential blurring between assets and outcomes. An illustrative example is provided by Leeds's much hyped strength in financial services, which might be perceived as a reflection of its underlying asset base: its supply of well-qualified potential employees; its reserve of suitable development sites and business accommodation; or even the various 'quality of life' factors or the 'business climate' which the city's advocates would claim to be of importance in helping to attract inward investors or skilled residents (see, for example, Leigh, 1995; Wong, 2001). At the same time, the effectiveness with which these assets have been moulded and marshalled by the city's policy elite – through regeneration interventions to ensure an adequate supply of land by tackling derelict or degraded land, or promotional work to attract incoming investment – might also be seen as an important element in supporting competitiveness. Such views on their own would not invalidate our reading of the dynamics of the competitiveness process. However, the city's very status as northern England's putative financial services capital could also be seen as an important asset in its own right: the city's continuing ability to lure financial services investment reflects its existing strength in that area. In other words, the assets–outcomes relationship is not a straightforwardly unilinear, causal one: competitive outcomes are conditioned by a variety of contextual assets, but themselves reinforce and help replenish a city's existing stock of assets.

A second conceptual subtlety centres on the means by which it is possible, in the context of a schematic model, to distinguish between the more 'organic' competitive outcomes which are the result of unfettered market processes, and those 'synthetic' outcomes which reflect intervention by government. Here, a particular difficulty in developing appropriate statistical measures of urban competitiveness is the enduring debate around different forms of competitiveness, some of them deeply polarised and highly politicised. In what ways, for example, might a statistical model embody, on the one hand, a view of competitiveness which views higher skilled employment as an essential ingredient in cultivating competitiveness, and, on the other hand, arguments that perceive competitiveness as based fundamentally upon less secure, low paid, lower skilled employment in areas characterised by lower levels of regulation, taxation and wage costs?

Related to this, thirdly, there are also debates regarding the significance that should be attached to different types of asset. Should one accord greater importance to particular types of asset, distinguishing between principal and secondary categories (and should this imply differential weightings in the context of a statistical model)? In this vein, some studies have attempted to recategorise assets to draw a distinction between 'traditional' determinants of firm location – land supply, business accommodation, local resident skills, transport infrastructure and so on – and those more ethereal factors ('quality of life' being one example) – of more questionable significance (Wong, 1998; Wong et al, 1999). Wong (1998), drawing on a survey of actors in the local economic development field, contends that this latter category of asset is less significant than the former in influencing competitive performance among firms.

How might urban competitiveness be measured?

The intricacy and complexity of the concept of urban competitiveness, as evident in some of the conceptual quandaries we highlight above, is reflected in the still meagre number of studies that try to build empirically upon the (by comparison) abundance of theoretically focused attempts to unpack competitiveness (see, for example, Cheshire and Carbanaro, 1996; Kresl, 1995; Kresl and Singh, 1999, and the chapters by Kresl and Boddy in this volume). We attempt to augment these pioneering studies by focusing on the major cities of England (and, where possible, the conurbations) and, in so doing, testing the utility of one potential approach to the conceptualisation and measurement of urban competitiveness. Our response to the multiple ambiguities concerning the definition and quantification of urban competitiveness has been to construct a set of indicators which capture as diverse a range as possible of the assets said to underpin competitive performance, drawing on a parallel qualitative study which canvassed the views of policy elites on the role played by different types of asset in attracting foreign direct investment to North West England (Wilks-Heeg et al, 1999). From this study, we have delimited four groupings of quantitative indicators that relate to the 'contextual' categories detailed in Figure 9.1.

The first category relates to the economic context underlying firm performance (Table 9.1). Here, we sought to ascertain the extent of variations between the places in the sample by exploring a number of indicators, looking at both the characteristics of individuals within each area and at the institutional infrastructure that supports firms. The stock of skills and qualifications was assessed through the use of indicators at three stages in the life-cycle: educational performance among school pupils, full-time education participation rates among school-leavers and job-related training undertaken by the working-age population. These offer an indication of the efficacy of policy interventions of various types – from attempts by government to increase higher education student numbers to the prompting for businesses to increase job-related training – in bolstering competitiveness. Conversely, the percentage of school pupils with no or low qualifications, and the proportion of unskilled employees, were included as liability indicators to show the extent of educational underperformance.

Paralleling these measures of individual resident characteristics, we also attempted to measure the quality of 'economic' assets in an institutional sense by exploring the characteristics of local knowledge-based institutions, on whose expertise firms potentially might call. In doing so, we drew on an array of studies which suggest the importance of university research capabilities for technology transfer purposes, for generating incubation units or spin-off companies, or for generating a flow of skilled graduates (see, for example, Robson et al, 1997).

Scores from the 1996 Research Assessment Exercise (RAE) conducted by the Higher Education Funding Council for England (HEFCE) were utilised as a proxy measure of the strength of university-based research (although such a measure arguably, and perhaps falsely, assumes that university research is geared directly to 'industrial' needs, rather than to international academic audiences weaned on 'pure' research). A score was calculated to cover the quality of research (if not its relevance to local economic needs) across what might be considered to be the key academic disciplines in terms of their role in underpinning competitive performance among firms: biological sciences and biochemistry; business and management studies; computer science; electrical and electronic engineering; hospital-based clinical subjects; and mechanical, aeronautical and manufacturing engineering. The composite indicator takes no account of the volume of research activity under these categories – although anecdotal evidence suggests that high scoring university departments often tend to be those with a suitably large 'critical mass' of staff – but does provide an indication of quality.

The second category of variable relates to the policy context underlying firm performance. This, as a number of authors note, presents particular difficulty in relation to a quantitative model. Kresl and Singh (1999), for instance, contend that the difficulty in quantifying policy and institutional influences on competitiveness necessitates qualitative exploration. Yet while it is undoubtedly the case that it is impossible fully to capture the precise intricacies of political, policy or institutional factors within a quantitative model of competitiveness, there remains some merit, if only as an exploratory precursor to subsequent qualitative assessment, for developing proxy measures that tentatively embrace institutional cohesion and policy effectiveness in their broadest senses. Two surrogate indicators – Single Regeneration Budget Challenge Fund (SRBCF) expenditure and European Union grant funding (both expressed on a per capita basis) – were selected to convey the volume of the broader array of policy resources directed towards cities within the sample, and to provide a preliminary indication of the proficiency of local policy actors (and the effectiveness of the wider configuration of institutional structures within which they operate) in attracting flows of discretionary grant funding. Although both indicators partly reflect levels of local social need – and Structural Fund resources, in particular, are based on an 'objective' process of determining area eligibility that is as much top-down as bottom-up – they may also provide an approximation of the aptitude shown by local policy makers in deciphering grant disbursement rules and bidding for funds (see, for example, Jones and Ward, 1997; Quilley, 1999) and, at a deeper level, of the cohesiveness of local institutional structures and approaches to local governance.

Capturing variations in the environmental context within which firms operate also presents difficulties, particularly in light of arguments which gainsay crude but pervasive assumptions that infrastructural development is a critical trigger for economic development (and foreign direct investment specifically, Peck, 1996). Notwithstanding this caveat, we explored a number of indicators of 'environmental' or physical assets. Road network density was identified as an indicator of the quantity of infrastructure available to firms. While it takes no account of the quality of roads, or of their efficiency in facilitating trade, a number of studies conclude that infrastructure continues to be perceived by firms – and by the foreign direct investors who have been seen by policy makers as central to economic development efforts in Britain – as of critical importance to their viability and profitability (Wilks-Heeg et al, 1999; Wong et al, 1999). A similar logic applies to the 'environmental' liability indicator selected. Large fractions of derelict land, another of the 'traditional' disincentives to industrial location, can be interpreted as indicative of a dearth of developable sites in a particular location, and therefore a disincentive to firm immigration and a potential constraint on in situ expansion.

Another aspect of the environmental context perceived to be of significance (particularly in helping to attract and retain skilled employees) is the quality of housing stock and, more specifically, the availability of affordable housing. Here, there is a need to devise a measure of affordability, which takes account of the longstanding disparities in house prices across regions. We do so by utilising data for average house prices (assuming a common mix of house type) and relating them to median gross earnings. The result is an indicator that conveys the affordability of housing stock: a high ratio could suggest the possibility that affordable housing may be limited in supply; a lower ratio could indicate that housing costs and earnings are less out of kilter (although it could also result in instances where the low quality of housing stock is reflected in depressed prices).

The final category of asset relates to the social context underlying firm competitiveness. Again, data were collected for a number of asset and liability indicators, on the assumption that competitiveness can be enhanced by cohesive social relations (which can help encourage the immigration of skilled labour, and limit its emigration). Once more, quantifying cohesive social relations is beset with difficulty, other than, somewhat unsatisfactorily, as the inverse of a variety of aspects of generally conceived social malaise. Our response has been to explore the use of data on electoral turnout as a generalised surrogate measure of cohesion, in light of arguments that the presence of high levels of citizen activism (whether in the form of membership of voluntary organisations, or of engagement with the formal political process) is associated with, and arguably underpins, wider social well-being and economic health (Putnam, 1993). There are again a number of cautionary qualifications in the use of turnout data – not least that buoyant levels of turnout may be associated as much with political instability and related voter disquiet, or with other localised electoral peculiarities, as with vibrant levels of civic engagement and underlying social cohesion – but turnout provides a measurable indication of one aspect of the social context within which firms operate.

Alongside civic engagement, two liability indicators were selected to capture the intensity of social problems, which could potentially constrain levels of competitiveness, both by generating demands on local taxpayers,

Table 9.1: Assets and liability indicators

Contextual category	Indicators
Economic context	1. % of pupils with 5+A*-C GCSEs, 1997 (DfEE)
	2. % of all 16-19-year-olds in full-time education, 1999 (LFS)
	3. % of all working age receiving job-related training, 1999 (LFS)
	4. Average RAE scores in key sectors, 1996 (HEFCE)
	5. % 15 year-old pupils with no/low GCSEs, 1997 (DfEE)
	6. % of all employment in unskilled occupations, 1999 (LFS)
Policy context	7. SRBCF grant funding per capita, outturn 1997/98 (DETR)
	8. European Union grant funding per capita, outturn 1997/98 (DETR)
Environmental context	9. Total road network length per sq km, 1997 (DETR)
	10. Mean house prices 1995-97/median gross yearly FT earnings (April 98) (Land Registry/Regional Trends)
	11. % area derelict, 1993 (DoE)
Social context	12. % electoral turnout, 1996 (University of Plymouth)
	13. % households on Council Tax Benefit, 1996 (DSS)
	14. Standardised Mortality Rate 0-64, 1997 (DETR/ILD)

Notes:

1. Sources are shown in parentheses.

2. Emboldened text denotes liability (as opposed to asset) indicators.

3. DfEE – Department for Education and Employment; LFS – Labour Force Survey; HEFCE – Higher Education Funding Council for England; DETR – Department of the Environment, Transport and the Regions; DoE – Department of the Environment; DSS – Department of Social Security; ILD – Index of Local Deprivation.

4. The average RAE score was calculated by taking seven disciplinary units of assessment, chosen because of their supposed importance to the local and regional economy: electrical and electronic engineering, mechanical, aeronautical and manufacturing engineering, business and management studies, computer science, hospital-based clinical subjects, biological sciences and biochemistry. For each of the universities in the respective conurbations, the RAE scores across the seven units of assessment were averaged.

and by inhibiting the immigration of skilled employees. Standardised Mortality Rates for residents of working age were used to indicate levels of ill health among residents, and to suggest areas in which the potential pool of employees may be limited by underlying problems of illness. The percentage of residents eligible for assistance towards (or exemption from) residential property taxes (Council Tax) was used as another means of identifying problematic social circumstances.

Alongside these four categories of asset, six outcome measures were selected. Where possible, these were chosen to capture circumstances at a later date than for the asset measures, on the not unreasonable grounds that there is likely to be a time lag (albeit of unspecified duration) between an asset's exploitation and the results being yielded in terms of firm performance. Of the six measures of outcome, three were chosen to convey the collective well-being of businesses in each city, and three to provide an indication of broad economic health across the sample. For the first category, numbers of firms registered for Value Added Tax (VAT) expressed as a percentage of total numbers employed (1999) were selected to provide a static indication of the relative health of local businesses generally, and of small firms (which account for the majority of registrations) in particular (following Robson et al, 1994). This is complemented by an additional indicator – net new business registrations as percentage of total stocks (1999) – which, following Coombes and Wong (1993), provides a dynamic measure of change across the cities. Alongside these measures of the buoyancy of the small firm sector, the ratio of public limited companies to conurbation population provides a measure of the extent to which the cities have different relative concentrations of corporate headquarter functions.

For the second category of outcome measure, indicators of competitiveness included were: GDP per capita (1998); office, industrial and retail rentals (1999) (on the assumption that high rental levels denote competitive property market circumstances rather than a paucity of supply of land and premises); and the percentage of unemployed economically active residents (1999) in each of the cities.

Data on both assets and outcomes were collated for what could be considered to be England's principal cities – Birmingham, Leeds, Liverpool, Manchester, Middlesbrough, Newcastle, Sheffield – and for their surrounding conurbations. Inner London was defined as an additional core city, and Outer London its broader conurbation. Bristol was included as a core city, but the surrounding Avon county excluded on the grounds of its non-comparability with the former metropolitan counties of England (or with Cleveland) which comprise the conurbations for the rest of the sample.

In the remainder of the chapter, we report on patterns across these cities and conurbations and explore the degree to which variations in their competitive outcomes can be attributed to corresponding differences in their asset bases.

Applying the urban competitiveness model in an English context

The preliminary supposition we sought to explore was that the nature of a city's asset base conditions competitive outcomes. As Figure 9.2 shows, this is a view that appears to have some merit in light of the generally positive association between the aggregate z-scores (used to standardise the different indicators in order that they could be summed) for assets and outcomes. Only two of the cities – Leeds and Manchester – suggest other than a directly proportional relationship between assets and outcomes. For Leeds, the data suggest that a seemingly strong asset base, relative to the rest of the sample, exists alongside competitive outcomes which are underdeveloped in comparison to the set of places overall. For Manchester, by contrast, the overall asset base, the data would suggest, is weaker than the mean for the sample, yet its outcome score is better than the average. One possible reading of this might be that while firms in Leeds have failed to capitalise upon a relatively strong stock of assets, aggregate competitiveness among Manchester firms is stronger than would be expected in light of the weaker asset base at their disposal. Manchester, it is possible to infer, despite an overall asset base not dissimilar to that of cities like Liverpool and Middlesbrough could be characterised by levels of competitive performance in line with the evidently better endowed Leeds.

This preliminary interpretation suggests that variations in competitive outcomes across the sample of cities are conditioned to varying extents by disparities in their underlying assets bases. Such a conclusion has inevitably to be qualified by an acknowledgement that the categorisation of cities according to their competitive performance is based on the happenstance of the mean values for the sample as a whole. Nonetheless, the analysis retains a degree of validity, not least, as Table 9.2 shows, since the amalgamation of asset and outcome indicators (to generate an overall measure not unlike conventional generalised measures of socioeconomic circumstances) yields a rank order across the sample which remains broadly

Figure 9.2: The assets and outcomes relationship

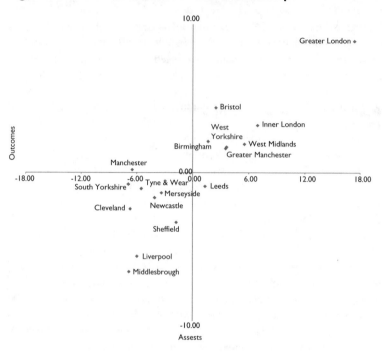

Source: authors

– but significantly, not entirely – unaltered from that produced on the basis solely of outcome measures.

The assets–outcomes relationship applies generally across the sample, but to varying extents for individual cities. This provides some potentially important pointers in terms of our attempt to identify cities that might be deemed especially competitive (or uncompetitive). In this respect, Liverpool and Manchester, neighbouring cities in North West England, provide a contrasting illustration. The data assembled lend some credence to standard interpretations – many of them developed in the absence of any systematic analysis of relevant data – of political and economic change in the two cities. Both cities, it appears, are characterised by relatively weak asset bases, but stronger competitive outcomes in Manchester accord some credibility to conventional readings of the city's history from the late 1980s onwards, which contend that improved economic fortunes had their roots in local political and institutional transformation of that time (although the extent to which this genuinely resulted in more effective

Table 9.2: Rankings for outcome and aggregate asset/outcome scores

City/conurbation	Assets	Outcomes*	Rank: outcomes	Rank: Assets + outcomes[†]
Greater London	17.3	8.9	1	1
Inner London	6.9	3.2	3	2
West Midlands	5.5	1.9	5	3
Bristol	2.5	4.4	2	4
West Yorkshire	3.6	1.7	6	5
Greater Manchester	3.5	1.6	7	6
Birmingham	1.7	2.1	4	7
Leeds	1.4	−0.9	10	8
Merseyside	−3.3	−1.4	12	9
Sheffield	−1.7	−3.4	15	10
Newcastle upon Tyne	−4.1	−1.7	13	11
Manchester	−6.5	0.2	8	12
Tyne & Wear	−5.5	−1.1	11	13
South Yorkshire	−6.9	−0.8	9	14
Cleveland	−6.7	−2.4	14	15
Liverpool	−6.0	−5.6	16	16
Middlesbrough	−6.8	−6.7	17	17

Notes:

* Columns 2 and 3 ('assets' and 'outcomes') show the aggregate values for the z-scores of the various asset and outcome indicators respectively.

[†] Columns 4 and 5 show the rankings (from 1-17) for each place within the sample based on aggregate outcome scores (column 4), and for asset and outcome scores from columns 3 and 4 combined (column 5).

exploitation of assets and minimisation of liabilities is unclear in the absence of qualitative assessment of the specific dynamics of the relationship between 'governance' and competitive performance among firms). For Liverpool, by contrast, the assets-outcomes analysis provides further confirmation of the apparent intractability and intensity of the long-term economic difficulties with which it is afflicted: it is a city (unlike Manchester) in which competitive outcomes are perhaps less healthy than might be expected, even given its relatively weak asset base.

There is a clear suggestion, which the examples of Liverpool and Manchester illustrate, that the strength of the assets-outcomes relationship is more marked for some cities than for others. It appears that there are some cities which perform particularly strongly (or weakly) in terms of

Figure 9.3: Residuals from regression of assets and outcomes

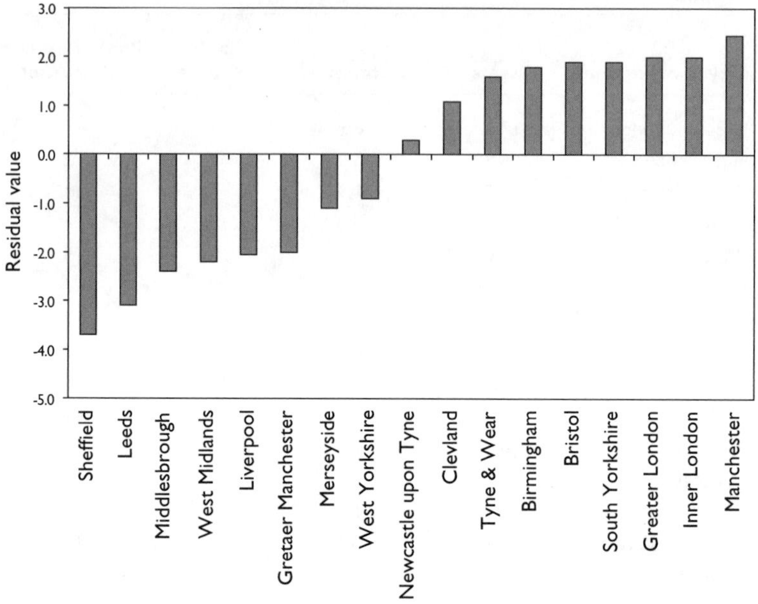

Source: authors

capitalising upon various types of asset. This contention can be explored further through a regression of outcomes and assets across the sample, the residuals from which lend further support to the notion that while asset bases generally provide a good predictor of competitive performance, there are outlier cities for which observed outcomes are markedly different from expected ones (Figure 9.3). Again, Manchester stands out as a notably 'competitive' city, not in the sense that its economic performance is especially strong, but rather that its outcomes are stronger than its asset base might lead one to expect. The reverse is true of Sheffield, for which the suggestion is one of notable underperformance: the city, it might be inferred from the data, has an underdeveloped asset base, but manages not even to harness that to good effect.

Data on assets and outcomes also shed further light on the relationship between core cities and their surrounding conurbations for the urban areas examined. The general pattern within the sample is one in which core cities tend to possess asset bases weaker than their encompassing conurbations, and the former tend, as a result, to have correspondingly less buoyant levels of competitive outcome. In this sense, the core-conurbation relationship across the sample as a whole confirms the extensively chronicled processes of decline characteristic of many core cities, and the relative well-being of their broader conurbations (see also, Turok and Edge, 1999, and the chapter by Begg, Moore and Altunbas in this volume). As Figure 9.4 shows, Birmingham provides the only exception to this general pattern of cores performing (in terms of the competitive outcome measures used here) more weakly than their surrounding conurbations, perhaps reflecting the particular influence of the city's buoyant commercial core on the retail and office rental outcome measure, as well as the historic residue of once vibrant manufacturing industry across much of the rest of the West Midlands. Likewise, Sheffield and, to a lesser extent, Newcastle, are the only cities in the sample that do not accord to the pattern of core cities possessing fewer and weaker assets than their conurbations.

Yet while the general pattern is, as expected, one of core listlessness and relative conurbation buoyancy, the degree of disparity varies across the sample. As Figure 9.4 shows, for some conurbations the degree of core-periphery polarity is particularly marked. In the case of Greater Manchester, for example, the acute difference between core and conurbation – in terms of assets, though only marginally so in terms of outcomes – reinforces earlier research which concludes that the contrast between employment decline in the core and growth in the outer districts

Figure 9.4: Assets–outcomes relationship: linkages between cores and conurbations

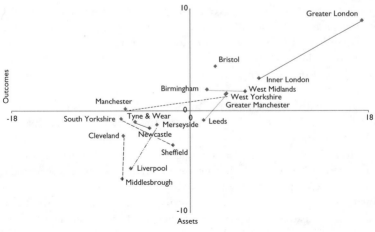

Source: authors

is more pronounced than in any other conurbation in Britain (Turok and Edge, 1999). Within Greater London, too, there is – somewhat more predictably – an acutely drawn contrast between core and conurbation circumstances. But by contrast, for other conurbations such as Tyne and Wear and West Yorkshire, circumstances in the core cities and conurbations differ much less markedly.

Conclusion

The model developed for this analysis represents one way of exploring patterns of urban competitiveness, taking account of both the strength of underlying asset bases and the effectiveness with which they have been harnessed. Conventional approaches to competitiveness, perhaps deploying sets of indicators not dramatically dissimilar to the outcome measures used here, might have generated a rather different (and perhaps more predictable) ranking of cities. However, such an analysis would not have said anything about the extent to which levels of competitiveness within different cities reflect the differential strength of their respective assets bases, or about the aptitude of local elites in marshalling and maintaining those assets.

It is this attempt to explore competitive outcomes in light of the context provided by economic, social, political and environmental circumstances in cities, which may provide scope for further investigation. The research on which we report here, in light of the multiple difficulties in attaching quantitative measures to the manifold subtleties of the competitiveness process, is necessarily tentative and exploratory. Nonetheless, it does provide a means of identifying cities at which more detailed qualitative research might be directed in order to explore the factors – not least in relation to different aspects of local governance – which render some places more or less competitive than their asset bases might otherwise suggest.

An illustrative example of the 'value added' that the assets-outcomes model potentially brings is provided by the results of our analysis for Liverpool, Manchester, Leeds and Sheffield, the four principal cities of northern England's trans-Pennine corridor. A conventional assessment of the cities' recent economic trajectories might well have reaffirmed the various stereotypes which attach themselves to each city: the seeming intractability of the economic travails of Liverpool and Sheffield, Manchester's partial and hesitant renaissance, and Leeds's generally healthier economic circumstances. Such a conclusion, though, would have provided only a partial picture. The assets–outcomes data on which we report here suggest, in some cases, rather different interpretations: that Leeds has more extensive assets than its Pennine neighbours, but capitalises upon them relatively less effectively; that Manchester, despite an unpropitious asset base, is a more competitive city than one might expect; that Sheffield and Liverpool have predictably underdeveloped asset bases, but the former city capitalises upon them to notably poor effect.

Clearly, such sweeping headline conclusions mask processes of competitiveness within the cities that are highly intricate and not easily amenable to quantification. Yet they do provide messages which, to some extent, chime against conventional narratives of economic change in each of the cities. In this sense, they provide conjectures towards which future research might sensibly address itself. At the same time, however, they also provide further illumination of some of the arguments emerging from earlier, qualitatively oriented studies of recent economic and political change. There might, for example, be some evidence from this study (albeit far from incontestable) to suggest that Manchester's widely trumpeted effectiveness in attracting policy resources (notably those allocated on a competitive basis) has played a role in creating the conditions within which economic performance can be maximised. The success of the numerous 'grant coalitions', which came to festoon the city's policy landscape in the 1980s and 1990s, and their particular faculty for decoding (and anticipating) grant entitlement rules, flagship event opportunities and so on, might be seen as reflecting an underlying cohesiveness in the city's political relations; in turn, this could impact on competitive outcomes through the revitalisation of the city centre, or through the multiplier effects generated by high-profile events or landmark developments.

It may be that factors such as this, which lie beyond the usual ambit of analyses of competitiveness, can help explain why some cities are more competitive than others. This raises potential pointers for local economic development policy makers, not least that future policy effort should gear itself towards restocking urban asset bases – a particular priority for those cities like Manchester, Sheffield and Liverpool with relatively under-developed assets – and that this has to encompass as broad a range as possible of different types of asset if genuinely competitive outcomes are to be engendered. Equally, for other cities like Leeds, the emphasis could sensibly be directed towards exploring why relatively strong endowments of assets are harnessed to apparently limited effect. In both cases, this is likely to necessitate policymakers looking beyond crude headline messages about economic performance and grasping the myriad factors that affect urban competitiveness.

References

Boddy, M. (1999) 'Geographical economics and urban competitiveness: a critique', *Urban Studies*, vol 36, no 5/6, pp 811-42.

Buckley, P., Pass, C. and Prescott, K. (1988) 'Measures of international competitiveness: a critical survey', *Journal of Marketing Management*, vol 4, no 2, pp 175-200.

Cheshire, P. and Carbanaro, G. (1996) 'Urban economic growth in Europe: Testing theory and policy', *Urban Studies*, vol 33, no 7, pp 1111-28.

Coombes, M. and Wong, C. (1993) *Developing a local environment index*, Sheffield: Department for Education and Employment.

Georghiou, L. and Metcalfe, S. (1993) 'Evaluation of the impact of European community research programmes upon industrial competitiveness', *R&D Management*, vol 23, no 2, pp 161-9.

Jones, M. and Ward, K. (1997) 'Grabbing grants? ... the role of coalitions in urban economic development', *Local Economy*, vol 13, no 2, pp 28-38.

Kresl, P. (1995) 'The determinants of urban competitiveness', in P. Kresl, and G. Gappert (eds) *North American cities and the global economy*, London: Sage Publications, p 45-68.

Kresl, P. and Singh, B. (1999) 'Competitiveness and the urban economy: twenty-four large US metropolitan areas', *Urban Studies*, vol 36, no 5/6, pp 1017-27.

Leigh, C. (ed) (1995) *The impact of inward investment projects on local economies in Yorkshire and Humberside*, Leeds: Yorkshire and Humberside Regional Research Laboratory, School of Geography, University of Leeds.

Peck, F. (1996) 'Regional development and the production of space: the role of infrastructure in the attraction of new inward investment', *Environment and Planning A*, vol 28, no 2, pp 327-39.

Porter, M. (1990) *Competitive advantage of nations*, London: Macmillan.

Putnam, R. (1993) *Making democracy work: Civic traditions in modern Italy*, Princeton, NJ: Princeton University Press.

Quilley, S. (1999) 'Entrepreneurial Manchester: the genesis of elite consensus', *Antipode*, vol 31, no 2, pp 185-205.

Rapkin, D. and Strand, D. (1995) 'Competitiveness: useful concept, political slogan or dangerous obsession?', in D. Rapkin, and W. Avery (eds) *National competitiveness in a global economy*, London: Lynne Rienner.

Robson, B., Bradford, M., Deas, I., Hall, E., Harrison, E., Parkinson, M., Evans, R., Garside, P., Harding, A. and Robinson, F. (1994) *Assessing the impact of urban policy*, London: HMSO.

Robson, B., Drake, K. and Deas, I. (1997) 'Higher education and regions', Report 9 to the National Committee of Inquiry into Higher Education (Dearing Commission), London: The Stationery Office.

Turok, I. and Edge, N. (1999) *The jobs gap in Britain's cities: Employment loss and labour market consequence*, Bristol/York: The Policy Press/Joseph Rowntree Foundation.

Wilks-Heeg, S., Deas, I. and Harding, A. (1999) *Does local governance matter to city competitiveness?*, Working Paper No 2, ESRC Cities programme, Liverpool-Manchester Integrated Case Study, Manchester: School of Geography, University of Manchester.

Wong, C. (1998) 'Determining factors for local economic development: the perception of practitioners in the north west and eastern regions of the UK', *Regional Studies*, vol 32, no 8, pp 707-20.

Wong, C. (2001) 'The relationship between quality of life and local economic development: an empirical study of local authority areas in England', *Cities*, vol 18, no 1, pp 25-32.

Wong, C., Baker, M. and Gallent, N. (1999) 'The north west', in M. Breheny (ed) *The people: Where will they work?*, London: Town and Country Planning Association.

TEN

The enhancement of urban economic competitiveness: the case of Montreal

Peter Kresl

Urban economies throughout the world are under extreme pressure to be active rather than passive. This involves anticipating and responding to the threats to existing activities and the opportunities for developing new activities following the openness of markets, deregulation of industries and dramatic changes in technology that are the hallmarks of globalisation. A proper response necessarily requires the engagement of the national level of government and the mobilisation of local actors in both the public and the private sectors. While the free market and the invisible hand can very effectively allocate resources, they generally take more time to act than is available in the high-pressured environment of inter-urban competition, and are to varying degrees affected by market imperfections. If we think back analogously to recent advances in international economic theory, there is often little to chose from between two potential suppliers of a good or two potential occupiers of a specific role in the global urban hierarchy. In this situation the prize sale goes to the one that is active while passivity leads to stagnation and marginalisation. Because of this, a coherent approach to strategic planning or to policy aimed at enhancing an urban economy's competitiveness is an absolute necessity if resources are to be efficiently allocated toward attainment of a clearly identified objective. In this chapter we will examine two basic approaches to competitiveness enhancement, and we will then apply them to Montreal – one of North America's most active and engaged urban economies.

Why Montreal provides us with a good case study

To begin with it is natural to ask the question – why Montreal? Las Vegas, Portland and Vancouver are getting better press coverage as North America's most interesting urban experiments. Los Angeles, Toronto and Atlanta have had more spectacular growth in recent decades. But it is cities like Chicago, Cleveland, and Montreal that have had experiences which are more difficult and less assured of success, and it is this kind of urban economy that gives us our best and most informative example of strategic thinking and accomplishment. Montreal is one of the most interesting cities from the standpoint of the objective of this chapter due to the following aspects:

• Its location is rather peripheral to the main areas of economic activity in North America – a bit north of the 'industrial heartland' – Boston to Chicago to Cincinnati to New York.
• Unlike Vancouver and Toronto, Montreal has no natural cross-border partner city.
• Montreal's constitutional and linguistic situation means it has unique advantages and disadvantages.
• For a North American city Montreal has been extraordinarily active in its planning, with a relatively strong role for government.
• The relationship between the city and the provincial government has been highly developed.
• Montreal has been made attempts to realise its 'international vocation' for at least twenty years.

I would argue that most other North American cities have been less actively engaged in their development and with less long-term consistency than Montreal, hence this is a relatively well-defined strategic approach to urban competitiveness that we can evaluate.

Montreal has been the centre of the 'quiet revolution' that has transformed the economic, political and cultural life of the province of Quebec since the mid-1960s. As the result of the emergence of a generation of leaders who sought to modernise the province, the church, formerly at the centre of society, has been replaced by completely secularised institutions and processes; a classic education has given way to the full curriculum of the modern university; thousands of French-speaking students have graduated from business schools and taken command of the economy; provincialism has given way to cosmopolitanism; and the debate over the constitutional status of the province has replaced conservative and romantic evocations of a proud past. As the primary city in Quebec, Montreal has been at the centre of all of these developments.

Another element in the development of Montreal has been the decline of the old east–west orientation of Canadian economic activity that was based on the forwarding of raw materials to Europe and the importation of European manufactured goods. What has emerged is a north–south orientation, with the United States replacing Europe (and more specifically the United Kingdom) as the primary external economic partner of Canada. This transition began with the conclusion of the First World War, but was accelerated by the exigencies of defence production during the Second World War, the completion of the St Lawrence Seaway, the Canada–US Auto Pact (1964), and most importantly the Canada–US Free Trade Agreement (1989) and the North America Free Trade Agreement (1994). Since Montreal was described as the prime city of the Empire of St Lawrence, this transition had its most powerful impact within this region. Montreal was also the first, and strongest, proponent in Canada for free trade with the US. The leaders of the city stake their economic future on a strategy of developing an extensive and powerful integration with the US economy, a strategy that has been consistently pursued for the past 20 years. Thus Montreal can be seen as one of the North American cities that has been most actively engaged in charting its own course.

Before examining the current competitiveness of Montreal we discuss the notion of urban competitiveness itself.

Approaches to strategic thinking about urban competitiveness

There are two rather different approaches to planning the enhancement of the competitiveness of an urban economy. The first is quantitative and comparative, while the second is qualitative or subjective and necessarily more focused on the characteristics of the individual urban economy itself. Each of these approaches is described briefly and then applied to the case of Montreal.

The quantitative approach

One cannot actually directly measure urban competitiveness but in this approach the author asserts that urban competitiveness is a function of three variables that can be used as 'indicators of urban competitiveness'. The variables used are: growth over a period of years; manufacturing value added; business services (as defined by the US Bureau of the Census); and retail sales (Kresl and Singh, 1994, 1999). (One could include employment growth, but this is unreliable since employment may increase or decrease depending on the labour and capital intensities of the expanding and contracting sectors.) Manufacturing value added is used because its rapid growth indicates investment in human and physical capital that will have a positive impact on the competitiveness of the city's industrial production. Business services are essential to any expansion or transformation of the city's economic activity. Retail sales grow if the city's residents have a rising income and if the city is attractive to non-residents for shopping, cultural events, dining and recreation. The variables are added up and the share of each in the total of the three is used as the weight for each variable in the calculation of a ranking of the cities in the survey according to their competitiveness. Once this ranking has been obtained, one can then do a regression analysis to find variables that 'explain' the ranking. Applications of this approach have generated sets of seven or eight 'explanatory' variables, and when two or three of them are, in turn, analysed, one has about a dozen variables that can be used to explain the competitiveness rankings. These variables are considered to be the 'determinants' of urban competitiveness.

The final step is to examine the place of an individual urban economy among the other economies in each of the variables. For example, the number of cultural institutions (a proxy for urban amenities) has emerged as one of the explanatory variables. One could then examine how an individual urban economy compares to its competitors according to this element of competitiveness (since attracting highly educated workers is generally taken to be a component of competitiveness enhancement in industrial economies). If the urban economy being examined is ranked low in cultural institutions this suggests that its position in the competitiveness ranking could be improved if more attention were paid to the richness of its cultural amenities. When an analysis is done of the urban economy's comparative position in all of the determinants of competitiveness, the results can be used to indicate where work has to be done and where that economy already has strength in relation to other urban economies. That is, the results can be used to guide policy makers in their strategic planning for economic development or competitiveness enhancement.

The advantages of the quantitative approach are that it is objective and also explicitly comparative. Many times an urban economy will take pride in building a new conference centre, but if competing economies are also building new conference centres it has gained nothing and may just be holding its relative position. The obvious disadvantage of this approach is that it requires comparable data for scores of variables for at least 15 or 20 urban economies. This data is available for the US and partially for Canada, but is utterly inadequate for any other part of the world. Not even the European Union has the data that would be required.

This approach may, however, be applicable outside North America. If one assumes that in our globalised economic environment (with its flows of capital, goods, services and even labour, free to move across national borders and with financial and other sectors being deregulated) all urban economies, at least in the G8 countries, are subject to the same competitive forces that confront North American urban economies. In this case, the variables that have been seen to have relevance in the US should also have relevance in these other entities. That is to say, if the number of cultural institutions and growth in per capital money income are significant variables in the US they could also be taken to be significant for urban economies in the EU or Japan. This will have some relevance in the study of Montreal that follows.

The qualitative approach

When the necessary data are not available or when local decision makers need to clarify the specific vocation or role of their city they will chose the option of a process that is more discursive, speculative and qualitative in nature. Here the primary requirement is an intimate knowledge of the city's strengths and weaknesses, a realistic appraisal of the city's current situation, awareness of the activities of competing cities and an understanding of the capabilities and ambitions of local institutions and individuals. The qualitative approach can be seen in Figure 10.1 (Kresl, 1992, pp 37-9). The 'ultimate objective' is in no way controversial, but it does explicitly draw attention to the fact that the city's leaders must see themselves as acting in a global, rather than a local or national, economic environment. Obviously this will have more relevance for some cities than for others. The first of two important decisions will be that of choosing to stake the city's future on a 'quantitative expansion' of the activities that currently characterise the local economy, or to initiate a 'qualitative restructuring' that will focus on the development of new activities. This decision will be based on the current condition of the city's economy. For example, when Chicago suffered the loss of employment in the steel and heavy manufacturing sector in the south east part of the city in the 1970s, a decision was made to focus on regaining jobs for the displaced workers utilising the skills they already had. This is

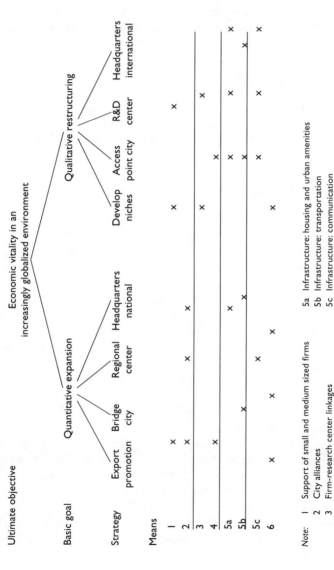

Figure 10.1: Strategic planning options: qualitative approach

Note:
1 Support of small and medium sized firms
2 City alliances
3 Firm-research center linkages
4 International linkages

5a Infrastructure: housing and urban amenities
5b Infrastructure: transportation
5c Infrastructure: communication
6 Specialized business services

Source: Kresl (1992)

an example of quantitatively expanding existing resources. By contrast, in Toronto the economy in the 1980s was very robust and wages rose to the point that traditional activities were no longer competitive. Here the decision was made to engage in a qualitative restructuring emphasising financial and other services.

When the basic goal is chosen, this will be done concomitantly with the determination of the 'strategy' to be adopted. Once the strategy (or strategies) has been chosen, the 'means', that is the programmes and projects required for the realisation of the strategy chosen, will also be determined. In Figure 10.1 the strategies indicated are not intended to be comprehensive. They are meant to be suggestive of the options that are available and may be somewhat different for each city. But it is the process of determining the basic goal and the strategy to be pursued that I want to offer for local leaders as an alternative to the numerical databased quantitative approach.

As indicated at the beginning of this section, there are certain advantages of the qualitative approach that make it most suitable for many cities. First, very few cities have access to the mass of data for a set of comparable cities required for the quantitative approach, although some of the conclusions of that approach may be usable by these cities. Second, and most importantly, the qualitative approach produces a characterisation of the vocation of the individual city and of its role in the global urban hierarchy that will be important not only in determining strategy and means but also in encouraging the local 'boosterism' that is crucial for developing the enthusiastic participation of local actors (Krugman, 1991, pp 30-3). Seeing itself as, for example, a 'point of access' or a 'headquarters' city will serve to unify the actions of all participants. On the negative side, the process of determining the city's central strategy may be distorted by the existing visions and commitments of major actors. A hard, realistic evaluation of a city's economic situation and its future prospects is often politically difficult and perhaps even costly to established leaders. Furthermore, a mere listing of a city's strengths and weaknesses, and the resulting set of economic characteristics that require attention, is more satisfying to a research economist or geographer than inspiring to the individuals and institutions asked to do the work.

Only cities that have access to the required data will have the luxury of choosing between the two approaches I have offered as alternative methods of strategic thinking for a city's competitiveness enhancement. But even for these cities it is probably best that the quantitative exercise be undertaken as a support activity for the processes of self-examination and strategic determination that comprise the qualitative approach. If done properly the two approaches should buttress each other.

Application of the two approaches to the situation of Montreal

The course of the Montreal economy has been greatly influenced by two forces that have had their effect over several decades: exogenous factors, and strategic thinking.

The *exogenous factors* include:

• The opening of the St Lawrence Seaway (in 1959), which allowed shallow-drafted ships to sail through the port of Montreal to the Great Lakes without transhipment to truck or rail. It was decades before the ship channel was deepened so as to allow ocean-going vessels to sail as far as Montreal, at which time the port began to experience a revival of sorts.
• Technological changes, which allowed transatlantic flights to avoid landing at Montreal for refuelling.
• The National Energy Policy of 1980, which had negative impacts on Montreal's oil refining activity.
• The continental-wide shift of economic activity from the north-east to the south and the west. This diminished Montreal's role as a financial and decision-making centre for Canada.
• Most important was the decision by the Canadian government to implement a free trade agreement with the United States (in 1989), and then with Mexico. This step had the effect of changing the spatial axis of Montreal's economic activity from east–west within the Canadian economic space, to north–south.

While many North American cities have experienced similar exogenous shocks, literally none has had Montreal's long experience with strategic thinking and planning. The provincial government of Quebec has issued a series of fairly consistent planning documents for both the provincial and Montreal economies beginning with 1979 (Provincial Government of Quebec, 1979a, 1979b, 1982a, 1982b) that have emphasised:

• Overcoming stagnation and stimulating productivity growth in the wake of the OPEC price hikes of 1973 and 1979.

- A restructuring of output away from producing traditional goods in outmoded facilities and toward goods that are intensive in high technology and innovation, and have high income elasticities of demand.
- The need to create a francophone workforce that could participate fully in the anglophone and modern new 'globalised' economy they would face.

The basic thrust was thus away from protectionism of existing activities towards development or creation of a comparative advantage in certain desirable directions and towards the emerging service sector. There was explicit recognition that a fundamental transformation of the economy of Quebec and, especially, of Montreal was necessary. Some steps to alter taxation, institutions and the budget were introduced to encourage movement in these directions.

This policy direction was supported by reports and policy recommendations of the Montreal Chamber of Commerce, private research groups such as Institut national de la recherche scientifique, and the Communauté urbaine de Montréal, as well as the government of Canada (Montreal Chamber of Commerce, 1985; Ministre des Approvisionnements et Services Canada, 1986; Thibodeau et al, 1986; Communauté urbaine de Montréal, 1989). As implementation of the Canada-US Free Trade Agreement approached (in 1989) there was general agreement in Quebec that the north-south orientation was the axis of the future and that Montreal had to develop its relations with the US even if that came at the expense of its ties to the rest of Canada. These aspects of Montreal's recent history suggest that this is an excellent urban economy for an application of both the quantitative and qualitative approaches to urban competitiveness.

The quantitative approach

While the data required for the competitiveness ranking of Montreal vis-à-vis other North American cities were available, one does experience difficulty getting much of the other data for the determinants of competitiveness for the relevant variables. The equation used for the competitiveness ranking was:

Competitiveness = .541(RS) + .371 (MVA) + .088(BS),

where the three variables are: RS = retail sales, MVA = manufacturing value added, and BS = business sales.

Data were only available for the limited period 1982-92. Later (1997) data are not yet published for the US and earlier data were not available for Canada. What this methodology captures is the movement of a city relative to other cities, and the governing assumption is that a city that is improving its relative position does so because it is increasingly competitive relative to other urban economies. As can be seen from Table 10.1, Montreal ranks at the head of Canadian cities for this decade, and is among the top one third of all the cities. Cities rise and fall in the ranking in a rather short time as the numerical gap separating cities five or ten positions apart is sometimes rather small. Thus a study that was able to utilise 1997 data might show Montreal in a somewhat different light.

Table 10.1: Competitiveness ranking of 40 US and 7 Canadian metropolitan areas (1982-92)

Ranking	City	Score	Ranking	City	Score
1	Charlotte	3.247	25	Cincinnati	1.876
2	Norfolk	3.205	26	Indianapolis	1.869
3	Orlando	2.617	27	San Diego	1.863
4	Atlanta	2.424	28	Minneapolis-St. Paul	1.862
5	Seattle	2.402	29	Milwaukee	1.842
6	San Francisco	2.321	30	Denver	1.830
7	Phoenix	2.294	31	Dallas	1.817
8	Hartford	2.267	32	San Antonio	1.802
9	Jacksonville	2.256	33	Chicago	1.740
10	Portland	2.238	34	New Orleans	1.725
11	Sacramento	2.221	35	**Edmonton**	**1.681**
12	Tampa	2.144	36	Philadelphia	1.677
13	Columbus	2.135	37	St. Louis	1.672
14	Detroit	2.110	38	Baltimore	1.655
15	**Montreal**	**2.041**	39	Pittsburgh	1.652
16	**Vancouver**	**2.033**	40	Los Angeles	1.650
17	**Calgary**	**2.019**	41	**Quebec**	**1.645**
18	Boston	1.966	42	Buffalo	1.605
19	Cleveland	1.958	43	Oklahoma City	1.561
20	Salt Lake City	1.956	44	Rochester	1.550
21	Kansas City	1.946	45	**Ottawa**	**1.458**
22	Miami	1.938	46	New York	1.446
23	**Toronto**	**1.897**	47	Houston	1.375
24	Memphis	1.888			

This very positive result comes as a surprise to many Montrealers whose thinking about the city has been dominated by the uncertainty that comes from the continuing constitutional debate, the difficult times the city experienced during the 1980s, and the rise of Toronto to Montreal's former position of primacy in the Canadian economy. The basic conclusion of all of the comparative research reported here is that Montreal is doing far better than its local psychology would indicate. The objectivity of comparative and externally based research is, of course, one of its primary advantages.

The research cited in Kresl (1992) and Kresl and Singh (1994) indicated that the following variables are significant as determinants of urban competitiveness:

- growth in per capita money income;
- research centres/manufacturing value added;
- growth in the percentage of firms with more than 100 employees;
- number in the labour force with more than an undergraduate university degree;
- share of engineering, accounting, research and management (EARM) workers in the total labour force;
- growth in the number of cultural institutions;
- growth in the capital stock for the (US) state;
- exports as a share of total output.

Several others were shown, in turn, to be determinants of the growth in per capita income and in the share of EARM workers in the labour force:

- growth in population;
- transport services;
- research centres/labour force;
- fiscal and regulatory climate;
- growth in the labour force;
- number of cultural institutions.

The limited availability of data makes it impossible to do a more extensive analysis of Montreal's position in relation to all 40 US cities, but data have been available for 24 US and 7 Canadian cities for some of the determinant variables. In Table 10.2 the comparable relevant series for both Canadian and US cities are given and it shows that Montreal's leaders can take comfort in the knowledge that their city ranks high among Canadian cities with regard to cultural institutions (taken as a proxy for

Table 10.2: Montreal and the determinants of competitiveness

Determinant variable	Montreal ranked in relation to 24 US and 7 Canadian cities	Montreal ranked in relation to 7 Canadian cities
Number of cultural institutions	10	2
Population growth 1996/1976	19	7
Research centers	15	1
Transportation services	18	3
Research centers/MVA	17	4

'urban amenities') and research centres. The relatively large size of its manufacturing sector reduces its ranking in research centres/MVA. Finally, the uncertainty that surrounds the constitutional situation and Quebec's preference for French-speaking immigrants has placed it at the bottom of population growth for Canadian cities, although Montreal is in the middle of all cities.

The qualitative approach

Application of the qualitative approach is much easier to do but is less objective in its conclusions; however, we also have the opportunity to compile data of great descriptive interest (albeit not directly analytically relevant to the quantitative approach). In this section of the chapter two different approaches to qualitative analysis of urban competitiveness are used: first, Montreal's situation is examined using the model described above (see Figure 10.1) and, second, Montreal is examined in the context of selected recent North American literature about urban economic development.

Montreal has been engaged in a process of modernisation that has been an official strategy of both the provincial government and the municipal authorities since *la révolution tranquille*, which began in the late 1960s. Quebec has become urbanised, industrialised, secularised, and internationally engaged in sharp contrast to its rural, catholic, and inward-looking past. Thus in the broadest sense Montreal has been characterised in its strategic thinking by 'qualitative restructuring', in the terms of Figure 10.1. First, there has been an explicit effort to promote the city as a centre of research and development, the success of which is attested to by Montreal's number one ranking among Canadian cities (as was noted in Table 10.2). According to the Gale Research yearbook, Montreal is home to 180 research centres, with Toronto in second place with 153 (Research Centre Directory, 1998). Related to this 'R&D strategy' are specific technology-intensive industries: Montreal has about 50 per cent of Canada's aerospace and biopharmaceuticals industries, and hosts the country's largest concentration of engineering consultancies. Montreal also ranks first among Canadian cities in higher education resources, being the only one with four major PhD-granting universities, and it is sixth among Canadian and US cities combined.

Second, the development of Montreal as an international centre has been a consistent strategy for at least two decades. In 1986 the federally sponsored 'Picard Report' (1986) pressed the view that Montreal should concentrate on attracting headquarters of international organisations (it was successful with IATA) and companies, and that the city should become 'un véritable carrefour international' (an authentic international crossroads). However, the north-south linkage was ignored and a diversification away from economic relations with the US was urged in favour of closer ties with Europe and Asia. This report was issued on the eve of the decision to implement a free trade agreement between Canada and the US so this aspect of the report was sadly out of date when it was issued. The Montreal Chamber of Commerce countered that 'Montreal will distinguish itself by becoming the bridge between Europe and North America ... the Montreal of Tomorrow will affirm itself as a Euro-American city of the first rank' – although with mixed results. Having lost its primacy to Toronto as Canada's primary financial and corporate decision-making centre, Montreal's leaders were clearly trying to reposition the city in the larger globalised economy. An international airport, Mirabel, was built but it was not successful in meeting the competition from Toronto for international flights and its own in-town airport, Dorval, for domestic flights, so it has been reduced to serving charters and air freight. Finally, Montreal International was established with the support of about 100 of the city's largest companies and all levels of government. Its objectives include the 'promotion of Greater Montreal on the world scene' as well as soliciting foreign investment and providing other services.

As Figure 10.1 shows, once a city's leaders have chosen one or more strategies, the means required to achieve that end are clear. In Montreal's case, the strategies are 'R&D Centre' and 'Headquarters: International'. An assessment of Montreal's experience in this regard would be far too complex to be discussed here, but it would entail an evaluation of the degree to which the various means have already been achieved, how competing cities have performed and what then remains to be done.

A second approach to a qualitative assessment of Montreal's competitive position can be cobbled together from a reading of literature that is unrelated to this city's situation. The first contribution is that of Jane Pollard and Michael Storper who differentiate, in addition to the service sector among 'intellectual capital industries' (those with high proportions of high-wage, non-production occupations), 'innovation-based industries' (those employing high proportions of highly skilled, technical labour), and 'variety-based industries' (those marketed by the diversity of their products (Pollard and Storper, 1996). In the first category they include industrial chemicals, electronics, financial services and research activities; in the second are biological products, aircraft, engineering and office equipment; and in the third they list food processing, printing, chemicals, construction equipment and routine manufacturing. Employment gains were strongest in services, decline was found in variety-based industries, and moderately strong employment gains were noted in the other two industry groupings. As has already been suggested, Montreal has strength in both 'innovation-based industries' and 'intellectual capital industries'. This is clear from the data presented in Table 10.3 in which Montreal is shown to have a number one ranking among Canadian cities in all areas of technology-related employment, except for communication in which it is second to Toronto. Thus in the Pollard and Storpor typology Montreal would be classified in the 'High Growth, Multiple Specialisation: Older High-skill, High-technology Centers' category.

The second reference to the literature is to the work of Ann Markusen. She asks why it is that, in the context of restructuring and de-industrialisation, some locations, 'sticky places', have shown resiliency in

Table 10.3: Technology-related employment, Canadian cities ranked among Canada-US cities (1995)

City	Information technology	High technology	Software and computers	Commun-ication	Rank among Canadian cities
Calgary	42	27	57	58	4
Edmonton	35	45	58	57	5
Montreal	7	10	8	15	1
Ottawa-Hull	58	35	27	56	5
Quebec	57	60	62	55	7
Toronto	9	16	19	10	2
Vancouver	45	23	21	54	3

their economic vitality in the industrialised world (Markusen, 1996). After rejecting the Marshallian and Italianate industrial districts models as inappropriate to North America, where highly interactive networks of many small local firms do not exist, she identifies three versions of districts that are relevant to North America. The 'hub-and-spoke district' comprises a small number of large firms that anchor the local economy and serve as the geographical centre of a web of suppliers. Seattle is an example of this, with Boeing, Microsoft and Weyerhauser as its anchors. The 'satellite platform' is 'a congregation of branch facilities of externally based multi-plant firms' with no command functions. Finally, the 'state-anchored district' is centred on one or more facilities such as military bases, a political capital, one or more universities, and regional health facilities. Markusen's advice to local authorities is that they 'assess their existing district structure accurately and design a strategy around them, rather than committing to a fashionable strategy of small firm networking within the region'.

Montreal, as can be seen in Table 10.4, is still a major corporate headquarters and decision-making centre in Canada, indicating that 'satellite platform' is not an apt description but 'hub-and-spoke district' is. Furthermore, Montreal's rich endowment in universities, research institutes, regional health facilities and cultural institutions makes it clear that the city's economy is also that of a 'state-anchored district'.

Table 10.4: Canadian corporate headquarters locations (1997)

Revenues	> $4.0 billion*	$2.0-4.0 billion	$1.0-2.0 billion
City and number of Headquarters			
Toronto	13	10	30
Montreal	11	9	14
Calgary	7	7	8
Vancouver	3	3	12
All others	6	3	14
Cumulative number of Headquarters			
Toronto	13	23	53
Montreal	11	20	34
Calgary	7	14	22
Vancouver	3	6	18
All others	6	9	21

Note: *This amount is the cut-off point for the Fortune 500 in the United States.

Source: The Financial Post 500, Toronto, 1998

In describing these two districts, Markusen says they share the following characteristics:

- the economic structure is dominated by a small number of large firms or government entities;
- scale economies are high;
- there is substantial intra-district trading;
- the labour market tends to be local, except for professional and technical workers;
- there is an evolution of unique local cultural identity and bonds;
- the public sector is highly involved in providing infrastructure.

In sum, the appropriateness of classifying Montreal as a combination of hub-and-spoke and state-anchored districts is suggested by the headquarters data presented above, the role of the public sector in infrastructure provision, the unique local cultural identity, the characteristics of the labour market, and the linkages of Montreal firms. Finally, we can note that Montreal service sector receipts (defined by Statistics Canada to include fire, business services, education, health, food and hotel, and miscellaneous) are the highest as a share of the total for Canada of any of the major cities – its share is 33.8 per cent and Toronto follows with 28.6 per cent. This confirms Montreal's identification as a 'hub and spoke district' and a 'state anchored district' as defined by Markusen.

The final approach examines the rise and fall of US metropolitan areas (Negrey and Zickel, 1994). They offer a typology of six forms based on the growth of population and manufacturing employment, presented in Table 10.5. Using data for 138 US metropolitan areas, they determined the following clusterings: Type I – 19, Type II – 1 (Boston), Type III – 38, Type IV – 11, Type V – 15, and Type VI – 54. Two thirds of the cities experienced: either a decrease in manufacturing employment and a less than national average increase in population (predominantly those cities in the traditional manufacturing areas in the North); or an increase in manufacturing employment and a greater than national average increase in population (exclusively cities in the South and the South West).

Data for Montreal show that it is the only one of Canada's major cities that can be classified as Type III. This category includes the US cities of Baltimore, Chicago, Indianapolis, Kansas City, Philadelphia, San Francisco and St. Louis (Table 10.6).

Table 10.5: The Negrey-Zickel classification of metropolitan areas

Type I: Classic Deindustrialising Centres (manufacturing employment decreased and population decreased).

Type II: No designator (manufacturing employment increased and population decreased).

Type III: Stable Centres in Transition (manufacturing employment decreased and population increased less than the national average).

Type IV: Innovation Centres (manufacturing employment increased and population increased less than the national average).

Type V: New Services Centres (manufacturing employment decreased and population increased greater than the national average).

Type VI: New Manufacturing Centres (manufacturing employment increased and population increased greater than the national average).

Source: Negrey and Zickel (1994)

Table 10.6: Canadian metropolitan areas and the Negrey-Zickel model

Area	Change in population % 1976-92	Change in manufacturing employment % 1976-92	Negrey and Zickel Type
Canada	21.4	—	
Calgary	67.0	−3.9	V
Edmonton	57.2	−10.3	V
Montreal	16.2	−27.8	III
Ottawa	40.7	−17.7	V
Quebec	24.0	−31.1	V
Toronto	46.9	−14.4	V
Vancouver	45.0	−19.1	V

One can use the information gained from these approaches to construct a table that is similar in nature and function to that of Figure 10.1. This is done in Table 10.7 in which the typologies of: Markusen – 'Hub-and-spoke' and 'State-anchored'; of Negrey and Zickel – 'Stable centres in transition'; and Pollard and Storper – 'High growth, Multi-specialities', are taken to be 'strategies', each of which requires a set of 'means' for realisation. These strategies are not in conflict, therefore one can sum the

Table 10.7: Strategic planning option from the literature: Montreal structures

Strategies means	Hub-and-spoke	State anchored	Stable centre in transition	High growth multi special	Number
Development and support of small and medium sized firms			X	X	2
Development of alliances with other cities	X				1
Establishment of effective links between firms and universities and research centres			X	X	2
Establishment and expansion of international linkages	X			X	2
Construction of infrastructure: housing and urban amenities		X		X	2
Construction of infrastructure: transportation	X		X	X	3
Construction of infrastructure: communications	X			X	2
Develop adequate specialised business services		X	X	X	3
Promote clusters or concentration of firms				X	1
Develop specialised manpower training		X	X	X	3
Attract large firm head offices	X			X	2

'means' horizontally so as to get a measure of the priorities one should attach to each of them. In this scenario the most pressing priorities for Montreal would appear to be providing an adequate transportation infrastructure, and both specialised business services and manpower training. Alliances with other cities and promoting clusters of firms would appear to be the least pressing. A detailed examination of the adequacy of each of the 'means' in relation to those of competing cities would be required before a plan could be designed to improve Montreal's competitive performance with regard to each of the strategies.

The column on the far right simply indicates that for the four strategies given alliances with other cities and the promotion of clusters of firms are less generally important than are, for example, development of a transportation infrastructure, or specialised manpower training.

What can we learn from this about city planning to enhance competitiveness?

Perhaps the first thing to note about this research on Montreal is the degree to which the results were counter to the expectations of the city's residents and leaders. It is very easy for individuals to develop a false sense of the competitiveness of their city if they concentrate on an internal discussion that feeds off their own misconceptions. Montreal does have a history of growth that is less exuberant than that of its neighbour, Toronto, or Calgary and Vancouver in the west. Furthermore, the question of language rights and the negative impact on investment of the uncertainties attached to possible separation of Quebec from Canada have cast a pallor of pessimism over the city. Objective, comparative research is freed from this self-perpetuating parochial mindset. Even with the constraint of limited data that precluded a full quantitative analysis, Montreal was found to be well placed among both Canadian and US cities in terms of economic competitiveness. Additional analysis of a qualitative nature highlighted some of the city's strengths relative to its competitors.

Further analysis of Montreal vis-à-vis other cities in North America would draw attention to sets of cities with which it has features, strategies or roles in common. While some of these cities would be competitors, it would be possible to develop mutually beneficial relationships of cooperation and common problem solving with non-competitor cities. This is an element of the 'Euro Cities' movement in Europe[1], and it is one that is sadly lacking in relationships among North American cities.

In a more general vein, it is clear that much can be learnt about a city's competitive position in relation to other cities by means of an essentially qualitative mode of analysis. An individual city can be placed in a variety of typologies or systems of classification, some of which will be more relevant than others. From this, an understanding of the most promising strategies for competitiveness enhancement can be gained, as well as sets of policy measures that must be enacted for realising a particular strategy. There may be conflicts among the potential strategies and the means required to achieve them – this is where a competent, objective analysis by local leaders in both public and private sector entities becomes invaluable. But in the absence of comparative quantitative data this exercise can become detached from a realistic appraisal and evaluation. As was true with Montreal, much data can be obtained to serve this purpose even though the data required to apply the comprehensive quantitative approach articulated here are not always, or fully, available. This does, however, highlight the crying need for national governments and multinational entities such as the European Union to devote both the resources and the political will to compiling more complete, comprehensive, and comparable data of the metropolitan area or, for the EU, the NUTS II level of aggregation. In the context of a globalisation of economic relations in which some powers and responsibilities for economic management have been devolved from national to sub-national governments this need is more pressing than ever. Interurban, indeed, intercontinental, competition for production facilities, roles in the urban hierarchy and jobs is becoming increasingly intense and accurate data are one of the tools local authorities require for strategic decision making.

Notes

[1] The best source for material on 'Euro Cities' is their website: www.eurocities.org

References

Communauté urbaine de Montréal (1989) *Economic overview of Montréal, 1988*, Montréal: Communauté urbaine de Montréal.

Kresl, P.K. (1992) *The urban economy and regional trade liberalization*, New York, NY: Praeger Publishers.

Kresl, P.K. and Singh, B. (1994) 'The competitiveness of cities: the United States', in *Cities and the new global economy*, Canberra, Australia: OECD and the Government of Australia, pp 424-46.

Kresl, P.K. and Singh, B. (1999) 'Competitiveness and the urban economy: twenty-four large US metropolitan areas', *Urban Studies*, vol 36, nos 5/ 6, pp 1017-27.

Krugman, P. (1991) *Geography and trade*, Cambridge, MT: MIT Press.

Markusen, A. (1996) 'Sticky places in slippery space: a typology of industrial districts', *Economic Geography*, vol 72, no 3, p 294-310.

Ministre des Approvisionnements et Services Canada (1986) *Rapport du comité consultatif au comité ministeriel sur le développement de la région de Montréal*. Ottawa: Ministre des Approvisionnements et Services Canada.

Montreal Chamber of Commerce (1985) *Montréal tomorrow: An international city*, Montréal: La Chambre de commerce de Montréal.

Negrey, C. and Zickel, M.B. (1994) 'Industrial shifts and uneven development: patterns of growth and decline in US metropolitan areas', *Urban Affairs Quarterly*, vol 30, no 1, pp 27-47.

Picard Report (1986) Pollard, J. and Storper, M. (1996) 'A tale of twelve cities: metropolitan employment change in dynamic industries in the 1980s', *Economic Geography*, vol 72, no 1, pp 1-22.

Pollard, J. and Storper, M. (1996) 'A tale of twelve cities: metropolitan employment change in dynamic industries in the 1980s', *Economic Geography*, vol 72, pp 1-22.

Provincial Government of Quebec (1979a) *Pour une politique québécoise de la recherche sceintifique*, Québec: Editeur officiel

Provincial Government of Quebec (1979b) *Bâtir le Québec*, Québec: Editeur officiel.

Provincial Government of Quebec (1982a) *Un project collectif: Le virage technologique, Bâtir le Québec Phase 2*, Québec: Ministère d'état au développement économique.

Provincial Government of Quebec (1982b) *Bâtir l'avenir*, Québec: Ministère de Communications.

Research Centers Directory, 24th Edition (1998) Detroit, MI: Gale Research.

Thibodeau, J.C., Pontbriand, M.-T. and Martineau, Y. (1986) *La postion concurrentielle de l'industrie manufacturière Montréalaise, 1971-1981-1991*, Montreal: Institut national de la recherche scientifique: urbanisation.

ELEVEN

Urban networks and the new economy: the impact of clusters on planning for growth

Philip Cooke, Clare Davies and Rob Wilson

Introduction

Today, competitiveness involves leveraging numerous different assets to give firms and support institutions for local areas advantage in a global not merely national contest. Thus, what was once relatively marginal to firm competitiveness, like the land-use planning system, moves on to the radar of competing firms in new ways. In an era when markets have been liberalised and state interventions are judged in terms of their market-friendliness, regulating market failures is something of a *terra incognita* for firms and policy makers alike. One such area concerns negative 'spillovers' or diseconomies of agglomeration that arise from rapid growth of economic activity in new places or old places where it has not previously been particularly pronounced. One such kind of location is the university town. Now that the value of scientific and other creative knowledge has been revalued upwards as global competitiveness entails more knowledge-intensive production for more discerning markets, university towns with global knowledge-competitiveness can be growth nodes. If they are blessed with medieval townscapes set in heritage landscapes such growth is both a source of political conflict and a lightning-rod for urban containment policy. New solutions to the sensitive issue of growth versus environment will be required in future. This chapter explores one candidate solution, which is to encourage controlled growth in urban networks.

The chapter involves exploring the validity of 'urban networks', meaning enhanced communications and facilities linkage between neighbouring towns and cities in furthering new economic growth without excessive negative externalities and sustainability implications. The focus is on 'Areas of Economic Pressure' in South and East England. In London and in smaller, knowledge-intensive urban economies like Cambridge and Oxford, there are intense economic growth pressures concerning politically strongly defended land and townscape heritages. In these 'knowledge economies' where indices of high-tech manufacturing and knowledge-based services (OECD, 1999) are high, quality of life is a major asset for firms seeking to recruit and retain highly qualified intellectual labour. Widespread shortages of software engineers, in particular, cause inflationary income-bidding, which raises costs of living and lowers the supply of intermediate skills in industry and public services due to the lack of affordable housing and inadequate transportation. A new approach to planning is long overdue to help resolve rather than exacerbate such tendencies and the urban networks concept is a strong candidate for supplying intellectual support for planning which accommodates economic growth without compromising goals of achievable sustainability. The latter notion, it will be argued, has been transmuted into an old and negative planning discourse of containment. Questions have begun to be raised about the capability of a planning profession that survived the retrenchments of the Thatcher era by a Gramscian, defensive 'war of position'. This stripped the ideology of planning to its bare bones, which were fundamentally anti-urban, anti-developer and anti-competitive, as enshrined in the heart of successive legislative planning milestones.

Urban networks and economic growth

This chapter is in tune with the thinking informing the recent European Spatial Development Perspective where urban networks are advocated as the means of securing polycentric and balanced spatial development rather than concentration in a few mega-urbanisation belts (see for example, Krätke, 2001). In the UK the deleterious effects of weakening planning at the expense of market forces are being felt severely by employees. These are increasingly endangered by inadequate and overcrowded railways bringing commuters to an overheated London labour market, and householders finding that expansion of urban growth into flood hazard areas is unsustainable. Urban networks, by design, exert a moderating effect on excessive commuting and inappropriate land development through enhancing the liveability of areas with growth prospects in rational but not excessively rule-bound ways. However, these cannot simply be created from a *tabula rasa*, they network and enhance existing settlements. Hence, to develop the application of the urban networks concept it is firstly necessary to assess the extent to which network potential exists among UK urban centres. It is clear that they scarcely exist in any obvious way in the UK, let alone displaying evidence of policy in support of them. Hence, this chapter explores the potential for managing competitiveness cohesively rather than being a description of accomplished fact. Moreover, to the extent that potential is found, it will be seen conceptually and concretely to take on different forms, for example institutional or physical.

In the research reported on here, potential was first assessed through analysing flows among towns and cities located polycentrically and judging the degree of city-effect or agglomeration potential they had through shared facilities like theatres, museums, hospitals, universities and retail facilities. Second, methods were deployed to enhance this research, using indicators like daily commuting and telecommunication flows, indicators of 'city-effect', and estimates of growth potential based on the presence of advanced economic activities like IT, biotechnology, research and knowledge-intensive services. From these analyses a long list of over 20 candidate urban networks was identified for Britain. In the full study we examined them in favoured and less favoured regions, which meant reducing the number to three that were subject to detailed investigation. The strongest of these, based on flow indicators, was found in North East England linking Newcastle, Gateshead, Sunderland and South Shields. The weakest in terms of flows but strongest in terms of growth was in the Thames Valley linking Reading, Swindon, Oxford and Newbury. The intermediate one was in South East Wales linking Cardiff, Newport, Bridgend and Pontypridd, distinctively hierarchical in network structure, with Cardiff strongly dominant. The other two had stronger lateral linkages. For the purposes of this paper, we shall discuss only the Thames Valley case, and the Oxford biotechnology cluster specifically, comparing its evolution with that of Cambridge, which one of the authors has studied independently (Cooke et al, 1999a). Both are environments that foster innovation and can be characterised as 'knowledge economies' set in heritage locations pressured by growth in the 'new economy' of biotechnology and ICT businesses. For obvious reasons, these are the forerunner places where economic pressure is greatest, where policy innovation is thus in greatest demand, and where experimentation may bring learning opportunities for policy adaptation and implementation elsewhere.

A key feature of urban networks is willingness for towns to sink historic differences and engage in collaboration for mutual benefit. This has become more prevalent in recent years in areas where it might be thought unusual. In the Thames Valley there are numerous partnership bodies and some experience of collaboration among unitary authorities on issues like transportation, economic development and tourism. The Thames Valley Economic Partnership manages economic development for former counties (prior to a local government reorganisation the mid-1990s) of Berkshire, Oxfordshire and Buckinghamshire and seeks to manage growth location in this 'Area of Economic Pressure'. Thames Valley Enterprise combines TEC, Business Link and the Chamber of Commerce for the equivalent area. Both are affected by the emerging Learning and Skills Councils and Small Business Administration franchises which divide former Berkshire, responsible for the economic development of the M4 corridor (the area around the motorway that runs between London and South Wales), from Milton Keynes, Oxfordshire and Buckinghamshire. According to TVEP and the South East England Development Agency (SEEDA, 1999) this points to an important potential new growth network linking Oxford, Milton Keynes and Cambridge. Although Cambridge is outside the South East Economic Development Agency remit, in neighbouring Eastern England Development Agency's area there has been discussion and a measure of consensus that in this knowledge-driven economy, it makes sense for Oxford and Cambridge to develop stronger links. In early 2000 the Oxford and Cambridge Partnerships, public–private partnership bodies, opened discussions on how this might be effected. In terms of input of policy ideas for implementing this, a disused railway could have been reopened if Railtrack could have been persuaded, something a cynic might suggest had slim prospects given the millennial travails of that unfortunate and, in late 2001, bankrupt firm.

Where local government expenditure is heavily controlled by central government, administrations are forced to compete for public allocations and in the 1990s this also forged the idea of partnership between diverse representative and private bodies because of the nature of the bidding rules of these contests. Partnerships compensated somewhat for the historic absence of *regional* governance bodies, as distinct from decentralised unitary administration in England that had meant there was no supervening influence offering leadership for strategy development above the local level. However, that changed in April 1999 when Regional Development Agencies (RDAs) were established, and the findings of this research suggest that this has opened up some divergence between the thinking of town planners in the Regional Government Offices and economic development professionals in the RDAs in some places. Especially in the heavily populated South East of England, the Government Regional Office sought to promote concentration of growth in four 'gateway' locations at Stansted, Crawley, Ashford and Milton Keynes. The Regional Development Agency in its first strategy documents promoted 20 or more 'knowledge-driven hubs' capable of network linkage. Not only were these rooted in knowledge economy businesses and research activities, they also had ambitions to strengthen such 'clusters' with a proposed Oxford–Cambridge axis, or through enhancing existing links such as Portsmouth–Southampton.

The central government Department of Environment, Transport and the Regions (DETR) – since reorganised – reached its judgement of Solomon by averaging the planners' upper and lower annual housing demand estimates, stressing brownfield over greenfield development sites, thus not compromising SEEDA's 'multiple hubs' strategy for fostering the knowledge-driven economy. This was cost-free to the DETR, since the Development Agency had to win the 'cluster challenge' contest run by the Department of Trade and Industry to build the cluster 'seed-crystals'. Since this was an all-England contest, SEEDA would never have been able to develop more than a few in the short-term. As 'clusters' were New Labour government industry policy, the DETR leant towards polycentrism, rather than major concentration in the 'gateways' proposed by Professor Stephen Crow as the optimal spatial strategy for South East England. It was helped in this by the professional support of the South East Regional Planning organisation (SERPLAN), representing the combined official views of local government chief planners. They supported SEEDA against the Government Office for the South East, who in traditional urban containment style were main champions of Crow's report (Crow and Whitaker, 1999).

Concepts, processes and policy rationale

As can be seen, in intellectual terms, the issue of urban sustainability has potentially serious competitiveness implications, already recognised by European urban theorists themselves seeking a 'third way' between sprawl and megacity development. The EU funded studies into alternative forms of urbanisation (Archibugi et al, 1996) and the most appealing to emerge was that of self-sustaining, polynuclear urban development, an approach which now fully informs spatial development thinking in the EU although it has no real purchase in policy terms since subsidiarity rules mean spatial planning is a second-level (member states) function. Nevertheless, all member states signed up to the ESDP at the Amsterdam Council of Ministers meeting in 1999, so in effect it is, in spirit if not yet in law, the new planning ideology of the UK. These conclusions were based on studies of successful urban economies (Andersson, 1986; Batten, 1995) which showed that the most successful urban settings in terms of growth, welfare and sustainability indicators were not large cities but those of modest population size, from 300,000 upwards; such settings normally consisted, spatially, of a key city and satellites; an open and external focus was normally exhibited in good land and air transportation, export-oriented firms, and the presence of at least one university; and administrative or commercial functions such as banking or insurance above the national norm. These characteristics broadly coincided with criteria being developed by the European Commission in their thinking on cities with the best potential for future success. These included: a mix of high added-value services and manufacturing; an educated and innovative workforce; a strong university research and design base; cultural and environmental quality; excellent international accessibility; and innovative urban governance (Parkinson et al, 1991).

Urban theory research by the likes of Andersson (1986), Westin and Östhol (1992), Batten (1995) and Batten et al (1998) showed that globalisation was causing 'an innovative class of polycentric urban configurations or network cities' (Batten, 1995) to come to the fore. They combined resources to improve efficiency and effectiveness in research, design, training and education, knowledge and cultural transactions and services, with creative urban managers often leading the associational effort involved (see also Henton et al, 1997). In Europe, London-Cambridge and Stockholm-Uppsala axes were characterised by excellent land and air links, telecommunications connectivity, and globally significant knowledge production, exploitation and commercialisation. Other embryonic or established urban networks, or as Andersson (1986) referred to them, 'creative regions', included the Randstad, the 'Flemish Diamond' of Brussels-Leuven-Ghent-Antwerp, and Heidelberg-Karlsruhe-Stuttgart as well as Bonn-Cologne-Düsseldorf in Germany. These last two German cases were designated BioRegios after a competition in 1995 run by the federal government to identify the three best locations to encourage the formation of clusters of biosciences research, exploitation and commercialisation. Their strong intra- and inter-urban networking cultures were key assets in helping secure their success.

Researching urban networks: some methodological points

The specific objectives of the project were, first, to review and seek to establish the extent to which urban networks exist in the UK. Building on Archibugi et al (1996) some 24 potential or candidate networks were identified. These formed the basis for a subsequent refining process that led the research team to identify the three already discussed for more in-depth investigation. The second objective was to seek to demonstrate intra-network connectivity using flows indicators like commuting, freight movements and business telecommunications traffic and, to the extent possible, catchment area profiles. This objective was achieved but the resources required to perform it as thoroughly as intended were unavailable. Flows data for travel-to-work movements proved the most robust indicator, backed up after an extremely lengthy process of eliciting data from British Telecom by telecommunications traffic. Freight data is collected privately at county level and the fine-grain required for urban analysis could not be achieved. Catchment area data on health and higher education facilities were accessed and used as indicator data for designating candidate urban networks in possession of facilities commensurate with exhibiting a city-effect (Cooke et al, 1999b).

A third project objective was to examine in detail three strong candidate urban networks in favoured, intermediate and less favoured regions, using secondary data to determine, particularly, innovation, cultural and environmental assets and liabilities. Fourth, barriers and opportunities to furtherance of urban network and inter-urban partnership building were to be explored through key actor interviews. Some 15 interviews were conducted in each region, 45 in all, and valuable findings were generated (see, for example, Cooke et al 1999c). Finally, objective five was to draw up strategic policy guidance for use by government in tackling urban issues through an urban networks approach. Surprisingly, this was achieved, first, through our involvement in the UK Minister of Science's Biotechnology Clusters task force, which enabled an initial Oxfordshire-Cambridgeshire comparison, and the invitation to contribute to the Minister's report on *Biotechnology Clusters* (DTI, 1999) by advocating Urban Networks for Innovative Cluster Areas (UNICAs) to deal with growth in heritage settings like Oxfordshire and Cambridgeshire. Thereafter this became a key feature of new Regional Planning Guidance for dealing with clusters issued by DETR in November 1999.

The South East of England was most strongly represented for commuting and telecommunication flows between candidate networks by south Hampshire, with Thames Valley (Oxford-Reading-Swindon-Newbury) third for commuting and second for business telecommunications interaction. Examination of indicators such as higher education places, expenditure on R&D, absolute and change data on high-technology employment 1991-96 and business buoyancy measured by change in stock of firms (VAT registrations and deregistrations) 1994-

97 led to the Thames Valley being the stronger of the two South East candidates for fuller investigation. This was clearly important in theoretical terms since the innovative environment was shown in the research literature to be a key feature in the tendency towards urban network development. Other research, such as that of Andersson (1986) and Batten (1995) showed Cambridge to be one of Europe's most creative cities in terms of the innovation indicators discussed above with its main network interactions towards London along the M11.

However, when explored in detail it became clear that much of Cambridge's interaction field for innovative activities is globalised as well as localised. Thus, Hinxton is concerned with maintaining and developing the commercialisation of genomics not just in the UK but near Cambridge. However, the partners in decoding the human genome are the Whitehead Institute, linked to MIT, in Cambridge, Massachusetts, and Washington University in St Louis, Missouri. The UK Treasury subsidised research and commercialisation partnership between Cambridge University and MIT underlined this. Figure 11.1 alludes to the third-generation mobile telephony technology 'Bluetooth', discovered by the Californian firm LSI Logic, and then acquired by Philips, with a mobile telephony research facility in Cambridge. A network of ex-Philips Bluetooth engineers now works for systems design houses like PA Consulting and Symbionics, which was contracted by Ericsson of Sweden to design its licensed application of the technology. Symbionics contracts out to local components and systems suppliers who, in turn, source specialist raw materials from traditional suppliers of such materials to Cambridge University research laboratories. To the extent that the local system extends outside Cambridge it is found mainly within easy reach, in neighbouring districts and Eastern England locations such as Huntingdon and King's Lynn and particularly in the science parks scattered in South Cambridgeshire (Cooke et al, 1999a).

For Thames Valley, in line with the urban networks project methodology, key actors were identified from local and regional government bodies and interviews with key economic development and planning actors were set up, beginning in late 1998. Key thematic issues included: networking activities engaged in, types of network, actors involved, mechanisms, barriers to and opportunities for networking; partnership activities by type, actor, form, function and so on; and governance of networking and partnership activities, modes of consensus formation, contestation and conflict resolution. Questioning then ensued on functional aspects of collaboration, coordination and competition in transportation, retail, economic development, tourism, culture and leisure, housing and education. Efforts were made to ascertain the extent of under- or overprovision or duplication as well as efficiency, complementarity and sharing of facility provision. This enabled a sense of the qualitative nature of networking and partnership practice to be formed, as well as gaining a clear picture of the receptivity or barriers to cooperative modes of policy development, both in the past and as anticipated in future, particularly in light of the strengthening of the regional level of policy formation during the late 1990s.

In Cambridge, a comparable approach was pursued for economic development actors, including firms, while the question of planning was focused on the issues surrounding Hinxton and related 'science parks in the green belt' conflicts. This was followed through secondary means, interviews with regional actors and telephone interviews with local authorities and the Cambridge Partnership. The Cambridge Partnership is an authoritative and innovative 'associational' model of urban governance, similar to the Austin, Texas, Joint Venture: Silicon Valley, the Massachusetts Technology Collaborative and other high technology, new economic community forms of civic entrepreneurship (Henton et al, 1997; Cooke and Morgan, 1998).

The nature of policy networking in cluster economies

For the Thames Valley network connecting Swindon, Oxford, Reading and Newbury, commuters between network nodes are almost universally low in intensity and balanced, except for 17 per cent of Newbury residents commuting to Reading and 6 per cent going the other way. Clearly, it might be thought that commuting in this sub-region is dominated by London, but apart from the Reading-Newbury nexus, these labour markets are remarkably self-contained with 71 per cent of the labour force living and working in the same node and less than 17 per cent travelling to work outside the network. The Thames Valley is perceived by policy actors to have a weak identity, but it displays higher policy partnership than might be anticipated, although in a nexus rather more circumscribed than originally postulated in the research. The first point to be made is that in terms of the development of policy partnership, regional boundaries probably always mattered to some extent but the establishment of the RDAs has underlined that significantly. Thus Swindon, on the eastern edge of South West England, equidistant between Bristol and Reading, is far more strongly aligned with the South West than the South East.

The only known collaboration by officers was research on R&D and financial services sponsored by the South East Economic Development

Strategy Group (SEEDS). Thames Valley officers noted little interaction, while recognising shared transportation (rail and road) and business links (Honda in Reading and Swindon; Rover in Swindon and Oxford; high-tech electronics in Swindon, Newbury and Reading). Indeed ten firms from Swindon, Reading, Newbury and Slough had produced a joint study on park-and-ride, suggesting business perceives greater commonality of interest than the governance parties. But moving to the Thames Valley itself, there was a high degree of policy partnership in the Berkshire-Oxford-Buckinghamshire (BOB) sub-region, represented by the Thames Valley Economic Partnership (TVEP) and Thames Valley Enterprise (TVE). It was in the latter, which encompassed the TEC, Business Link and Chamber of Commerce, that the view of the Thames Valley's lack of identity was expressed the strongest. The TEC had nine sub-boards, there are no common media but rather 15 weekly and 1 (Reading) daily newspapers, 10 radio stations and 3 distinct TV broadcasting areas.

With the demise of the TEC in 2001 and the franchising of a Learning and Skills Council (LSC) as well as a local Small Business Service (SBS), BOB is being transformed into MOB (Milton Keynes-Oxford-Buckinghamshire). Berkshire disappeared following local government reform and the establishment of six unitary authorities, but it is a distinct LSC and SBS franchise. Milton Keynes, though, joins Oxfordshire and Buckinghamshire, thus underpinning a perception, promoted by SEEDA and welcomed by TVEP, that the next growth axis for the sub-region lies north eastwards towards Cambridge. To some extent this vision fits in with the promotion of Milton Keynes by the Government Office for the South East as a further-to-be-developed growth pole, especially for accommodating residential development. But the knowledge-driven economies of the two university towns in all probability will be the engines of growth, and whether Milton Keynes will be attractive to such labour remains to be seen.

TVEP has, since set-up in 1994, been mostly M4 Corridor focused and, acting as the economic development arm of local government, has been managing inward investment. Unemployment fell from 10 per cent in 1994 to 2 per cent in 1999 and new arrivals like Oracle, employing 3,500 at Reading, and other Enterprise Resource Planning software firms clustering nearby, such as SAP at Basingstoke, Baan, PeopleSoft and J.D. Edwards – at the time the world's top-five, known as 'JBOPS' – is testimony to the assistance TVEP has been able to contribute. Further, with a major shortage of advanced software engineers, TVEP and TVP have been involved in assisting Newbury Further Education College in attracting a £27 million INPAQ software engineering design facility.

Hence, despite a perceived lack of socio-cultural identity, enterprise support and industry work in a well-networked manner, including upwards to SEEDA for which the South East's 76 economic partnerships like TVEP are key interlocutors.

Cambridge and, more widely, Eastern England, its Government Office, RDA and TEC-Business Link for Cambridgeshire are different from Thames Valley in demographics, economy and policy disposition. The perception among the policy community is that Cambridge is small, rather remote, with uneven development and social exclusion problems affecting the Fens, into which the UK's Silicon Valley has been parachuted, it sometimes seems. Support for development of business clusters is an aim of EEDA and the now defunct CambsTEC Business Link (CTBL, responsible for Cambridge City, East Cambridgeshire, Huntingdonshire and South Cambridgeshire). Cambridge has spawned two fully functioning clusters, first in IT and more recently in biotechnology. These have the three key cluster characteristics of localised vertical and horizontal inter-trading, market specialisation and at least informal network governance mechanisms (Porter, 1998). Thus, the policy community has a clear understanding of the socio-technical mechanisms involved in clustering, and the specific characteristics of knowledge-driven clusters. The potential for developing others, such as engineering, food and distribution has also been explored by CTBL, bidding for the LSC franchise, and similar aims are expressed in EEDA's regional strategy.

However, there is also recognition of the need to spread some of the economic benefits from Cambridge to the less favoured areas, notably Fenland. A recent decision of St John's College to build a new 'incubator' facility at Littleport near Ely in the north east of the county suggests recognition of the fact that there is less hostility to expansion in the north and east of the area than to the south, within easy distance of the M11 and London, but where green belt land is also perceived to be under threat. As we shall see below, there are localised moves with respect to transportation strategy, in which Cambridge Partnership is active, to evolve a decentralised network approach to managing economic growth. The scale of this thinking is beginning to extend from the old county level to that of the East of England region as awareness increases of the economic complementarities between universities and industries from Essex to Norfolk, not to mention the housing and labour markets of towns such as Stevenage, from where medium-skilled labour is increasingly recruited to meet Cambridge's skill shortages.

The Oxfordshire biotechnology cluster

Until recently the UK's largest indigenous biotechnology firm, British Biotechnology was a spin-out from the American firm Searle (part of Monsanto) of High Wycombe (near Oxford), when the latter closed its UK operations in 1985. Two research directors established British Biotech and by 1992 it had become the UK's first publicly floated biotechnology company. Its site at Cowley is close to other Oxford-based biotechnology ventures such as Oxford Glycosciences, Oxford Molecular and Xenova. In 1997 British Biotech was Europe's leading biotechnology company in terms of market capitalisation and R&D investment, and second to Qiagen of Germany in employment, with 454 employees.

At the other extreme, OGT is a spin-out from Oxford University, which retains a 10 per cent stake in the firm, set up in 1995 to manage income from DNA microarray patents. Other Oxford firms of significance in biotechnology include Oxford University spin-out Oxford GlycoSciences, the world's leading proteomics firm, now partnered with Incyte Pharmaceuticals of California, Oxagen (functional genomics) based in nearby Abingdon, and therapeutics company Oxford Molecular. Other firms in the extended Oxford cluster, which is aligned down the A34 corridor, are near Abingdon and Didcot on the Milton Science Park and include Prolifix, a cell cycle control therapeutics firm, Oxford Asymmetry in bioinformatics and Cozart BioSciences (immunodiagnostics). A number of newer firms are located at Oxford Science Park, including Progenica (diagnostics), Oxford Therapeutics (drug development), Oxford BioResearch, Kymed (biopharmaceuticals) and Evolutec (drug discovery). Other centres such as the Medawar Centre and Abingdon Science Park also house biotechnology firms.

The Institute of Molecular Medicine at the John Radcliffe Hospital, Oxford (part of Oxford University's Clinical School), is a leading research institute which spins out new firms, notably specialising in oncology and AIDS/hepatitis vaccines, in partnership with Isis, the Oxford University technology licensing and spin-out support organisation, private investors and venture capitalists. Oxagen, in Abingdon, is a recent spin-out from the Wellcome Trust Centre for Human Genetics in Oxford, and Prolifix was spun out from the Medical Research Councils' National Institute for Medical Research in London. Yamanouchi Research Institute is the first privately funded biotechnology research institute to be established in the area (1990). On-site is BioTecNet, a biotechnology incubator. In 1999, Oxfordshire BioLink, a network association for the industry, was established.

Oxford has some 50 biotechnology firms and 200 supply, service or intermediary firms and organisations. It has most of the features of a cluster, though still relatively small, including rising costs of industrial and domestic property, congestion, and shortages of venture or other kinds of investment capital (partly caused by the negative British Biotech effect upon investor confidence). A study by Mihell et al (1997) showed that of 40 biotechnology firms identified in 1995 (50 in 1999), 9 out of 12 interviewed were spun-out from the university or other public research base, and all firms interviewed had grown swiftly in employment and revenues in the previous five years. Collaborations among local firms and with both the local science base and more distant pharmaceuticals firms are central to firm strategy, though local networking between firms was not as developed as the other links, signifying the comparative immaturity of the cluster. At the time of the survey, in 1996, 2,200 were employed in the 40 firms identified, and new firms were forming at a rate of three to four per year.

The Cambridge biotechnology and IT clusters

Estimates by the CambsTec Business Link (CTBL) suggest that high technology employment in the Cambridge area was some 38,000 in 1998, an increase of 5,000 since 1995. This accounts for 11 per cent of total employment, 70 per cent of which is in Cambridge City or South Cambridgeshire. The two science parks on the Milton road (Trinity and St John's) house some 150 firms but, while the presence of Cambridge University is important, Garnsey (1995) estimated that only 20 per cent of all high technology firms in the area were spin-outs from it. Other research laboratories are also sources of new firms, for example the Medical Research Council's Molecular Biology Research Laboratory has 12 in biotechnology, and the Babraham Institute some 20 or so.

Cambridge's core biotechnology industry consists of some 50 firms and the broader cluster (venture capitalists, patent lawyers and so on) probably consists of just over 200 firms, including the core biotechnology ones. The growth in number of biopharmaceutical firms was from 1 to 23 over the 1984-1997 period, an average of just under 2 per year, but the rate was 4 per year in the last two years of that period. Equipment firms grew from 4 to 12 during 1984-97, and diagnostics firms from 2 to 8. Key firms include Cambridge Antibody Technologies, one of the 12 spin-outs from the Molecular Biology Laboratory, Chiroscience, a start-up originally based at the Babraham incubator, Cantab Pharmaceutical, Brax Genomics, Churchill Applied Biotechnology and American offshoots

Chiron and Amgen. Many of the UK firms originated in Cambridge research laboratories and retain close links with them.

The infrastructure support for biotechnology in and around Cambridge is impressive, much of it deriving from the university and hospital research facilities. The Laboratory of Molecular Biology at Addenbrookes Hospital, funded by the Medical Research Council; Cambridge University's Institute of Biotechnology, Department of Genetics and Centre for Protein Engineering; the Babraham Institute and Sanger Institute with their emphasis on functional genomics research; and the Babraham and St. John's incubators for biotechnology start-ups and commercialisation, are all globally recognised facilities, particularly in biopharmaceuticals. However, other important research institutes in the 'green bio' field of agricultural and food biotechnology are also located in the Eastern region, such as the Institute for Food Research, John Innes Centre, Institute of Arable Crop Research and National Institute of Arable Botany. Thus in research and commercialisation terms, Cambridge is well-placed in biopharmaceuticals; and with respect to basic and applied research, but perhaps less so in terms of commercialisation of agro-food biotechnology. Within a 25-mile radius of Cambridgeshire many of the specialist biopharmaceutical firms are found with which commercialisation development by smaller start-ups and R&D by research institutes must be co-financed. Firms like Glaxo Wellcome, SmithKline Beecham (in 2001 merged as Glaxo SmithKline), Merck, Rhone-Poulenc Rorer, Hoechst Pharmaceuticals (in 2000 merged as Aventis) in the 'big pharma' category are represented and, in the specialist biopharmaceutical sector, Amgen, Napp, Genzyme and Bioglan inter alia. Thus, on another of the criteria for successful cluster development, namely access within reasonable proximity to large customer and funding partner firms, Cambridge is, again, fortuitously positioned.

Finally, with respect to 'agro-food bio', Aventis, Agrevo, Dupont and Unilever are situated in reasonably close proximity to Cambridge. Hence the prospects for linkage, though more occluded by public concerns about genetically modified organisms than in the case of health-related biotechnology, are nevertheless propitious in locational terms. Cambridge is relatively well blessed with science and technology parks, though the demand for further space is significant. At least eight of the key therapeutics or 'biopharmaceuticals including vaccines' firms are located on the Cambridge Science Park itself. St John's Innovation Centre, Babraham Bioincubator, Granta Park, the Bioscience Innovation Centre and Hinxton Science Park have all been recently completed, are under construction, or under planning review. Most of the newer developments are taking place within a short commuting distance of Cambridge itself, on or near main road axes like the M11, A11, A10 and A14. This is evidence of the importance of *access* for research-applications firms to centres of basic research, also reinforcing the point that not everything concerning biotechnology must occur 'on the head of a pin' in Cambridge City itself.

The final, important, feature of the biotechnology landscape in Cambridge and the surrounding Eastern region is the presence of both informal and formal networking between firms and research or service organisations and among firms themselves. Cambridge Network Ltd was set up in March 1998 to formalise linkages between business and the research community, connecting both from local to global networks in a systematic way. It is mostly IT focused, though some of this spills over into biotechnology, given its demand for IT equipment and opportunities for IT delivered patient and clinician data services through, for example, telemedicine or bioinformatics. Of more direct relevance to the biotechnology community are the activities of the Eastern Region Biotechnology Initiative (ERBI). This biotechnology association is the main regional network with formal responsibilities for newsletters, organising network meetings, running an international conference, website, sourcebook and a database on the bioscience industry; providing aftercare services for bio-businesses; making intra- and international links (for example, Oxford, Cambridge, MA, San Diego); organising common purchasing, business planning seminars; and government and grant-related interactions for firms.

The Cambridgeshire IT cluster is larger, with some 245 firms, 98 of which were established in the 1990s. During 1995-97 computer services companies accounted for 42 per cent of all new high technology start-ups. Software engineering and systems design accounted for 112 firms, employing approximately 2,000, around 30 specialist Internet and Web design firms, and some 25 computer, communication and components hardware research and production companies. The remainder are in computer consultancy and computer aided design. Figure 1 gives a flavour of a part of the Cambridge IT cluster based on interviews conducted in 1999.

This graphic is illustrative of the kinds of interaction occurring between a randomly selected group of Cambridge IT and electronic engineering firms. At the high value-added end, interacting substantially with the university and the Cambridge Network, are systems design firms like Cambridge Advanced Electronic (CAE) and Symbionics. These are also intimately connected professionally and socially with large, specialist

Figure 11.1: Aspects of the Cambridge IT cluster

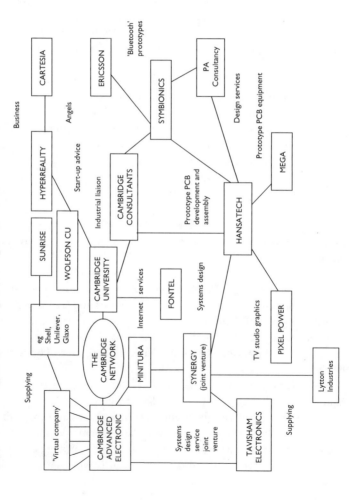

consulting houses such as PA and Cambridge Consultants. CAE animates networks of partner firms and in 1999 established itself as a virtual firm, with neither industrial premises nor overheads but a network of contractors based in Eastern England, Russia and Turkey. At a different node in the network, Hypereality, a computer games firm, has weak ties to the university but strong ties to its community of Internet games developers. Local business angel funding was accessed through the chamber of commerce and some start-up advice from the university's Wolfson commercialisation arm. The sub-network previously alluded to, involved in Bluetooth technology, links PA, Cambridge Consultants, Symbionics, Hansatech, and Mega in the supply chain to Ericsson. But Hansatech, as a speciality systems producer, links in to numerous other customers and suppliers in the Cambridge area. Thus, it produced, in September 1999, computerised control motherboards for a Formula 1 motor racing constructor alongside the Bluetooth boards for Ericsson (and Electrolux). These are the kinds of knowledge 'spillover' effects that give clusters a competitive edge with respect to productivity, innovation and new firm formation, three key indicators of business competitiveness (Audretsch and Feldman, 1996; Porter, 1998).

Urban networking responses to cluster growth

The unique feature of high tech cluster growth in the contexts described is the character of the locations and the nature of the economic impulse. These are knowledge-based industries, the key resource for which is created in two of the world's oldest universities set in medieval, heritage townscapes with World Heritage status. Surrounding both are areas of protected landscape ranging from green belt to areas of outstanding natural beauty. There are numerous Sites of Special Scientific Interest and well-organised conservation lobbying groups protective of the status quo. Thus, encapsulated in these two sites are many of the contradictions of growth economics and sustainability politics that arise with particular force in the knowledge-driven economy. Because such localities are clearly in the focus of UK government thinking and policy for the new economy, it is around them, but more particularly Cambridge, that some of the sharpest recent planning conflicts have arisen.

At the regional level encompassing Oxford, SEEDA, through its 'hubs' approach, is seeking to demonstrate the virtues of collaboration as a competitive weapon. Hubs are distinctly 'knowledge driven', involving universities, MOD research and the like. Hubs will be promoted in part through the South East Portal, involving various websites, information on business, tourism, universities, industries, training and learning opportunities. The Oxford–Milton Keynes–Cambridge 'network' is based on cooperative as well as competitive thinking and the need for integration in the absence of 'community', coherent local authorities, poor communication and rail-links. Oxford city is perceived by SEEDA as a 'go-ahead' for this approach, Oxfordshire is motivated by an anti-growth sentiment to the extent that it left the Thames Valley Economic Partnership, of which Oxford City remains a member. Thames Valley Economic Partnership remains an important supporter of Oxford in the policy development scene and one that fully endorses the SEEDA growth axis proposal involving a rail link between Oxford and Cambridge, taking in Milton Keynes, and ultimately linking to Channel and North Sea ports like Southampton and Harwich/Felixstowe. Despite this, there is a perception that such a link could also be valuable if extended to Abingdon, in strengthening growth potential towards Swindon.

In terms of economic development, Oxford City council and the county council are perceived to have differing objectives, but despite the fact that they don't always see eye to eye the two authorities work together on numerous issues, for example, the city is the highways agent for the county. The economic development department of the county council is not perceived to be very structured and, on the planning side, is thought to be more inclined to put housing into Oxford and make Oxford a housing centre, whereas the City council is more concerned with maintaining a balance. The attitude towards development within Oxfordshire held by the county council is that they accommodate whatever is reasonable to accommodate providing it's not detrimental to the environment and doesn't overturn the green belt.

The Oxfordshire Structure Plan sets out a broad strategy for development in the county and names Banbury, Bicester, Didcot and Witney as the preferred locations for new development. The policy aims to protect the green belt around Oxford by directing growth from Oxford out to the four node locations which do not suffer from the same growth pressures. This will be achieved by restricting the provision of further land for employment-generating development in Oxford while providing land for such uses in the four target areas. In addition, housing and major new shopping developments will be directed towards Banbury, Bicester, Didcot and Witney. The policy of promoting these four towns as areas of future growth rather than the city of Oxford accords with urban network theory in that growth is directed to the nodes of a network to take pressure off a large agglomeration. For development of the biotechnology cluster, the Oxford-Newbury axis along the A34, taking in Abingdon and Didcot, is the favoured direction. The large Milton industrial estate, which links those two towns has a recently completed technology park at its heart, housing biotechnology and IT firms like Oxagen, Prolifix and Psion, while Oxford Glycosciences is among six biotechnology firms on Abingdon science park. With prospects of further growth in Banbury and Bicester, closer to the M40, the embryonic urban network signified by park and ride bus interchanges may quickly develop into a decentralised high-tech urban system based on sustainability and new economy principles.

In Cambridge, as we have seen, the city is smaller, development more compact, but the knowledge-based clusters are larger than in Oxford. Similarly though, under relatively relaxed development control conditions up to 1997, the spread of new technology parks to accommodate growth was to the south. Thus, Peterhouse Fulbourn, Babraham, Abington and Hinxton are all village-based science or technology parks between the A11 and M11 routes. While Babraham and Abington were subject to planning refusals, they were eventually approved following design-related communication with South Cambridgeshire planning authority. But the Wellcome Trust's application for a 40,000 sq m extension to its research campus in the Cambridge green belt was turned down after being called in for review by the Secretary of State for the Environment, John Prescott, in 1999. Permission was given for 24,000 sq m of extended incubator and nursery space for small start-ups seeking to commercialise the decoded human genome data. The South Cambridgeshire and DETR rationale was claimed by District Chief Planner Gareth Jones not to have been NIMBY-ism ('not in my back yard') but concern about rural infrastructure for what was perceived to be a development to attract large pharmaceuticals firms. Wellcome Trust's belief is that the DETR inspectorate was misled into believing pharmaceuticals firms would build large facilities on such a site rather than small research-led units. Discussions between South Cambridgeshire and Wellcome about a prospective 30,000 square-metre compromise were resolved at the end of 2000.

The difficulty of expanding southwards on land owned or acquired for speculative development of technology parks has meant a switching of attention northwards. A new town with a population of 60,000 was advocated by the East Anglian regional planning guidance panel to be built to the north of Cambridge. The Cambridge Research Park at Landbeach has been built in the same direction and now St John's College will build its new incubator near Ely, also to the north. Park and ride bus facilities have been established, three to the south, one to the north of

Cambridge city. But these are unlike those in Oxfordshire by being set within the outskirts of the city. Urban networking potential of the kind embryonically visible in Oxford is less apparent presently. However, it may develop if Cambridge's new town gets built and if a green infrastructure plan advocated strongly by the Cambridge Partnership is adopted. Then organised decentralisation of growth linked with modestly upgraded transportation links would mean an urban network form of solution to the 'planning for growth' dilemma in Cambridge (Greater Cambridge Partnership, 1999).

Conclusions

These are instances of satellite cities not far from the metropolis of London that demonstrate remarkable urban competitiveness because of their status as 'knowledge economies'. Such places are shown in the analyses of OECD (1999) to be the most competitive in terms of GDP growth, income levels and labour shortage of all kinds. They are also congested, expensive spaces that generate their own negative 'spillovers' in terms of agglomeration diseconomies. They will continue to be growth magnets needing judicious planning that promotes growth without jeopardising sustainability. In 2001, the re-elected Labour government announced steps to revise the UK spatial planning system to take account of these concerns by, for example, investigating the costs of public participation, also suggesting a reassertion of parliamentary sovereignty over significant development decisions. However, competitiveness requires careful regulation if it is not to descend into a war of all against all. Urban networks offer an approach to tackling the growth/sustainability trade-off in ways that are neither purely state nor market driven. Thus, it is clear that pressures from urban growth caused by cluster development in knowledge-based industries places new kinds of pressure on the planning system. Whereas in countries where space is abundant and growth is relatively minimally regulated, the US being the most obvious case, growth either sprawls along highways like Route 101 in Silicon Valley or is slightly more managed in growth points along Route 128 and now I-495 around Boston, this is impossible in highly regulated South East England. But knowledge-driven economic growth is occurring more and more in relatively few knowledge-intensive university cities. Indeed, both Oxford and Cambridge are in precisely the sort of highly regulated, even in large part 'anti-growth' environment that presages future problems. Thus the new economy has brought forth a new dilemma that, to some extent, sets planners and economic development professionals at odds. The former emphasise sustainability and self-contained living and working locations, the latter seek to stimulate growth while recognising the diseconomies of agglomeration associated with overheating regional economies like Thames Valley.

A question routinely asked of such developments concerns the extent to which they are confined to satellites of major metropolitan areas like London. In another form the question is posed as to whether urban networks have anything to offer declining cities and regions. There are at least three ways of answering this on the basis of the research we have conducted. First, economic growth of the kind in Cambridgeshire and Oxfordshire is contingent upon academic entrepreneurship, early market entry and critical mass of new economy business sectors that create spillovers and attract enterprise and innovation support services. Second, where markets are weaker but there is clear potential for growth, enterprising public policy of an associative kind may be a suitable substitute. Thus, in Scotland these propulsive industries have been assisted considerably in university cities like Dundee where globally significant research is related to a cluster-facilitation strategy backed by partnership funding (see Cooke, 2001). Firms related to such embryonic clusters have located to nearby towns like Perth as well as Dundee, diffusing growth. And third, even in difficult regional economies like Northern Ireland, venture capital finds investment opportunities in new firms based on the exploitation of excellent telecommunications and Internet software research in syndicated investment partnerships involving banks and economic development agencies. An example is a network of incubators and the planned Northern Ireland science park, which involve Belfast, Coleraine and Derry. Hence the issue is not whether innovative environments can function as urban networks but why so few development specialists have researched policies such as those mentioned for outer parts of the UK and which may represent the beginnings of a sea-change in policy formulation. The key elements include entrepreneurship (academic or otherwise), enterprising public strategy, and private, equity-based financing rather than yesterday's model of creating grant dependent life-support systems for less favoured regions (Cooke et al, 2001).

A 'social translation' (Callon, 1991) of this into a spatial development perspective, established in theory and practised in some continental European cases, is to seek to build up or build on partnerships between neighbouring smaller cities to encourage polycentric linkage in the form of urban networks. These prevent coalescence of built-up areas but facilitate functional collaboration such that, at their most fully developed, they share facilities and, through integrated transportation, share the possibilities of self-sustaining, sustainable growth. In the process they become places with a preferable quality of living and working life to the large cities for which lengthy and stress-inducing, not to say dangerous, commuting is necessary. The 'urban overload' of the latter may even be substituted by the 'city-effect' that collaboration and benign economies of scale among smaller cities can produce in terms of social, cultural, health and educational facilities. We saw that, interestingly, such partnership relations were originally induced to some extent but are now rather well developed in institutional terms, in line with the experiences of other innovative environments such as the 'associational' high-tech locations of the US. Thames Valley Economic Partnership and the Greater Cambridge Partnership are both successfully merging private and public interests and now acting as key interlocutors for the new regional economic strategy professionals in their respective Regional Development Agencies.

In embryo, it can be seen that in both Oxford and Cambridge, growth is beginning to be accommodated in locally decentralised forms that take on urban network potential as the necessary improvements in integrated transportation evolve. From the theoretical viewpoint, however, it is noteworthy that the scale of such potential networks is small compared with those written about elsewhere. On the other hand, until recently, the strategic level for developing such proactive thinking was also small. As the RDAs have emerged, there has been an increase in the number of network proposals, such as that linking Oxford and Cambridge as a new potential growth axis countering the over-concentrated corridor in the Thames Valley. This would be an excellent focus for a new approach to planning for growth in the new economy, and the fact that public transportation connections are being placed above private ones is testimony to the compatibility of urban network thinking with sustainability criteria. This is also seen by the green transportation proposals being pursued or implemented in Oxford and Cambridge themselves.

References

Andersson, A. (1986) 'The four logistical revolutions', *Papers of the Regional Science Association*, vol 59, pp 1-12.

Archibugi, F., Cooke, P. and Lichfield, N. (eds) (1996) 'The integration of cities into their regional environment', report to EU DG12 ACT-VILL programme, Rome: Planning Studies Centre.

Audretsch, D. and Feldman, M. (1996) 'Knowledge spillovers and the geography of innovation and production', *American Economic Review*, vol 86, pp 630-40.

Batten, D. (1995) 'Network cities: creative urban agglomerations for the 21st century', *Urban Studies*, vol 32, pp 313-27.

Batten, D., Conti, J. and Thord, R. (eds) (1998) *Networks in action*, Berlin: Springer.

Callon, M. (1991) 'Techno-economic networks and irreversibility', in J. Law (ed) *A sociology of monsters: Essays on power, technology and domination*, London: Routledge.

Cooke, P. (2001) 'Biotechnology clusters in the UK', *Small Business Economics*, vol 17, pp 43-59.

Cooke, P. and Morgan, K. (1998) *The associational economy*, Oxford: Oxford University Press.

Cooke, P., Huggins, R. and Browne, J. (1999a) *Cluster development potential in Cambridge*, Cambridge: CambsTEC Business Link.

Cooke, P., Wilson, R. and Davies, C. (1999b) *Urban networks in Britain: Concept, indicators and analysis*, Working Paper No 1, 'Cities' programme, 'Urban networks as innovative environments' project, Cardiff: Centre for Advanced Studies.

Cooke, P., Davies, C. and Wilson, R. (1999c) *Economic development hubs or a spoke in the wheel?*, Working Paper No 2, 'Cities' programme, 'Urban networks as innovative environments' project, Cardiff: Centre for Advanced Studies.

Cooke, P., Roper, S. and Wylie, P. (2001) *Regional innovation strategy for Northern Ireland*, Belfast: Northern Ireland Economic Council.

Crow, S. and Whitaker, R. (1999) *Report on planning and growth in the South East*, Guildford: GOSE.

DTI (Department of Trade and Industry) (1999) *Biotechnology clusters*, London: DTI.

Garnsey, E. (1995) 'Cambridge's high tech success: Growing high technology industry from the science base', *New Economy*, vol 3, pp 262-5.

Greater Cambridge Partnership (1999) *Congestion ahead – which way to turn*, Cambridge: GCP.

Henton, D., Melville, J. and Walesh, K. (1997) *Grassroots leaders for a new economy*, San Francisco, CA: Jossey-Bass.

Krätke, S. (2001) 'Strengthening the polycentric urban system in Europe: conclusions from the ESDP', *European Planning Studies*, vol 9, pp 105-16.

Lambooy, J. (1998) 'Polynucleation and economic development: the Randstad', *European Planning Studies*, vol 6, pp 457-66.

Langlois, R. and Robertson, P. (1995) *Firms, markets and economic change: A dynamic theory of business institutions*, London: Routledge.

Markusen, A. (1996) 'Sticky places in slippery spaces: a typology of industrial districts', *Economic Geography*, vol 72, pp 293-313.

Mihell, D., Kingham, D. and Stott, M. (1997) *The development of the biotechnology sector in Oxfordshire: Implications for public policy*, Oxford: Oxford Innovation Ltd.

OECD (Organisation for Economic Co-operation and Development) (1999) *Science, Technology and Industry Scoreboard 1999: Benchmarking knowledge-based economies*, Paris: OECD.

Parkinson, M., Bianchini, F., Dawson, J., Evans, R. and Harding, A. (1991) *Urbanisation and the functions of cities in the European Community*, report to DG16, Brussels: European Commission.

Porter, M. (1998) *On competition*, Boston, MA: Harvard Business School Publishing.

SEEDA (South East England Development Agency) (1999) *Building a world class region*, Guildford: SEEDA.

Westin, L. and Östhol, A. (1992) *City networks and the search for regional potential*, Working Paper 13, Umeå: University of Umeå.

TWELVE

Policies to uncover the competitive advantages of America's distressed cities[1]

Edward W. Hill and Jeremy Nowak

Introduction

This chapter is not about public policies directed at poverty alleviation: it is about re-establishing the competitive viability of distressed central cities. It discusses public policies that reconnect fiscally distressed cities to their regional economies through the fundamentals of economic development: land, labour and capital. The reason for this focus is that cities can help relieve the poverty of their residents only if they foster economic opportunity. The problem with too many central cities and fiscally distressed older (formerly) industrial and residential suburbs in the United States is that they have institutional structures, redistributive practices and political cultures that are more appropriate to the market positions they had in the 1940s and 1950s when most business transactions had to be completed within their municipal boundaries (Peterson 1981).[2] Evidence is presented in other chapters of this volume that British cities are also subject to the accumulation of these economic sclerotic features (see: Bailey, Docherty and Turok, and Begg, Moore and Altunbas).

Outdated institutional structures, practices and cultures of fiscally distressed cities, combined with changes in transportation and telecommunications technologies, have eroded central cities' competitive positions. Distressed cities must become competitive in terms of tax costs and the bundle of services they offer to residents and business in order to regain their historic role as generators of opportunity, income, and wealth – these are the foundation of a competitive future. If changes are not made, city governments will continue to be managers of decline as their cities' competitive position continues to erode, and connections to their regional economies remain tenuous.

In this chapter we explore the financial difficulties of extremely distressed American cities. The particulars of the intergovernmental system of taxation in the US differs from those of other nations in regard to local governments' authority to assess taxes on business, the relatively low level of participation that the national government has in financing the operations of local government, and the relatively large role local governmental authorities have in paying for services to low and moderate income families.[3] Despite these differences our findings about what is required to regenerate distressed cities in the US are applicable to any local government; the specifics about how they can be implemented will differ.

Method

Our recommendations draw on observations made from two sets of cities in the US. We drew on summaries of 16 roundtable discussions with over 300 participants that were organised by the mayors who were members of Ohio Governor Bob Taft's Urban Revitalization Task Force during the Fall of 1999 (Ohio Department of Development, 2000). These represented a cross-section of Ohio's cities that were fiscally challenged in the early 1990s. We also conducted more than 30 half-hour/hour conversations with key decision makers and observers in the four older cities in the greater Philadelphia region in late January and early February 2000: Philadelphia, Pennsylvania; Wilmington, Delaware; Camden, New Jersey; and Chester, Pennsylvania.[4] Similar political and economic problems were identified in both sets of discussions. We then inductively formulated a set of policies from our analysis of the interview material.[5]

The two smaller cities in the greater Philadelphia region, Camden and Chester, are representative of the most problematic of America's distressed municipalities. These are highly distressed cities that lost their ability to regenerate their tax bases and are not large enough to make it on their own. They are cities that have failed economically and fiscally. We saw that these two cities have desirable physical assets, but those assets are weighed down by abandonment and tax and political structures that repel investment. The market properly values these assets; however, the value of these assets could increase markedly if placed in a different political and competitive context. The question is: how to create that context?

An introduction to Camden, New Jersey: a failed city

We use the case of Camden, New Jersey, throughout this chapter to demonstrate our ideas because in many ways it is an extreme case of a fiscally distressed city. The state of New Jersey took over the administration of the city a few months after we had completed our interviews and the sitting mayor was indicted and convicted of a laundry list of corrupt practices. Recent data paint a very bleak picture of Camden. The record of its municipal leadership is chilling. – four of its last five mayors were either indicted or convicted for corruption. Yet, economic reality in this formerly industrial city – once the home of the RCA Corporation, active dockyards, and still the headquarters of Campbell Soup Company – is colder still. In the year 2000 Camden had a population of nearly 80,000, down 22 per cent from its 1970 population. Early releases from the 2000 Census of Population show that:[6]

- Nearly a majority of the city's residents are not of working age: 38 per cent are younger than 20 (the US average is 28.6 per cent) and an additional 7.6 per cent are older than 64 (the US average is 12.4 per cent), resulting in 54.4 per cent being between the ages of 20 and 64 (the US average is 59 per cent).
- A little over 4 per cent of the city's population is institutionalised; many reside in a riverfront prison operated by the state of New Jersey.[7]
- Single females head 58.2 per cent of those families with children under the age of 18. The US average is 21.9 per cent.
- Of all households (defined as singles, families and non-family residential groupings) in the city of Camden, 9.6 per cent have a child under the age of 18 who is not the child of the household head (for example, the child is living with a grandparent, other relative, acquaintance or living alone). The US average is 3.3 per cent.
- African-Americans make up 49.8 per cent of the population and Hispanics 38.8 per cent.

Given these facts it is no surprise that in 1997 46.3 per cent of the city's residents lived in households with incomes that were below the poverty level.[8] The average for all central cities in the US was 18.7 per cent and the average for all residents in metropolitan areas was 12.7 per cent.[9]

Poverty is a result of people interacting unsuccessfully with the labour market. The 1990 Census estimated that 50.3 per cent of Camden's adult population (age 25 and older) terminated their education without earning a secondary school diploma, giving them an extreme disadvantage in the labour market.[10] Despite this disadvantage Camden's residents did benefit from the strong performance of the economy during the decade of the 1990s. The US Bureau of Labor Statistics estimated that the unemployment rate in Camden dropped from 20.8 per cent in 1991 to 11.4 per cent in 2000 (for comparison: the entire region's unemployment rate was 7.0 per cent in 1991 and 4.0 per cent in 2000). However, the decrease in the official unemployment rate over the ensuing decade grossly overstates the degree of economic success experienced by the city's residents.

The good news is that the number of unemployed residents living in Camden dropped by nearly half from 1991 to 2000. But the way the decrease occurred is odd. The number of people employed increased by only 466, while the number unemployed dropped by 3,539.[11] This means that 3,100 people left Camden's labour force over the decade, a decline of nearly 10 per cent. In other words, as employment prospects improved migration of the employed out of the city took place.

In this chapter we focus on the operation of property markets in Camden because that is where economic regeneration leaves its most lasting footprint – in the effective demand for housing and commercial properties. Cities have a limited set of assets to trade in the economy for income: they have land and they have labour. While labour is mobile, land is not. Camden's housing market is more distressed than the labour market because families with the means to do so leave the city. The median sales price of a home in the five-county Philadelphia metropolitan area in 1999 was $124,800. This is contrasted with the typical $20,000 to $45,000 sales price of an occupied row home in Camden (a vacant building has nearly no value).[12] The 2000 Census shows that 18.8 per cent of the city's housing units were vacant; the US average for all metropolitan areas is 7.2 per cent. A large portion of the city's residential building stock is in such deplorable condition that it cannot be rated for a loan (with or without a governmental guarantee). Residential building permit data further demonstrate the absence of a viable housing market. No building permits were issued for new residential construction from 1991 through 1996. In 1997, 16 permits were issued, 14 in 1998, 13 in 1999, and 5 in 2000. This is a total of 48 building permits with an average value of $69,200; all were supported by non-governmental organisations.[13]

Six development principles and six obstacles to their implementation

The challenges faced by municipalities such as Camden are daunting, but they come down to one question: how can extremely distressed cities become fiscally and economically viable? In this section we state six development principles that, if followed, will enhance the competitive positions of central cities. The principles are followed by a discussion of the institutional barriers that block meaningful reform. We then present a practical set of fiscal and management reforms in the final section of the chapter that encompass the development principles and respond to the obstacles.

Principle one: cities must be reincorporated into their region

There are two reasons why distressed cities should strive to be fully reincorporated into their regional economies (Hill et al, 1995). First, distressed cities will become places of opportunity only when their assets are competitively linked to their regional economies. They can do this by creating environments in which city assets are part of three self-sustaining, self-organising markets – housing, labour, and business locations – where the city provides valued services and can assess taxes to support its operations. Second, fiscally distressed cities have limited financing capacity and often do not have the fiscal ability to support critical investments in infrastructure that were made over the decades. Older central cities have accumulated regional assets (water and sewer plants, recreational facilities, ports and airports, museums, stadiums and convention centres) that are regional anchors, yet are often financed solely by the municipality. Another geographic mismatch occurs between the regional economy and municipal government when it comes to paying for courts, jails, and health care and other services for the poor. Now that the region has grown beyond the city's borders, funding for these assets should move to a higher level of government, possibly a special government that replicates the economic region or the state (Barnes and Ledebur, 1998).

The city's motivation for reincorporation should be clear enough as long as the political quid pro quo for reintegrating is not considered, but why should higher levels of government care if a failed city is reconnected to its region, especially if initially costs will be shifted to higher levels of government? The reason for state and federal involvement in the affairs of these places is pragmatic: in the long run subsidy costs will decline if distressed cities have self-sustaining economic structures. Currently higher level governments are locked into a strategy of pouring money into municipal coffers to keep basic services functioning, because the current stream of subsidy does not fix fundamental problems. The only way to fix the fundamental financial problems of distressed municipalities is to fully integrate them into the economic region. Camden offers a stark example.

According to our interviewees, the city of Camden raises about $30 million a year in local taxes and other revenues. At the same time, the city has combined municipal and school budgets of $330 million. The cost of operating Camden's public schools is about $250 million. Assume that, due to the low incomes of those enrolled in the school system, the entire school budget comes from the state. This leaves all of the locally generated revenue to be applied against the municipality's operating budget of $80 million. At a minimum, then, the state provides $50 million each year just to plug the city's structural operating budget deficit, leaving the city with no capital budget. This $50 million annual budget infusion from the state to the city is equivalent to the annual payments on a $714 million non-reducing bond issue.

Nearly three quarters of a billion dollars of the state's wealth is tied up in the equivalent of a bond whose principle will never be reduced: a bond that restrains the state of New Jersey's ability either to reduce taxes or invest in productive activities: a bond that just maintains the current low level of municipal services. Under current practices there is no possibility of the state of New Jersey ever extracting itself from this perpetual operating subsidy. The state of New Jersey needs a realistic, sustainable, exit strategy from the subsidy it provides to just one failed local government. The municipality's obstacles to integration are considered latter in the chapter.

Principle two: competitiveness

In the absence of a competitive package of residential goods the capacity to retain an economically diverse residential base dwindles. In the absence of a cost-competitive package of business services, businesses will locate elsewhere. The competitiveness principle requires that cities come to terms with the fact that they must place generative policies aimed towards wealth creation ahead of redistributive policies, which are best located with national government. As city leaders inherit a political culture defined by the needs of constituencies with limited choices, there is understandable pressure to pursue redistributive policies, even within the context of a shrinking municipal fisc. The irony is that over the long haul the pursuit of extremely redistributive policies hurts the very people those policies are intended to help because the ability of cities to generate opportunity is hindered when resources leave in response to non-competitive cost structures.

The impact of capitalised tax values and competition between municipalities was demonstrated in 1999 when all the properties completed by a community development corporation (CDC) in Camden were reassessed. The original tax bill of $1,500 (3.3 per cent of market value) on the typical row house was increased to $2,200 (five per cent of market value). Assuming a seven per cent discount rate, the market value of the properties decreased by $10,000 because of the $700 increase in property taxes. The competitive benchmark for Camden is the neighbouring town of Pennsauken, which taxes properties at 3.5 per cent of market value compared to Camden's five per cent rate. In addition to Camden's high property tax rate, properties in Camden need to be priced *lower* than in Pennsauken because of differences in the quality of public services. The reassessment took $10,000 of potential increase in property values away from homeowners, leaving a $2,000 gap before the prices are equalised with its competitor municipality.

In sum: Camden did not have a strongly competitive housing product once safety and public services are factored into the equation. Once the city increased its property taxes the value received by residents did not justify the taxes charged and they moved. The lesson from Camden is that even low-income families have residential choices as to the municipality they live in. In Camden, they voted with their feet (Hirschman, 1970).

Another lesson to be learnt is that municipalities that violate the competitiveness principle do not have a preordained right to succeed. They can fail. Under ideal circumstances the city would be disincorporated, but there is no unit of government that will take the resulting pieces either through municipal annexation or as unincorporated territory. The reason is that the city – either in whole or in parts – is a fiscal liability.

Principle three: build from strength, competitive advantage, and reward; not from weakness, need, and entitlement

The idea that cities should invest and build from strength is often controversial, due to constituent need and the programmatic orientation of urban politics and bureaucracies. Building from strength requires a strategic orientation, turning public subsidy into public investment (as the regeneration of Montreal described in Chapter Ten by Kresl shows). As an economic tool, subsidy must be viewed as a short-term economic input, not as a permanent programme. The use of subsidy must be organised around building up to a zero-subsidy market, rather than establishing subsidy as a way of doing business. In the absence of this orientation, cities become captive to economic development constituencies that attempt to compensate for structural inefficiencies with public dollars. Building from strength, rather than towards strength results in a fundamental change in the perspective of public policy, moving the emphasis away from need and entitlement, toward opportunity and investment.

Camden's problems are deeply rooted at the neighbourhood level (highlighting the significance of social factors – see the chapters by Boddy and by Potts), and the city's constant struggle to raise money puts a cap on housing values. However, a well thought out strategy that provides value to residents and builds from strength can turn around failing neighbourhoods. Camden is a neighbourhood that is anchored by a Catholic Church. The heart of the neighbourhood is composed of 1,200 housing units and is the focus of a church-sponsored community development corporation (CDC). In the mid-1990s one sixth of the units in the neighbourhood (200 properties) were abandoned, and the average value of the properties was $20,000, for a total market capitalisation of $24 million. In the last four years the CDC has tracked down the owners or heirs who had walked away from approximately 170 of the properties and directly negotiated purchases (they found that the city could not handle condemnation proceedings). It has rehabilitated and sold about 70 formerly abandoned houses and another 30 or so that were on the verge of being abandoned. Early in 2000 only 30 abandoned houses remained. The result is that the neighbourhood's market capitalisation has more than doubled to $54 million, with an average house value of $45,000.

The director of the CDC told us that the CDC decided to:

> "go against the traditional urban strategy, which is to find the most bombed-out part of your neighbourhood and invest there – which just did not make any sense. We thought we should look at where the market is semi-viable and invest [there], and then move from strength to weakness, as opposed from weakness toward strength. Because by the time you come out of stabilising your weakness, your strength is now probably weaker than at the point when you started.... And we think that [what] really just happened [in turning the neighbourhood

around] was that we invested at a rate greater than disinvestment [occurred]. We think that is all it is."

Principle four: private sector employment is more valuable than public sector employment

One of the primary roles of a city government –if not the primary role – is to ensure that private sector opportunity takes hold and grows. Cities must be in the business of opportunity creation and asset building, rather than being the custodians of a public sector workforce. We are not presenting an argument against public employment per se, but we emphasise that local government should be a service providing machine, not a job creation machine. (Later in this chapter we argue that an effective local public sector is a necessary condition for meaningful integration of a distressed city into its regional economy.)

More importantly, city government cannot be viewed as an obstacle to responsible private initiative. The taxpayer needs to be able to understand how the process is operating and why it is operating in a particular fashion. This requires that public services have four major attributes – relevance, predictability, transparency, and efficiency. Services, permits and inspections that the city requires must be relevant to the operation of businesses and public health and safety. The process of complying with regulations, licensing, and permitting must be predictable, easy, and performance based. These processes need to be transparent to the customer. Finally, city services and the issue of permits need to be reasonably priced in terms of both fees and formal and informal transactions costs. A non-partisan fiscal analyst pointed out the importance of this principle when he told us:

> "Until Philadelphia realises that the city is not a transfer machine we are, or will be, loaded down [with excess costs] that stand in the way of meaningful tax reform ... [this] government values public sector jobs more than private sector jobs."

Principle five: fiscal crises can motivate change

A financial crisis is a requirement for major change because most mayors cannot lead a city to make fundamental reforms without one. Different mayors use financial crisis in vastly different ways. Most do only enough to salvage the municipal bond rating and make temporary use of additional state funding or new taxing authority. Fewer mayors are able to catalyse longer term reform and strategic action – changes in management and labour relations, the institution of new productivity measures, reworking of the overall cost competitiveness of a city, and the introduction of new forms of civic participation. Too many mayors run out of steam once the immediate crisis has passed; these are mayors who, after receiving the well-earned accolades from editorial pages, return to the daily transactional and ceremonial demands of office.

Balancing the books is a necessary, but not sufficient, condition for turning around a city. Bruce Katz (2001), Director of the Center on Urban and Metropolitan Policy at the Brookings Institution wrote:

> "One can balance the books but still lose a city. Just ask Ed Rendell, the former mayor of Philadelphia. He heroically brought Philadelphia back from the brink of bankruptcy in the early 1990s only to find that it wasn't enough. The middle class still left, the new-economy firms still moved 30 miles away, the neighbourhoods still declined."

Principle six: work must pay

Cities are the places with the highest levels of concentrated poverty and the most deeply entrenched levels of welfare dependency and single parent households. Therefore, city competitiveness is based, in part, on workforce development and the creation of entry-level jobs. Workforce development encompasses not only job training, but also childcare, information networks and a transportation system that connects low income neighbourhoods to areas with jobs. These jobs must offer above poverty rate salaries (after taxes and transfers), a minimum floor of benefits, and some longer term career advancement possibilities – if not in that specific job at least as part of a broader, well-recognised job ladder. The key two points are:

- a competitive city strategy for high poverty cities requires private sector growth;
- local government should not interfere in the wage setting mechanism of the labour market.

While government cannot easily regulate any of this in a global marketplace, there is an important role for federal and state governments in helping make work pay. In the US context, federal and state governments can expand the earnings tax relief for the working poor, expand childcare and housing allowances, target transportation investments to strategies that connect low income workers with regional job growth, deal directly with the lack of medical insurance for millions of families, and provide incentives to promote the right workforce investment strategies. These issues speak to mainstream values that resonate across political lines.

Knowing what should motivate reform and the principles that work in healthy cities is an important, but insufficient base for change. If the principles outlined above are the thesis for uncovering cities' competitive advantages, the obstacles described below are the antithesis.

Obstacle one: history and lack of public administrative talent

City government and political culture are in many instances captive to historical expectations and operating systems that are hard to unravel or transcend. Distressed cities have histories of redistributive politics, including the use of public sector operations and contracts as jobs machines, which are deeply entrenched. Moreover, distressed cities have operating bureaucracies whose personnel and strategies reflect decades of decline and low expectations about performance. In these cases lower levels of municipal bureaucracies have forgotten the habits of getting things done, at the same time upper-level leadership has perfected the skills of managing decline and of catering to locally generated demands for petty income redistribution. These bureaucracies are often undercapitalised and not held accountable for their output.

While bureaucratic problems are frequently blamed on frontline workers, they are really the fault of decades of bad management practices coupled with outdated regulations. The pressure for reform is thwarted by the politics of dealing with organised labour and civil service regulations that have the protection of the jobs of current employees and the maintenance of the current bureaucratic structures as their primary goals, not the competitive viability of the city. However, meaningful administrative reform depends on making new arrangements with public sector unions, not on making workers into scapegoats.

There is a silent administrative erosion in declining cities, one that is more evident in smaller distressed cities than in large metropolitan centres, and it is a commonly echoed obstacle to growth. While the problem in large distressed central cities may be one of bureaucratic bloat and an uncompetitive regulatory environment, the problem in smaller distressed cities is more difficult. In smaller cities the bureaucracy is too small and it has forgotten how to get things done due to a lack of leadership and competence; and the financial resources required to build competence back into the civil service is also lacking. A mayor of a smaller distressed community told us:

> "At its heart [this city] is not a competitive place for either businesses or residents. The bureaucracy here is not bloated, but it is incompetent."

The management talent is simply not available to run major public sector agencies for two reasons. First, these cities often cannot offer competitive salaries to attract competent administrative talent, especially at middle and upper management levels. Second, people are unwilling to make a career in public service in distressed cities because the political environment is often too unstable or too unappetising.

When probed, what appears to be corruption in public service is really the end result of incompetence, mismanagement, and a regulatory system that does not function. A developer we interviewed in the Delaware Valley said:

> "There is no ducking it, corruption creates instability and that kills investment. However, 80 per cent of what looks like corruption is really incompetence. It is the lack of capacity – the lack of staff."

A functioning public sector is a precondition to reconnecting distressed cities to their regional economies and providing the seedbed for development and opportunity. The irony is that if the second principle is that valuing private employment is more valuable than public sector employment, then having a well-functioning public sector bureaucracy is necessary for achieving that principle.

Obstacle two: tax structure

Many distressed cities have backed themselves into, or have been backed into, a slow growth, high cost corner compared to other municipalities in their region. It does not matter who is blamed for non-competitive tax structures; the point is they exist and many cities do not have enough countervailing advantages to make it worthwhile for businesses and residents to bear these costs. The problem is that in the absence of radical tax reform, enabled by higher levels of government, most cities cannot take the short-term risk of making significant tax cuts in anticipation of growth. Lowered bond ratings and bankruptcy will arrive before the jobs and tax revenues. Additionally, without the real support of the state and federal governments, the real estate and financial markets will not trust the politics behind the lowered tax rates in the absence of immediate employment growth. Investors will act as if the cuts are a temporary expedient that will change as soon as revenue becomes tight – and they will be correct.

Obstacle three: lack of private catalytic leadership

Cities must learn to work with business and civic coalition networks that function as the keepers of a long-term opportunity agenda. The value of these networks is that they are not organised around short-term political horizons and they provide linkages into non-governmental resources, ideas and relationships. The problem that many central cities face is that the traditional sources of private sector leadership have either disappeared or are changing in the face of increased competitive pressures in private sector markets.

In mid-century, corporate leadership typically came from large national corporations, utilities, department stores, locally owned news outlets and large privately held firms. What they had in common was that they could catalyse a civic agenda by providing either political muscle or strategic funding, based on the personal involvement of the firm's chief executive officer. Today, an independent base of locally rooted corporate leadership is increasingly rare. One CEO told us that his personal involvement in civic affairs could not match either his own or his predecessor's efforts during the early 1980s because of pressure generated by the stock market, a smaller staff with less time for civic activities, and more business-related travel for the CEO.

Private sector leadership is increasingly coming from service businesses, such as real estate development, law, and accounting firms that have business relationships with the central city. Being dependent on a city administration for income makes it hard for these firms to stand against political winds. Another expected source of leadership is large, place-bound, non-profit institutions such as hospitals and universities. The problem is that they cannot write a cheque to political campaign funds. Administrators of higher educational institutions can offer a neutral and catalytic presence, but they cannot provide the same type of political muscle that comes from the private sector because they are so dependent on the public sector for either land or money.

In the future, either different forms of intermediation will develop or else the long-term civic agenda will become increasingly difficult to maintain. In some metropolitan areas leadership comes directly or indirectly from community foundations. In others, it comes from not-for-profit development organisations and other civic intermediaries (whose funding is somewhat independent of the local public sector) in conjunction with private sector leaders. Local foundations, civic intermediaries and elite leadership in the form of politicians and the private sector form a municipality's civic infrastructure – its real social capital. The questions to be answered, and they will be answered differently in different communities, are: Who is the keeper of the long-term civic agenda? Where is catalytic political and economic power located? Is the leadership group permeable or has it ossified? If leadership has ossified, the community will have lost civic, political, and economic flexibility. With that loss will come an increased inability to lead social and economic change.

Obstacle four: land costs and assembly

In the US, there are limited funds available to accumulate, clear, and retitle abandoned land in cities. It is difficult to find the 'typical' cost of acquiring and clearing urban land. There have not been enough viable commercial land development deals in Camden to use that city as an example, so we draw on the commercial record in metropolitan Cleveland, Ohio.

Much of the cost in redeveloping land depends on whether or not it is in the central business district, the degree of environmental remediation that is involved, the cost of clearance, and the difficulty of assembly. In a number of sites in two places, MidTown Corridor in Cleveland and an industrial redevelopment area in the city of Euclid (a former heavy industrial city to the east of Cleveland), the recent cost of acquiring and clearing an acre of land ranged from $200,000 to $300,000, while the cost of developing former farmland on the edge of the metropolitan area ranged from $25,000 to $50,000 an acre.[14] The $150,000 to $275,000 cost differential represents the difference in annualised profits at a 15 per cent rate of return of $22,500 to $41,250 an acre, not including other operating cost differentials that may favour the suburban site – such as crime and insurance. There is also the question of offsetting subsidies, where greenfield sites routinely receive some sort of heavily discounted subsidy for infrastructure such as gas, water, roads and highway access, and inner-city sites typically receive loan financing, if anything, to rebuild the same utilities. From the viewpoint of a firm we need to ask if the city site represents at least $22,500 per acre in additional profit? From a financial perspective, the answer is, most often, No.

The challenge for the development organisation is to bring the land cost down to the point where it can compete with greenfield sites. The economic dilemma is to ask if there are sufficient social efficiency gains and internalised external costs and benefits to warrant the steep public subsidy.

Obstacle five: concentrated poverty and social isolation

The social geography of many metropolitan regions reinforces urban isolation. As many cities become the repository of high levels of concentrated poverty as well as having majority non-white constituencies, their symbolic and social capital depreciates. Concentrated poverty sets off a chain reaction that strains public institutions, repels investment and reduces the impact of middle class consumer demand for political accountability (Jargowsky, 1997). As this occurs, smaller cities fall completely off the radar screen of businesses location decisions and major investment flows. This severing of civic connections and normative expectations works against the required sense of urgency and political will required to reform and reintegrate cities into regional economies. Severed connections to the region reinforces the call for redistributive politics, the politics of entitlement and confrontation, because isolated political communities see the public sector as their only source of income and opportunity.

Obstacle six: lack of state and federal political will

Non-competitive, fiscally challenged cities require long-term coordinated action from both state and federal governments. In the absence of a long-term, focused partnership, cities receive a patchwork of categorical aid with limited expectations for changing economic performance or focus. In other words, the tradition of state and federal aid to cities has become a major part of the problem in reintegrating cities into their regions. A new partnership requires that central cities be reintegrated into their regional economies and that tax structures and service levels be competitive with their suburbs. How can this task be accomplished?

A new partnership

State, federal, and county governments can help reconnect distressed central cities to their regional economies only as long as there is sufficient political will to do so. However, the proposals we offer are so disruptive to the current state of redistributive local politics that we expect that, initially, they will only be adopted by cities in response to an extreme municipal fiscal crisis. Currently, there are a number of severely distressed smaller urban municipalities that could immediately benefit from the policies we are proposing.

Meaningful reform will only take place with the aid of an outside agent, working with a tough operating agreement, so that local politicians can shift the blame for necessary, painful restructuring to that agent. The agent needs to be the domestic equivalent to the International Monetary Fund. No matter where the agency is located in the national government, it is critical that it have the ability to execute a rigorous operating agreement with the participating city and its state government. The agreement must have clear sanctions, including triggers that will end the federal government's participation in the fiscal reorganisation of the city, if the city or state does not fulfil its commitments.

The key to reintegrating distressed central cities into their regional economies is to create an economic environment that supports private sector productivity, and through productivity enhancement, job creation.

Step one: reforming the tax structure

The new partnership must begin with a public commitment to municipal tax reform. The state and federal government's major role in the partnership is to guarantee the city's flow of tax income over a ten-year period, so that it can undertake a radical reduction in its tax rates. This ten-year window gives tax reform a chance to succeed and, perhaps more importantly, allows the city to implement its own staffing reforms in a way that does not ask public employees to bear the entire burden of reconnecting the city to its regional economy. We recognise that real estate developers and businesses will not respond immediately to a radical reduction in tax rates for two reasons. First, it will take time to assemble, clear, and retitle an inventory of marketable land (a point also made in relation to British cities in the chapters by Gibb, Mackay and White and by Bramley and Lambert). Second, it will take time for business to understand and believe the changes that take place – especially in the way the city is administered. The increase in local tax revenue that is triggered by the full package of reforms is not likely to be evident until the programme is well into its fifth year.

Cities should abolish all business taxes that inhibit the location of start-up firms or taxes that discourage investment in productivity enhancing equipment or practices. The second group of commonly assessed business taxes that should be abolished is taxes on real property. A tax on the market value of land should be used as a substitute for business property taxes, coupled with the broader use of business improvement districts or tax increment finance districts to pay for major infrastructure investments. Land taxes have several advantages over property taxes as a means of maintaining the competitive position of a city's economy (Brown et al, 1997). First, land taxation discourages speculative land banking. Second, land taxes are an incentive to place as much capital on property as is economically justifiable because non-land forms of real property are not taxed. Third, land taxation provides a strong incentive to the city government to engage in practices that preserve the value of land. Fourth, land taxes provide a powerful incentive to maintain properties. The counter-argument against land taxes is that the value of land, or ground, rents are difficult to calculate (Anas, 1998; Mills, 1998; Solow, 1998).

Local personal taxes commonly take three forms: sales taxes, wage or income taxes, and property taxes, with the last being the most common. For the purposes of taxation, many states and cities classify rental properties in excess of two or three units per parcel as a business. All residential property – be it owner or renter occupied – should be treated on an equal basis for purposes of local taxation. This can be done through a real property tax. Such taxes have two components – a land tax and a tax on the value of the structure. The land component of the residential property tax should be assessed on an equal basis with the business land tax, again providing incentives to develop in neighbourhoods with low land values and providing incentives to prevent speculative land banking. The second component of the tax would be on the value of the structure to pay for purely residential services.

Not many central cities are allowed to assess resident and non-resident wage or income taxes, but for those places that can, these taxes are an important source of municipal income and are a politically acceptable form of redistributive regional governance. Wage taxes allow cities to receive revenue for services provided to non-resident workers, but they should not be raised to uncompetitive levels and they should not be assessed on either capital gains or on stock options.

Step two: reforming public administration

We have observed dynamic, competent, mayors who have attracted talented staffs and have made a great difference in the attitudes, performance and perceptions about their cities. The problem is that they do not have either the financial resources or institutional flexibility to hire enough people to turn around the performance of the city. They can only work at the margins of reform.

Public administration reform in central cities should begin with a management improvement task force that reviews the operations of city departments and investigates whether the different products and services offered by city departments are genuinely necessary. Attention should also be paid to the city's overall staffing levels benchmarked to employment levels of other, similar sized cities. We are by no means certain that a task force would find that every struggling city is hampered by a too-large workforce; their problem is not a bloated bureaucracy, but a bureaucracy that is too small and lacking in competent senior-level management. This would be the result of years of fiscal blood-letting and an environment of political and employment instability and penury that makes it difficult to hold onto competent mid- and senior-level management. It is critical that a managerial improvement task force identify where the city's bureaucracy is too small.

A second piece to the reform puzzle is for the state to make a commitment to fill the managerial hole. Most distressed municipalities provide a professional environment that is too risky to attract all but the most daring public professionals. To attract the necessary talent the state may have either to loan executives to the city for an extended period or give newly hired professionals the chance to move into the state's civil service system.

The task force should also comment on management practices and the types of capital equipment used in the performance of work and the levels and types of skills and training required to carry out tasks. It is important that employees and their unions be involved in these reviews, as employees know more about the ways their jobs are, and can be, performed than anyone else.

The issue of public sector corruption is, like the issue of staffing, difficult to address. Often, what appears to be corruption to someone who works with city departments is incompetence or the reaction to incompetence as people try to get around a dysfunctional bureaucracy. Another source of corruption is the breakdown of fiscal controls and an inattention to the day-to-day management of the city. The task force should address managerial breakdowns. Financial controls and issues of corruption should be dealt with in a vigorous audit of the city's operations. There should be an understanding that prosecutions, if required, should not drag on forever and that petty corruption should be handled administratively so that the city's business can resume as quickly as possible.

Step three: assembling land and renewing infrastructure

It is difficult to see how distressed central cities can revive their economies if they do not have an inventory of land on which to build, as has been shown in the Scottish context in the chapter by Gibb, Mackay and White in this volume. Cities need to clear and assemble properties into marketable parcels, and do so without lengthy court procedures. Too many abandoned parcels are on outdated small plots with cloudy titles (see, also, the chapter by Bailey, Docherty and Turok in this volume). There is a legal need for procedures that allow cities to take title to land quickly once it falls into some legal definition of 'abandoned property' (for example., once property taxes become delinquent by more than 6 to 12 months), coupled with the ability to combine abandoned properties and retitle them as parcels of marketable size. Funds to demolish abandoned structures and to fill foundation holes are necessary parts of this activity.

Federal and state funding to recycle abandoned urban land, along with the joint ten-year guarantee of municipal finances, are powerful incentives that federal and state governments have to entice cities to embark on this programme of economic and political renewal. It is impossible to rebuild the fiscal base of a municipality if there is nowhere to place the new activities.

Step four: making work pay

Key to any opportunity agenda is the ability to make work pay, and therein lies a role for government. We will not enter the argument about the minimum wage here – that is a federal issue. We do think that expansion of the Earned Income Tax Credit (EITC) to state and local taxes is the correct mechanism for making work pay without interfering with market-based wage setting mechanisms. The advantage of expanding the EITC is that it can be tightly targeted at adults with dependent children. In addition, there can, and should, be a state-federal partnership in the expansion of this part of the competitive cities agenda.[15]

Towards a ten-year fiscal experiment

We offer this proposal to spark debate and discussion, and intend it to be viewed as the basis for a voluntary experiment with a new partnership between city, state, and federal governments. At the heart of the experiment lies state government, because state governments have the most to gain from reconnecting distressed central cities to their regional economies.

Making distressed central cities economically viable is the only hope that states have of staunching the unceasing flow of operating subsidy that pours into distressed cities.

Our research has led us to conclude that fixing the real competitive disadvantages of distressed cities – outdated tax structures, broken political cultures, uncompetitive staffing levels, vacant and abandoned land, and an inappropriate array and mix of public services – requires the kind of radical experimentation described above and is evident in cities such as Montreal (see Kresl's chapter in this volume). Cities cannot address their competitive disadvantages on their own. Higher levels of government have to become partners with cities in reform. We acknowledge that these proposals involve some degree of risk and an enormous amount of change in inter- and intra-governmental relationships. But for extremely distressed cities there is little left to lose.

Notes

[1] This paper was sponsored by the Center on Urban and Metropolitan Policy of the Brookings Institution. The Annie E. Casey Foundation, the John S. and James L. Knight Foundation, the Reinvestment Fund, and the Urban University Program of the Ohio General Assembly provided financial support for our research. We thank Iain Begg, Bruce Katz and Harold Wolman for their comments on earlier drafts of this chapter. Jennifer Bradley and Susan Petrone have helped us with the structure of our argument.

[2] The exceptions are global cities such as Washington, DC, and New York City whose fundamental problems when they went bankrupt were political and managerial. These are cities that have assets that cannot be replicated easily elsewhere in their regions and they can charge redistributive rents in the form of relatively high municipal tax rates.

[3] There are considerable differences in the ability of local governments to tax residents and businesses in the US. In the US the constraints on local taxation come from state government, not the central government. This is because state governments approve the form, but not most rates, of municipal taxation. This results in a great deal of variation in the structure of local taxation across American cities. The most common form of personal and business taxation is the local property tax, which is assessed on the value of both lands and buildings. In 1997 there were 87,400 local governments in the US; 40 per cent of them are special service providing districts, another 16 per cent are school districts, the bulk of the

remainder are municipal corporations (US Census Bureau, 2000a, Table 490). All of these local governmental units have some form of taxing authority.

An analysis of the structure of taxes in the 38 largest cities in the US in 1996 was undertaken to show this variation. Revenue transferred from the federal government to these cities in that year averaged 7.2 per cent of total municipal general revenue and revenues from the cities' own sources averaged 74 per cent, with tax revenues accounting for 41.2 per cent. Kansas City, Missouri, generated the highest share of its municipal revenue from local tax sources with 57 per cent and Memphis, Tennessee, the lowest at 19.9 per cent. Property taxes average 18.2 per cent of total municipal revenue for the group of 38 cities (Honolulu was highest with 42.2 per cent and Columbus, Ohio, was lowest at 3.4 per cent), sales and utility tax revenues accounted for 14.3 per cent and other tax sources averaged 8.7 per cent (Columbus, Ohio, was highest at 45.3 per cent and Dallas was lowest at 0.9 per cent). In five of these large cities 'other tax sources', primarily locally assessed wage or income taxes, accounted for more than 20 per cent of local government revenues: Columbus, Cleveland, Philadelphia, Kansas City and Washington, DC. (Calculated by the authors from Table 520, Statistical Abstract of the United States, 2000.) There is also a large range in the residential property tax rates charge in America's large cities. The highest rate recorded is 4.59 per cent of value in Bridgeport, Connecticut, and the lowest was 0.49 per cent of value in Honolulu (US Census Bureau, 2000a, Table 517).

There have been large changes in the structure of municipal taxation in the United Kingdom as the central government has attempted to restrain local government spending by increasing the share of local revenues that comes from central government. Central government increased the national Value Added Tax (VAT) from 15 per cent to 17.5 per cent in 1991 to pay for increased grants to local government (Adam et al, 2000, pp 26-27). The council tax is the only local tax in the UK and provides 20 per cent of total local spending. The council tax was instituted in 1993 (replacing the poll tax) and it is based mainly on the value of occupied dwellings. To calculate this tax dwellings are placed into categories based on their assessed values. Local governments then determine the tax rate that will be charged to all dwellings within a given category, making the tax more progressive than the US property tax (where the same tax rate is typically applied to all properties). Tax exemptions are provided for vacant dwellings, armed forces barracks, and student dormitories and a 25 per cent tax reduction is given to dwellings occupied by a single person. The national government stripped local authorities of their ability to tax businesses in 1990. There is a national business property tax (called the National Non-domestic Rates) based on an estimated market rent for the business property. Business property owners are charged a uniform national tax rate on the estimated market rent. All business properties are reassessed every five years. In 1990, 1995 and 2000 the tax increase was phased in if there was a major increase in the estimated market rent. Exemptions exist for unoccupied buildings, small rural shops, and agricultural land and buildings (Adam et al, pp 15-16, 26).

[4] We were particularly intrigued by Philadelphia's regional economy because its four older cities performed very differently from 1993 to 1996, while being part of the same regional labour, housing, and business location markets (Brennan and Hill, 1999). The city of Philadelphia recovered from its brush with near-bankruptcy and fiscal crisis that began 1991. Despite the city's newfound fiscal stability, it experienced a 1.1 per cent decrease in private employment from 1993 to 1996, while the number of private sector jobs in its suburbs increased by 5.4 per cent. Wilmington, located a 30-minute drive to the south of Philadelphia, presents a different picture of the competitive position of cities. From 1993 to 1996 the number of jobs in Wilmington increased by 29.6 per cent, in contrast to job growth in its suburbs of 0.6 per cent. Camden, New Jersey (Philadelphia's first eastern suburb), and Chester, Pennsylvania (a formerly industrial city that overlooks Philadelphia's airport on its southern border), represent the hardest set of urban economic problems.

[5] Hill was a member of Ohio Governor Taft's task force and Nowak is CEO of The Reinvestment Fund, which is a financial intermediary located in Philadelphia. They were brought together to work on this issue by Bruce Katz, the Director of the Center for Urban and Metropolitan Policy of the Brookings Institution, to bridge the learning that was generated by the work of the Ohio Task Force and by the substantial investments the Reinvestment Fund has made in the distressed real estate markets of the four Philadelphia area cities.

[6] The US data are from the US Census Bureau (2001). The data for Camden were obtained from New Jersey Municipal Demographic Information (2001).

[7] The US Census enumerates prisoners by their place of residence, no matter how involuntary their residential choice. Therefore, federal and state prisoners are counted as residing in their prison, not in the municipality from which they were sent. How this counting affects the finances of the city where the prison is located and of the 'sending' city is discussed in Kulish (2001).

[8] The 1997 poverty estimates are from the US Census Bureau's Small Area Income and Poverty Estimates and were obtained from the US Department of Housing and Urban Development, State of the Cities Data System: http:// www.socds.huduser.org.

[9] The US statistical concepts of a metropolitan area (MA,) Metropolitan Statistical Area (MSA), Consolidated Metropolitan Statistical Area (CMSA) and its component Primary Statistical Areas (PMSA), and New England Consolidated Metropolitan Areas (NECMA) – a form of CMSA – have no statistical equivalent in the UK. The definition of a US metropolitan area is complicated but its essence is that it is centred on a core city (municipal corporation) of at least 50,000 population (or a contiguous urban area). The MA will include the core city and the county in which the core city is located and all contiguous counties where at least 15 per cent of the employed workforce commute into the central county or counties that are contiguous to the central county. The exact definition is in US Census Bureau (2000b). This memorandum also defines a central city. The concept behind the MA is a functional urban economy, based on a labour market. The MA is intended to be centred on a core city and includes the surrounding area that is economically linked to that city. These definitions will change in 2003 and the new definitions can be found in US Office of Management and Budget (2001). Wolman and Goldsmith (1992, pp 51-4) discuss the differences in the US and UK treatment of urbanised areas. The British concept of conurbation is more restrictive than the US MA, as the UK definition only includes the seven largest concentrations of population in the nation. Wolman and Goldsmith (p 53) found the term 'metropolitan counties' not to be equivalent to a metropolitan area in the US because they are political jurisdictions and are too large.

[10] The average for central cities in the US was 26.7 per cent and the average for all residents of US metropolitan areas was 23.1 per cent.

[11] The resident labuor force in Camden dropped from 34,509 in 1991 to 31,379 in 2000 while the number of employed residents only increased from 27,334 to 27,800 (an increase of 466), meaning that the number unemployed (those actively seeking work but not employed) went from 7,175 to 3,539, a drop of 3,130. Since the number employed increased by 466 then 3,130 people dropped out of Camden's labour force. Since those with newly acquired income have expanded residential choices, we assume that many of those 'missing' were employed and moved outside of the city with their increased income. The data are from US Department of Housing and Urban Development, State of the Cities Data System, http://www.socds.huduser.org

[12] The median metropolitan sales price was from Table 1202, Statistical Abstract of the United States 2000. The range of values of non-abandoned, or non-vacant homes for Camden was obtained from interviews and a review of investments in the city made by The Reinvestment Fund.

[13] Building permits in the bordering lower middle class municipality of Pennsauken can be used as a basis of comparison. In 2000 Pennsauken had a population of 35,737 and issued 12 single-family building permits with an average value of $107,000. The city of Cherry Hill, a wealthier neighbour of Camden's with nearly 70,000 residents in 2000, issued 45 permits with an average value of $132,000. These buildings were constructed through the private market and conventionally financed. Data on new residential construction permits are collected by the US Census Bureau and distributed by the State of New Jersey through its website, http://wnjpin.state.nj.us/OneStopCareerCenter/LaborMarketInformation/

[14] The development of the corporate headquarters of Applied Technologies in the MidTown Cleveland area cost $500,000 an acre, but the site assembly included obtaining properties with operating businesses.

[15] Crediting both the employer and employee portions of federal social security taxes to low wage workers on a sliding scale can expand the current EITC. At the same time the social security accounts of these low-wage earners can be credited for these earnings by either making the appropriation from the federal government's general fund or by increasing the upper income limit on the social security tax and redistributing these funds to the accounts of low -wage earners. States and cities should also help make work pay for low income individuals by creating state and local EITCs where state and local wage and income taxes are credited for low wage earning adults.

References

Adam, S., Chennella, L., Dilnot, A. and Roback, N. (2000) A *survey of the UK tax system*, Institute for Fiscal Studies Briefing Note 9, http://www.ifs.org.uk/taxsystem/taxsurvey.pdf

Anas, A. (1998) 'Commentary' in D. Netzer (ed) *Land value taxation: Can it work and why?*, Cambridge, MA: The Lincoln Institute for Land Policy.

Barnes, W. R. and Ledebur, L. (1998) *The new regional economies: The US common market and the global economy*, Thousand Oaks, CA: Sage Publications.

Brennan, J. and Hill, E.W. (1999) *Where are the jobs? Cities, suburbs, and the competition for employment*, The Brookings Institution, Center for Urban and Metropolitan Policy, Survey Series, http://www.brookings.edu/ES/urban/hillfa.pdf

Brown, H., Smolka J. and Smolka, M.O. (1997) 'Capturing public value from public 'investments', in H. J. Brown (ed) *Land use and taxation: Applying the insights of Henry George,* Cambridge, MA: Lincoln Institute for Land Policy.

DETR (Department of the Environment, Transport and the Regions) (2000) Local Government Financial Statistics (England), http://www.local.detr.gov.uk/finance/stats/lgfs/chapter5.pdf

Hill, E. W., Wolman H.L. and Ford III, C.C. (1995) 'Can suburbs survive without their central cities? Examining the suburban dependence hypothesis,' *Urban Affairs Review,* vol 31, no 2, pp 147-74.

Hirschmen, A.O. (1970) *Exit, voice, and loyalty,* Cambridge, MA: Harvard University Press.

Jargowsky, P. (1997) *Poverty and place,* New York, NY: Russell Sage Foundation.

Katz, B. (2001) 'Escape from Connecticut's cities', *The Hartford Courant,* 8 April. http://www.brookings.edu/views/op-ed/katz/20010408.htm

Kulish, N. (2001) 'Since census counts convicts, some towns can't get enough', *Wall Street Journal,* 9 August.

Mills, E.S. (1998) 'The economic consequences of a land tax', in D. Netzer (ed) *Land value taxation: Can it work and why?,* Cambridge, MA: Lincoln Institute for Land Policy.

New Jersey, Municipal Demographic Information from the 2000 Census of Population (2001) http://www.wnjpin.state.nj.us/OneStopCareerCenter/LaborMarketInformation/lmi25/sf1/dp_municipal_2000.xls

Oates, W. (2001) *Property taxation and local government finance,* Cambridge, MA: Lincoln Institute for Land Policy.

Ohio Department of Development (2000) *Ohio urban revitalization: Policy agenda and task force report,* http://www.odod.state.oh.us/urban.asp

Peterson, P. (1981) *City limits,* Chicago, IL: University of Chicago Press.

Solow, R.M. (1998) 'Commentary', in D. Netzer (ed) *Land value taxation: Can it work and why?,* Cambridge, MA: Lincoln Institute for Land Policy.

US Census Bureau (2000a) *Statistical Abstract of the United States,* interactive edition, http://www.census.gov/prod/www/statistical-abstract-us.html

US Census Bureau (2000b) Revised standards for defining metropolitan areas in the 1990s, memorandum, November, http://www.census.gov/population/www/estimates/mastand.html

US Census Bureau (2001) *Profile of general demographic characteristics, 2000.*

US Census of Population and Housing (2001) http://www.census.gov/Press-Release/www/2001/2khus.pdf

US Office of Management and Budget (2001) Urban area criteria for Census 2000 – proposed criteria; *Federal Register* notice (28 March, 2001), http://www.access.gpo.gov/su_docs/fedreg/a010328c.html, corrections to the original notice: http://www.access.gpo.gov/su_docs/fedreg/a010727c.html, US Census Bureau's web page on these changes. http://www.census.gov/geo/www/ua/ua_2k.html

US Office of Management and Budget (2000) Standards for defining metropolitan and micropolitan statistical areas, *Federal Register*, 27 December, vol 65, no 249, http://www.census.gov/population/www/estimates/notice001227.pdf

Wolman, H. and Goldsmith M. (1992) *Urban politics and policy: A comparative approach*, Oxford: Blackwell.

THIRTEEN

Managing urban development: land-use planning and city competitiveness

Glen Bramley and Christine Lambert

Introduction

This paper is concerned with the operation and impacts of planning on patterns of urban development and city (region) competitiveness. Land-use planning is one of the most important, possibly now the most important, form of regulatory intervention in economic activity and development in Britain. Indeed, some prescriptions for improving Britain's competitive economic performance draw particular attention to planning (McKinsey 1998).

Most of the literature on planning and urban development tends to be written from 'within the system'. That is, it tends to (a) adopt a normative stance, reasoning from certain desirable goals to proposed practical measures, and (b) take for granted features of the British planning system as normal/natural. In this paper we are trying to take a step back from this, and to look at the system more objectively, as an essay in 'political economy' which looks for some general regularities in the way that this decentralised politico-administrative system operates.

International comparisons may draw attention to this aspect of differences in the operating environment, without necessarily understanding the actual differences between land-use regulation regimes and ways in which these are changing. The way British land-use controls work is significantly different from systems operated in the US or elsewhere. Also, regimes in all countries are responding to environmental and political challenges, such that past assumptions about regulatory environments may no longer hold (see, for example, the US debate on urban growth controls (Danielsen et al, 1999; Downs, 1997; US Department of Housing and Urban Development, 1999).

Property markets and urban development have a significant impact on urban competitiveness (see also the chapter by Gibb in this volume), especially in relation to how planning deals with different sectors of development, location and land use. In the wider competitiveness debate planning is of interest for a number of reasons. Theories of urban economic performance (for example Krugman 1995) draw attention to the role of elastic labour supply in enabling potentially growing sectors and clusters to expand and realise the advantages of scale, agglomeration and dynamic change. This in turn requires elasticity in the supply of new housing or in the ability of workers to commute from nearby settlements. Research on locational decisions of firms and businesses shows some evidence of an increasing emphasis on 'quality of life' (Bramley 1999b, citing GCVPJC, 1997, Table 9). This directs attention to the role of planning in promoting high quality living environments and city centre environments offering a range of cultural and other amenities. Patterns of land release for housing and related density policies, relative to patterns of commercial development and other land uses, have a significant influence on patterns of travel behaviour and the associated environmental and congestion costs. Planning is also an increasingly important mechanism in relation to the financing and provision of infrastructure.

The chapter begins by outlining a framework for analysis. This takes the form of a set of general propositions about the operation and impacts of planning on patterns of urban development and city competitiveness, derived from prior knowledge and past research. These propositions are grouped under three broad headings: planning policy stances, planning implementation and planning impacts. The available empirical material is then used to illustrate, test and refine these general propositions. Our focus is more on planning decision making and procedures and about the kinds of biases and development outcomes that these produce, and rather less on impacts in terms of city and regional performance. However, we can offer some hypotheses and speculations on these, together with some partial evidence.

The chapter draws empirically on a variety of sources. These include research in two of the city-regions included in the ESRC Cities Research programme (Central Scotland and Bristol). These examples are of interest because the cities involved offer contrasting economic contexts. In UK terms, most of Central Scotland is more typical of the northern, economically declining regions of England, although there are marked internal, east–west divisions (between Edinburgh and Glasgow) in terms of prosperity and demographic growth (Bailey et al, 1999). Bristol is an example of a relatively affluent southern city, with significant growth pressures, economic and demographic, emanating from its role as regional capital and key node on the dynamic M4 corridor. There have, historically, been significant differences in the institutional arrangements for regional/ sub-regional planning in the two areas, but post-1996 evolving patterns in both areas are characterised by increasing fragmentation. In addition to these case study examples, we refer to material on the South East region produced in the context of regional planning/monitoring, of interest because of the high profile of recent debates on the accommodation of urban growth in this area.

A framework for analysis

We use a relatively simple framework for analysing the influence of planning on urban development, following Bramley (1998, 1999b). The key assumption underlying this framework is that localities differ substantially, but much of this variation is likely to be systematic. Although we have an increasingly prominent set of national planning policies (Tewdwr-Jones 1996), there is significant scope for discretion in the British planning system and local interpretation in the application of national policies. Indeed, local discretion within an overall comprehensive power of control is the fundamental feature of the British planning system (Grant 1992; Cullingworth and Nadin 1997). However, differences in the regional or local context may offer different opportunities in terms of policy choices and the leverage or bargaining power available to planning authorities in their relationship with developers.

The framework distinguishes three broad levels in the planning-development process:

- *The policy stance of planning*, distinguishing degrees of promotion/ restrictiveness in general and selectively between different forms of development.
- *The implementation of planning*, dealing with instruments and mechanisms set in a legal, policy and institutional context.
- *The impact of planning on development outcomes*, and wider impacts in terms of markets, environmental conditions, social equity and cohesion.

This framework may be used as a loose set of headings for more detailed propositions and hypotheses, and as a way of characterising the differences between localities and over time. For a more extended discussion of these aspects of planning see Bramley (1999b). For the purposes of this paper we derive a set of more general propositions and hypotheses about policy stances, implementation and impacts, which are then tested against the available empirical evidence.

Policy stances

Planning decisions are made primarily at local level, though national policy provides an important context in terms of both general policy prescriptions and in setting the 'rules of the game'. We first review key features of evolving national policy before commenting on systematic tendencies in local policy stances.

A national commitment to 'urban containment' is a long-standing and well-documented feature of the British planning system (Hall et al, 1973; Evans, 1991), seeking generally to constrain urban expansion. While there was some loosening of controls and selective attempts to deregulate urban growth in the 1980s, the planning system escaped any fundamental reform (Bramley and Lambert 1998). It can be argued that very often containment policies reflect an alignment of national and local policy predilections.

On the other hand, certain features of the system promoted nationally have also facilitated development. Historically, new towns and town expansions were a key tool in accommodating growth, though these have fallen out of favour in recent years (apart from the use of Urban Development Corporations in some inner city areas in the 1980s). Another important tool in recent years has been the use of demographic household projections to establish targets at regional and local level for land release for housing and related purposes (DoE, 1996; Bramley and Watkins, 1996; Breheny and Hall, 1996). Taken together with housing land availability targets and monitoring arrangements in place since 1980, these could be seen as a tool to ensure at least a minimum if not a generous supply of development land despite potential reluctance from some local authorities (Evans, 1991).

Current policies from national government are generally tending to reinforce urban containment and consolidation. A series of Planning Policy Guidance Notes (especially revised PPG 3 on Housing, DETR, 2000, and revised PPG 13 on Transport, DETR, 2001), and the report of Rogers' Urban Task Force (DETR, 1999) emphasise the benefits of compact cities, recycling of urban brownfield land and restraining car use. These policy shifts reflect one side in an ongoing academic debate about planning for 'compact cities' (Jenks et al, 1996). There have in effect been some moves away from the top-down prescription of household forecasts and housing numbers, adoption of targets for housing development on brownfield land and sequential testing for housing sites, to reinforce urban containment (DETR, 2000). At the same time, land availability targets and monitoring have been weakened, at least in England.

One difficulty with such prescriptions is that they run the danger of coming up against conflicting economic development and growth trends. These show a strong tendency to decentralisation to the outer parts of cities (Breheny, 1999). The policy also flies in the face of trends for many people to demand more space as incomes rise (Hooper et al, 1998) or to choose less urban residential environments (Champion et al, 1998).

Another important point about these national policy changes is a tendency for selective application, to housing, but not to business-related development. Household projections and related housing development requirements and environmental impacts have generated a high level of political controversy (DoE, 1996). Conversely, business-related development arouses less discussion, and there is much less national policy prescription. In this respect, national planning policy is tending to reinforce local policy stances, discussed below.

With more political resistance to housing and a more prescriptive planning and management regime applying in the planning for housing arena, there are dangers therefore of restraint biting in selective ways on housing as opposed to employment. This might limit the ability of housing to develop alongside jobs, leading to labour market imbalances, longer journeys to work and exclusion. We return to this point in the conclusions to this paper.

The second key general point to be made here is that there may be systematic variations in the stance of planning between affluent, middle class (high demand) and poorer, more working class (low demand) areas (see Bramley 1998, 1999b; and the chapter by Hill and Nowak in this volume). The former areas are likely to be more attractive, with residents who value environmental amenity more highly and who are likely to be owner occupiers with a stake in local residential property values. The latter areas' populations and political representatives will be more interested in promoting job and housing opportunities.

Summing up, it is possible to make the following general propositions about planning policy stances:

- There are systematic variations in the stance of planning between high and low demand areas. More affluent areas tend to apply more restrictive planning policies and emphasise environmental quality criteria more

strongly. Areas with a history of industrial decline may be particularly willing to accommodate new economic development without much regard to its environmental or wider impact.
- There is a degree of selectivity in the system, such that authorities tend to apply more restriction on new housing development than on new business development.

Implementation

Implementation processes are important partly because of the decentralised nature of planning controls, giving a key role to local elected authorities, but also because planning is fundamentally a regulatory response to private developer initiative. Major reviews of planning implementation in the 1980s demonstrated a systematic difference between areas of greenfield development, where negative regulation could be effective, and areas of urban regeneration, where the lack of instruments for 'postitive planning' and the direction of investment in infrastructure made implementation problematic (Healey et al, 1988; Cullingworth and Nadin 1997). Significant innovations such as the imposition of Urban Development Corporations could be seen as a response to these problems (Imrie and Thomas 1993).

Implementation of planning may be conditioned by a variety of factors: standard operating procedures; local fiscal conditions; the overall level of demand and development pressure; or by institutional arrangements and administrative boundaries. Examples of 'standard operating procedures' include the use of household projections and housing land availability guidelines as mentioned above. Another important example concerns the role and coverage of local development plans. Important changes, generally referred to as 'the plan-led system', were introduced at the beginning of the 1990s, essentially giving greater primacy to the provisions of local plans in development control decisions while requiring all authorities to have up-to-date, district-wide local plans in place (Tewdyr-Jones 1996). The administrative framework for planning was significantly affected in some areas by local government reorganisations in the mid-1980s and again in the mid-1990s.

Again, on the basis of previous research and prior reasoning, we can put forward the following propositions:

- The plan-led system offers more potential for coherent and predictable patterns of development, but this may be undermined by short-time horizons, review timetables and opportunism. In particular, decisions on major new economic developments may be strongly driven by opportunism in relation to particular sites, with future urban forms often shaped by such decisions.

- Political actors in planning are averse to the political risks associated with defining longer term settlement strategies and tend to resist commitment to long-term plans.
- The removal of (sub)regional tier planning authorities in more urbanised areas has weakened the ability of planning to apply strong strategic priorities between areas. Central cities are often under-bounded and lack direct control over many of the major developments within their functional regions.
- Fiscal motives are less important determinants of planning decisions in the UK than in the US and other countries because of equalisation mechanisms, but they may still play some role, for example, through planning agreements.
- Fragmentation of both planning and infrastructure provision and current funding mechanisms militate against coherent planning of infrastructure.
- Land availability monitoring arrangements for housing have in the past ensured some continuing supply of housing land, but recent policy changes may undermine this feature of the system.

The impact of planning

The planning system may have a wide range of impacts on development patterns and markets, with wider ranging economic performance, welfare and social equity and environmental effects. Here we concentrate on selected impacts that seem to have the most bearing on the 'cities and competitiveness' issues. The issues relate to the housing and other development markets, labour supply imbalances and travel and commuting patterns.

Impacts are more clearly an area where market forces drive outcomes within the constraints set by planning. It is important, also, to note that these impacts derive in part from the systemic local-level features of the planning system that we saw above. However, they also reflect the fact that Britain has moved away from comprehensive and proactive forms of regional economic policy of the kind practised up to the 1970s.

The following propositions are made and elaborated later in the chapter:

- Planning (because of selective restraint and related implementation issues) will tend to exacerbate inter-regional/inter-local housing and other property market differentials. Over-heating versus decline/ abandonment is the most obvious impact in the housing market.

- These patterns may be accompanied by a shift of both social profile and economic specialisation 'up-market' in the most attractive areas, and a downward spiral in the least favoured areas. There may be a qualitative divergence in job profiles between these different areas, with affluent areas concentrating more on higher quality jobs while the jobs on offer in the weaker areas are of a poorer quality.
- Selective restraint of housing versus jobs will lead to inadequate housing provision relative to job growth, leading to growing labour scarcity in growth areas. This could have various impacts on inflation, business costs and performance, or commuting patterns. Conversely, pools of underemployment are likely to build up in less favoured areas.
- Longer distance commuting from less to more constrained areas will expand.
- In addition, an emphasis on dispersed and peripheral locations for most new economic development will increase car dependency among workforces, business travellers and consumers. This will create problems of congestion, pollution and greenhouse gas emissions, and as such adversely affect the achievement of the government's espoused environmental goals.

Empirical evidence

In this section we draw on empirical evidence from a variety of sources to comment on, test and refine these propositions. The discussion is structured according to the framework outlined in the previous section, commenting in turn on planning policies, implementation issues and wider impacts of planning.

Planning policies

Variations in the stance of planning

The proposition here is that there are systematic variations in the stance of planning – more restrictive in growing, affluent areas and more permissive in declining areas. There are important issues here about how restrictiveness should be measured, and previous studies (Cheshire and Sheppard 1989, 1997; Cheshire et al, 1998) have perhaps over-relied on a single indicator, the success rate of planning applications, which may be misleading. As Bramley (1998) points out, this might be affected more by demand than by policy or implementation factors, with high rates of refusal in areas with large numbers of speculative applications where developers are 'trying it on'. This study concluded that the best measures of planning policy are land areas subject to formal constraint, structure plan provision levels and land available with planning permission or allocated in local plans. More subjective and informal indicators (attempts to characterise the apparent policy stance of different planning authorities) are less powerful predictors of outcomes.

Overall, policies are found to be most restrictive, at least for housing, in economically buoyant and affluent areas. This includes areas with a recent history of high growth and an overheated economy (for example, Berkshire) and tightly constrained historic towns (for example, Oxford, Bath). Least restrictive/greatest promotion of housing development was found in areas of long-run economic decline and low income, together with some new/expanding towns, which still promoted growth, and also in some rural areas away from London. There is also some evidence in other case studies of local political reaction in former growth areas leading to cyclical patterns (Boddy et al, 1997).

Recent debates in planning policy, which have surfaced particularly in the context of reviews of Regional Planning Guidance, would suggest that this proposition is generally plausible, with intense controversy mainly occurring in southern England. Part of the political and policy response to this controversy has been to signal a move away from the dominance of statistical household projections (so called 'predict and provide'), with more emphasis on flexibility and responsiveness to local circumstances, especially environmental constraints (DETR, 2000).

The evidence of the city studies included in the ESRC programme would also tend to lend support to this proposition, though this is based on qualitative evaluation of planning policy stances rather than quantitative measurement. Anti-growth sentiments in the Bristol area are currently strong, manifested in structure plan targets for housing land release set at levels well below needs implied on the basis of demographic forecasts (JSPTU 1998). However, this is happening in a context where the city region, and especially its suburban districts, have for something like a 30-year period experienced significant growth of both population and employment, suggestive of a backlash against the perceived negative impacts of past growth. In central Scotland, on the other hand, many authorities have a history and self-perception of industrial decline, making them generally more positive towards development than southern England authorities. Only in a couple of affluent suburban authorities adjacent to

Glasgow are there fairly pronounced growth restriction sentiments, although there are signs of such sentiments arising in Edinburgh and parts of its hinterland. Broadly, the evidence supports the general proposition, but reinforces the point about cyclical patterns in high growth areas, and also indicates that there may be regional differences in policy which are being accentuated post-devolution. The recent English policy shifts (DETR, 2000) have not been directly replicated in Scotland. It points also to the need for further research that attempts to systematically measure planning policy stances and relate them to wider socio-economic and environmental conditions.

Planning for housing versus jobs

The second issue explored is that there is some structural imbalance in the way that planning authorities react to business development as opposed to housing. The former is seen as positive, improving job opportunities for local people. The latter is perceived as negative and a threat to local environmental qualities, of benefit mainly to housing developers and non-local households moving into the area (Evans, 1991). The motivation to support employment development might be expected to be most powerful in areas which have experienced economic decline and unemployment, but it is suggested that this attitude has become prevalent in most areas, including prosperous parts of the country (Bramley, 1999b). Economic development has become a major function in most areas, and local authorities and their partner agencies tend to be more proactive in relation to economic development, in contrast to a more reactive stance in relation to housing.

Some more general evidence supports this proposition. The amount of land allocated for industrial use in particular typically exceeds likely requirements in the short to medium term, justified on the basis of providing a range and choice of sites (based on case study interviews). This weakens planning control over the location and form of development, exacerbated by changes in the use classes orders which govern different zonings, motivated by a desire to accommodate modern 'high-tech' industry (Wotton-Jeffries 1991, CRU, 1994). On the other hand housing land supply has been subject to much tighter management, albeit with housing land availability requirements to ensure some continuing supply in most areas.

Recent national policy change in England might be expected to reinforce differential policy stances between housing and jobs. The downgrading of statistical projections, brownfield land targets and sequential testing apply selectively to new housing development (DETR, 2000). There is extensive discussion of the development and environmental impacts of housing development, but very little discussion of the use of land for non-housing purposes, although all other uses combined are quantitatively almost as important. Table 13.1 (see columns 1 and 2), based on the analysis of Land Use Change statistics, shows that non-housing development accounted for half or more of land changing to urban uses in high growth counties. One impact of the recent policy changes may, however, be to change the presumption away from employment uses on previously developed land within urban areas, and in favour of housing. This may in turn displace more jobs from urban to greenfield sites.

A common feature of planning policy aims in both the Bristol area and central Scotland is to shift patterns of employment growth and development in order to deal with growing problems of sub-regional imbalance in terms of economic performance and unemployment. In the case of Bristol the emphasis is on shifting employment growth away from locations north of the city – effectively the western end of the dynamic M4 corridor – towards central city locations and areas south of the city. In central Scotland the policy aim is to encourage more employment development in the west relative to the east, and in Glasgow relative to other areas. In both cases, however, there are grounds for questioning the feasibility of these strategies, and risks that housing-employment imbalances are exacerbated.

In Bristol, employment land supply north of the city is relatively generous, a legacy of earlier policy decisions from which local policy makers are now reluctant to depart despite the shift in policy. The recent identification by the Regional Development Agency of strategic employment sites for the region is notable for its emphasis on sites north of Bristol. The recent panel report on draft Regional Planning Guidance also points to this area, extending east towards Swindon, as the main driver of the regional economy of national and international significance (Panel Report – South West, 2000). In Bristol city centre the capacity for development is limited, with employment uses increasingly coming into competition with housing; in 1999, for example, almost 30 per cent of city centre commercial space take-up was for conversion to residential use.

In Glasgow there is a high supply of vacant urban land but much of this is derelict and funding for remediation is inadequate (Bailey et al, 1999). Some would argue that past central government policy favoured Scotland's new towns, and more recent initiatives (including an Enterprise

Table 13.1: Land use change in high and low growth counties in England (1993)

County	Region	All	Changes to urban uses HA/100,000 Non-housing	Share from rural (%)	Housing on previously urban land (%)
High growth					
Lincolnshire	East Midlands	51	20	70	24
Cambridgeshire	East	50	30	57	37
Oxfordshire	South East	45	25	56	28
Wiltshire	South West	44	28	68	32
Cumbria	North West	43	30	65	25
Hereford and Worcs	West Midlands	42	21	70	31
North Yorkshire	Yorkshire	41	20	55	35
County Durham	North East	40	27	42	38
Hertfordshire	East	39	25	51	60
Kent	South East	39	24	35	53
Warwickshire	West Midlands	39	24	52	37
Low Growth					
Staffordshire	West Midlands	21	10	37	35
Lancashire	North West	21	10	40	41
Hampshire	South East	21	7	36	49
West Midlands	West Midlands	19	13	9	68
Tyne and Wear	North East	19	11	18	59
Nottinghamshire	East Midlands	19	9	48	47
Avon	South West	17	11	44	28
Greater London	Greater London	9	5	10	80

Note: Final column based on average of 1990-94.
Source: DETR (1998b, Tables 8.2, 8.4, and 8.7)

Zone) focused more on peripheral districts affected by the closure of a major steel works. The most dynamic areas in central Scotland are Lanarkshire and West Lothian, which share the characteristics of being centrally located relative to the main population centres, with space for expansion and access to government subsidies. In these two areas, both jobs and housing are promoted. However, it is arguable that Edinburgh is the key motor for Scotland's economy, with financial services and other knowledge-based industries at the fore. Although anti-growth sentiments are less extreme and widespread in Scotland, there are elements of this now affecting policy both within Edinburgh and in its hinterland.

The experience of regional planning in the South East also suggests that a policy of restraining 'hot spots' and shifting growth to 'cooler' areas (east of London or further north) may not be feasible given current government policy assumptions regarding economic growth. This was the gist of the panel report on the draft strategy prepared by the joint regional planning body SERPLAN (Panel Report – South East, 1999). A local case that symbolised this dilemma appropriately, was the decision by Newbury Council to approve a major greenfield development by Vodaphone in the context of the district with the lowest unemployment rate in Britain. We return to this issue of inter-authority competition and its impact on patterns of development in the next section, which discusses implementation issues.

Implementation issues

Short-termism/opportunism

Since 1990 development decisions have, in theory, been 'plan-led' (Tewdyr-Jones 1996). Some of the tendencies of decision making in the 1980s, where decisions made on appeal to central government resulted in some loosening of controls over out-of-town business parks, should be checked by this. In addition, there is a greater general commitment to 'more sustainable' patterns of development that generate less car-borne movements. Plan-led development provides some potential for more coherent and predictable patterns of urban development, though in practice decisions may still be driven by more short-term or opportunistic motivations.

Some of the specific decisions on development are driven by opportunities that present themselves within relatively short-time horizons. Many of these relate to the availability of particular 'windfall' sites generated by the restructuring of industry or major public land users. Alternatively they relate to unanticipated opportunities to capture some major piece of inward investment. The companies involved here may have strong bargaining power and can largely dictate the kinds of sites and premises that are available. Increased competition between areas may tend to reinforce opportunism. Examples of this can be observed in both central Scotland and the Bristol area. Local authority land ownership may be a further factor reinforcing opportunism. Some of the major retail and commercial developments to the west of Edinburgh were effectively promoted by the local authority as a landowner. On the other hand, the opportunity to realise gains from land disposals may, like planning agreements (discussed below), provide incentives to permit development in areas where otherwise anti-growth sentiments tend to dominate (Boddy et al, 1997).

The challenge for planning is to have a longer term vision of the urban form that these individual decisions will contribute towards. However, in practice extended review timetables for development plan preparation mean that many areas lack plan coverage.

Short-term perspectives are reinforced by the local politics of planning, with elected members in areas under growth pressure reluctant to face the opposition likely to be generated by an explicit long-term vision of how growth should be managed. This is the case in the Bristol area, and the South West region more broadly, where plans have been criticised for failing to make explicit the locations where development will be accommodated (Panel Report – South West, 2000). In areas with weaker economies local politics may be more likely to translate into territorial competition, for jobs especially, but also housing on greenfield sites that may attract better-off owner occupiers. There is some evidence for this in northern English conurbations, where there is a tendency for all districts to over-allocate land for new housing development. This weakens already fragile inner urban housing markets (Bramley et al, 2000). There are also examples of this in Central Scotland, where greenfield or green belt releases are promoted as a way of attracting higher income residents.

Weak strategic/sub-regional planning

The last 20 years have seen a retreat from strategic planning at regional and sub-regional levels. In part this was a deliberate reflection of ideologies championing market forces and downplaying the role and capabilities of the state. Subsequent rounds of local government reorganisation in the 1980s and 1990s targeted regional and higher tier authorities, particularly in metropolitan and urban areas, for abolition, and metropolitan area-wide structure planning tends to have been a victim of these reforms (Thompson, 1995). This trend was reinforced by the decline of traditional regional policy and by fiscal policy which greatly reduced the role of the public sector in new investment in sectors such as housing and transport.

The structures which remain for regional planning, such as the regional planning bodies in England, and the joint structure plan arrangements in larger cities (including the Glasgow and Clyde Valley and joint arrangements in the former Avon county in the Bristol area) are characterised by bottom-up processes and a consensual mode of decision making which arguably militates against strongly proactive planning decisions (Breheny, 1991). The situation is probably worse in areas like Greater Edinburgh, where is there no legally agreed joint arrangement for the production of the structure plan.

This issue is significant because such higher tier arrangements provide the potential for limiting the impact of inter-authority competition in declining areas striving for economic development, as noted above. They can also contain the tendency in more affluent areas for a locally based anti-development sentiment to take precedence over strategic responses to the development challenges facing growth regions. It can be argued that the recent dispute about housing land provision in South East England (Panel Report – South East, 1999) is illustrative of this strategic problem, and similar issues can be observed in the South West (Panel Report – South West, 2000).

However, there is also evidence that the effectiveness of sub-regional and regional joint arrangements varies somewhat with the wider context. Joint arrangements such as the Glasgow and Clyde Valley structure plan team would seem to have a greater capacity for delivering an agreed strategic vision for the sub-region, than similar arrangements in the Greater Bristol area (Kumar and Paddison, 2000), possibly because of the legacy of stronger and more effective regional arrangements. It may also be a product of less anti-development sentiment overall and less controversy about strategic principles. However, in this area significant roles are played by local enterprise companies (LECs) which in some areas (notably West Central Scotland) operate separately for the central city and for major chunks of its hinterland. The areas of difficulty currently appear to centre on retailing, characterised by strong developer demand and a degree of inter-authority competition, and transport where the problems reflect privatisation and sheer lack of resources.

In Scotland, the system has to some extent been living off the capital provided by the former regional authorities (disbanded in 1996). The Scottish Office/Executive has so far been reluctant to intervene in a strongly proactive way; rather there is some criticism of a tendency to defer decisions and pass them back to the local level. This arises in relation to major greenbelt incursions and major transport infrastructure decisions. The Scottish Executive is in the process of developing a national economic development strategy, but it has been suggested that land-use planning does not occupy a significant role in the emerging framework (Lloyd, 2000). Regional Development Agencies in England have been in place since 1999, but have limited powers and resources, relying largely on partnership and voluntary cooperation with other agencies. How far they will develop the spatial aspects of economic strategy, and be prepared to intervene in the process of preparing Regional Planning Guidance, and how this will relate to housing, is as yet very unclear.

Where cities are tightly bounded (as is the case in Bristol and in Glasgow) they lack direct control over development and development opportunities in their hinterlands. The impacts of this may also vary somewhat with the wider context in economic and political terms. On the one hand edge-of-city jurisdictions may strive to achieve more independence of action and more self-sufficiency in central place functions, increasing the possibility of inter-jurisdictional competition in sectors such as employment, retailing and leisure. There is some evidence of this happening in the Bristol area in the 1980s and in Glasgow and Edinburgh more recently. In economically weaker cities, like Glasgow, this has been associated with a degree of 'hollowing out' of the central city. A different response, possibly more typical of growing, more prosperous areas, is for edge-of-city jurisdictions to oppose development. In Bristol growth pressures necessitate additional large-scale development (particularly housing) in neighbouring authorities, but there is significant resistance to this. The territorial politics of the city-region have not, so far, found a way of coming to terms with the strong functional linkages between the city and its hinterland.

Difficulties in assembling the finance for major infrastructure investment, discussed in the next section, contribute to difficulties in decision making, especially where projects require cross-border cooperation, and possibly cross-subsidy (and where sensitive political issues like road tolling are involved). Public transport access to the burgeoning edge cities around Bristol, Edinburgh and Glasgow is a particularly problematic issue.

Infrastructure

Urban development depends upon the provision of a wide range of infrastructure, which is (traditionally) publicly or collectively funded. Infrastructure and financial limitations may significantly constrain development, while in the longer term the shape of urban development can influence the cost-effectiveness of infrastructure networks. Recent decades have seen a substantial reduction of the capacity of local government to fund new infrastructure, together with innovations in financing (through the Private Finance Initiative, now Public-Private

Partnerships) and the privatisation of significant infrastructure providers (water, energy and telecommunications).

In general fiscal motives to promote development are not a strong feature of British planning, in contrast with the US (see the chapter by Hill and Nowak), though powers which allow planning authorities to negotiate with developers for contributions to infrastructure improvements may provide some positive incentive. Public expenditure constraints mean that planning mechanisms (planning agreements and obligations) have become more important in enabling specific developments to happen and in providing wider benefits (open space, social housing, for example). The use of planning agreements is, however, unevenly applied, partly reflecting policy and legal uncertainty about its legitimacy (Healey et al, 1993). In addition, wide differences in the scope for 'planning gain' reflect the underlying economics of development in different areas, the level of land values and the potential gains contingent on the grant of planning permission. Thus, we would expect more exploitation of these mechanisms in parts of the South, than in the North or Scotland. What is sought and obtained through planning agreements may also depend on the foresight and expertise/skills of planning authorities.

One possible effect of an increasing reliance on private developer contributions for infrastructure is to affect patterns and the scale of land release. In Bristol during the 1980s, for example, the release of some very large ex-urban sites for housing and employment was conditioned partly by the need to generate large amounts of 'planning gain' to pay for necessary infrastructure, traditionally in the form of road building. This implies giving developers some long-term certainty over levels of development, sometimes straining the time-scales of development plans.

On the other hand, the inadequacies of infrastructure in growth areas in the Bristol sub-region – the road network, public transport and social/ community facilities such as health/education – have led to accusations that the planning authorities were somewhat incompetent in their negotiations with developers. A perception that urban development has not been well managed, especially in terms of infrastructure provision, now underlies much of the local resistance to further development in the Bristol area and elsewhere (Boddy et al, 1997).

In Scotland, the use of planning agreements as a lever in provision or funding of infrastructure and community facilities has been less strongly developed. This may reflect the economics of development, the policy stance of central government, the availability (until recently) of public investment resources, or the level of awareness of the local authorities. There are clearly local variations in the willingness and ability of otherwise similar authorities to negotiate over these matters. This risks accusations of inequity as well as incompetence, and may reinforce calls for standard development charges. However, such a system of uniform 'taxation' would provide less motivation to local authorities to facilitate development.

While the situation has certainly changed for infrastructure provision and financing, there has been relatively little research on what the impacts of these changes are, in terms of the kinds of planning decisions which are made, or how costs are apportioned. For example, are costs of servicing greenfield land lower than the costs of reusing urban sites, and is this a hidden subsidy? Preliminary evidence for Scotland suggests that this is not necessarily the case. Further changes are also anticipated, particularly in transport, with moves to allow local authorities to introduce road-pricing mechanisms to help fund transport improvements.

Monitoring land supply

The current catchphrase to summarise the approach to planning in England is supposed to be 'plan, monitor and manage' (as opposed to the previous but discredited 'predict and provide'). However, there are some doubts about whether the system is doing enough either in the way of forward planning or in the way of monitoring. One specific aspect of monitoring concerns the supply of readily available land for housing development. Since 1980 local authorities have been required to maintain registers of housing land at site level available for development, and to ensure that they had at least a five-year supply of such land. It is unclear if this requirement remains and, if so, how it will operate, with the shift of emphasis to 'urban capacity studies'. Although the new policy guidance (PPG3; DETR, 2000) seeks to monitor additional aspects of new housing provision, such as density, type and affordability, it is not clear how it monitors basic adequacy of land supply. By contrast, in Scotland annual land audits and five-year supply requirements still apply under the relevant planning guidance (NPPG3 and PAN38).

Table 13.2 provides some indications that by the late 1990s available land supply was actually becoming quite scarce in South East England. Available land was only 84 per cent of a five-year requirement in 1998, compared with 159 per cent six years earlier (SERPLAN, 1992). This table also indicates that the 60 per cent brownfield target will be difficult to achieve in this region, and that unidentified ('windfall') sites constitute a significant part of the supply (thus limiting the extent to which development is 'plan-led').

Current research on housing land supply in Scotland indicates that the high-demand Edinburgh and Lothians area shows persistent evidence of shortage of supply. This may be attributed in part to delays in implementing the major development areas like the South East wedge identified in plans. In the Bristol area there is sufficient available housing land in the short term, but significant uncertainties surround the longer term options for development. Formal constraints (Greenbelt and 'Areas of outstanding natural beauty') cover 75 per cent of the former Avon county area and significantly restrict the scope for further urban expansion.

Wider impacts

Housing and other property market impacts

Over time restrictive planning policy would be expected to raise house, and especially housing land, prices (Evans, 1991; Eve and the University

Table 13.2: Housing growth and land supply indicators for South East counties (1995-2000)

	Planned growth dwelling pa 1991-2006	Planned residual dwelling pa 1995-2000	Available 5-year supply % of residual 1995	Available 5-year supply % of 1998*	Sites within built-up areas %	Uniden- tified sites %
Hampshire	5,790	7,325	94	71	47	26
Kent	5,800	6,320	103	96	55	21
Essex	5,510	5,450	114	85	44	1
Hertfordshire	3,330	3,370	137	103	51	13
West Sussex	2,520	4,335	75	71	46	28
Bedfordshire	2,470	3,490	105	76	71	32
Buckinghamshire	3,330	3,450	89	99	74	15
Berkshire	2,670	2,865	96	88	50	20
Surrey	2,375	2,435	109	99	80	24
East Sussex	2,350	2,795	119	110	48	26
Oxfordshire	2,500	2,570	118	86	39	2
Isle of Wight	535	Na	Na	164	na	20
Regional Total	39,150	44,400	114	84	52	18

Note: *1998 refers to latest available year, 1997 in two cases, 1996 in one case.

Sources: SERPLAN (1996) *Housing land and structure plan provisions in the South East*. SERP 128, Tables 1, 2, 3, B; SERPLAN *Housing completions and commitments in ROSE 1996 to 1998*. SERP 506, Table 2

Table 13.3: House price levels and change (1995-99)

	Standardised average house price		
	1995	1999	Change %
Government office region			
North	51,602	59,367	15
Yorks and Humberside	53,456	60,889	15
North West	55,058	65,312	18
East Midlands	49,054	61,568	25
West Midlands	57,521	74,451	29
South West	63,574	88,367	38
East	59,241	79,446	32
South East	79,853	116,264	44
London	136,768	212,472	58
England	69,304	95,155	33
Collapsed Shaw-Region Classification			
Northern cities	55,604	66,149	19
Northern industrial	47,422	56,051	18
Northern suburban	59,190	75,043	26
Northern rural	55,515	67,310	21
Southern urban	70,601	99,836	41
Southern suburban	79,475	114,488	42
Southern rural	60,872	84,977	38
Inner London	153,312	238,875	61
Outer London	111,314	171,854	54

Source: Land Registry

of Cambridge, 1992; Monk and Whitehead, 2000). Some recent work provides model-based estimates of the impact of planning restrictions on house price levels and/or density levels (Bramley 1999a; Bramley and Watkins, 1996; Cheshire and Sheppard, 1989, 1997).

If, as we suggest, there is a systematic relationship between prosperity and the policy stance adopted, and further biases in policy implementation, then we would expect planning to have the effect of reinforcing inter-local or inter-regional house price differentials. Recent data on house price levels and changes (see Table 13.3) shows that house prices were already much higher in London and the South East in 1995. As the general increase in house prices has progressed in these areas, and also in the South West, this has resulted in much higher proportionate and absolute increases, implying a widening of differentials. This pattern is similar to that observed in previous economic upswings in the 1970s and 1980s.

One impact of strong housing demand and land supply constraints in cities like Bristol and Edinburgh is to shift more housing development into city centre areas, often building at high density. This is already happening, including through the conversion of vacant office buildings and dockside development, mainly catering for certain niche markets: more up-market; childless professionals; and 'empty-nesters'. Other groups, including middle income families, may be forced to look further afield. There is also a possibility that housing will come into stronger competition with other land uses, especially employment, within the urban area. Thus, the market may reinforce policies described earlier in shifting economic activity outwards while consolidating residential development in the central city. In this way, cities can be seen as tending to turn 'inside out'.

Interviews with economic development officers and property agents in Bristol suggest a tightening of commercial and industrial property markets. Hence, lower value activities are being squeezed out of central city locations, through the conversion of secondary office space to housing (initially catering for the student market, but more recently for the general needs market). In some suburban areas lower value manufacturing and distribution are more threatened. This, together with the housing market effects noted above, may contribute to a broader up-market shift for the local economy and housing market.

Labour market imbalance and travel and commuting patterns

Selective restraint of housing versus employment may translate into growing labour scarcity and ultimately higher costs in high demand areas. Table 13.4 provides evidence of the widening disparities in labour market conditions between different regions of England in the 1990s (see also Turok and Edge, 1999).

Part of the adjustment to the problem of labour market imbalance at the city-region level is through longer distance commuting from less to more constrained areas. In both Bristol and Central Scotland there is certainly likely to be growth in longer distance commuting. The commuting hinterlands of all the included cities increased in the period 1981 to 1991, but reliable data post-1991 is scarce. Job growth in Bristol and in Edinburgh exceeds growth in the labour force, and activity rates in both cities are already high. In the Bristol area there has certainly been a growth of commuting from the south of the sub-region – a 'soft'

Table 13.4: Selected employment indicators by region and type of local authority

	Job growth		Unemployment rate		Non-employ ment
	Total	Male	All	Long-term	
	1993-99 %	1993-99 %	1998 %	1998 %	1992-99 %
Government office region					
North East	0.2	−1.4	6.7	3.2	32.8
Yorkshire & Humberside	0.8	−1.3	5.8	2.5	23.5
North West	0.0	−2.2	5.5	2.5	25.9
East Midlands	5.6	3.1	4.1	1.7	20.3
West Midlands	6.5	7.4	5.2	2.2	22.7
South West	4.7	5.4	3.7	1.5	20.1
East	4.9	5.2	3.5	1.4	17.3
South East	7.3	8.2	2.9	1.1	17.2
London	4.4	4.3	7.0	2.7	25.4
Collapsed Shaw-Region type					
Northern cities	2.5	0.4	6.7	3.0	26.6
Northern industrial	0.4	−1.0	6.0	2.7	27.1
Northern suburban	7.1	7.5	3.0	1.3	18.2
Northern rural	2.9	−0.5	3.3	1.3	19.8
Southern urban	−1.0	−1.8	5.1	2.1	22.7
Southern suburban	9.6	10.8	2.2	0.8	15.0
Southern rural	3.8	4.6	4.2	1.6	21.0
Inner London	3.2	2.3	9.3	3.7	30.1
Outer London	5.9	7.1	4.0	1.4	19.0
England	4.2	3.7	4.8	2.0	22.2

Source: Bramley et al (2000)

area in terms of previous housing development, but less attractive for employment. Commuter-oriented communities can also be seen developing at considerable distance from the main cities in Central Scotland.

There are equal grounds for concern about the rapid development of 'edge cities', mainly in the last ten years. As a general measure of divergent patterns of job and housing development, in the Glasgow and Clyde Valley Structure Plan area, while around 70 per cent of new housing is built on brownfield land, 70 per cent of the best employment sites are greenfield. It is clear that the retail, office and industrial parks rapidly developing in these areas are designed for high levels of car access, and most workers, business travellers and shoppers reach these places by car. Local planners report the difficulties of providing satisfactory public transport access to these kinds of developments, exacerbated by the deregulated and privatised bus system which is reluctant to institute new services ahead of manifest demand. New transport policies promoting public transport (plus cycling/walking) and restraining car use are being promoted now in Edinburgh and Bristol, but it is unclear how effective these will be.

Conclusions

We would argue that current features of urban development, driven mainly by market forces but mediated by a decentralised planning system, and characterised by certain biases and limitations, could be damaging to competitiveness in the long term.

In high growth areas there is likely to be an inadequate supply of housing, leading to house price inflation, housing exclusion (affordability problems), labour shortage constraints on economic growth and a rise in longer distance commuting. Increased polarisation is likely to arise between favoured areas, including some cities such as Bristol and Edinburgh, which compete more in up-market (high earning, high value-added) sectors, and less favoured areas which compete for lower paid, less secure employment and public subsidies.

The increased role of 'edge cities' together with the growth of longer distance, mainly car-based commuting, accompanied by inadequate public transport alternatives, must be adverse for long-term environmental sustainability. At the same time these trends will do little to help more deprived groups trapped in urban areas connect with the areas of greatest economic opportunity.

City-regions that fail to deal with the resultant transport and environmental problems will suffer from longer-term deterioration in their competitive appeal as locations to live, work and invest in. Differences in institutional capacity to plan in the broad sense may account for future stories of cities that did or did not succeed in building on their earlier success.

What policy innovations would help to counter these problems? Stronger regional planning machinery must be a key candidate here, tying together local authorities, Regional Development Agencies and central government. There is a case for longer term plans allied to spatial development strategies, albeit with phasing mechanisms, rather than the current trend to short-termism. Longer-term plans require a commitment to a future settlement strategy, but offer greater assurance of quality infrastructural provision and of avoiding problems of a strangulated labour supply.

There is a case for reformulating planning 'rules of the game', in relation to housing land supply and jobs-housing balance; authorities should not be allowed to plan for more jobs than the number of extra workers they are willing to house (the implementation problems of this attractively simple idea should not, however, be underestimated). In addition, the provision of affordable housing (including intermediate low cost home ownership options) can be promoted through planning and has a valuable role in maintaining the availability of labour of different kinds to service regional economies (Monk and Whitehead, 2000).

Economic and fiscal instruments related to development are being debated currently in the context of emerging urban policy in Britain (DETR, 1999). Arguably, these have evolved and may need to evolve further in ways that capture more of the gain in land and property values for investment in infrastructure, but in a fashion which facilitates development rather than simply acting as a tax. In less favoured, declining urban areas, such instruments have less to offer and subsidy is required to counter the implicitly negative development values on many brownfield sites, although an imaginative use of tax breaks and recycling mechanisms may be helpful. More generally, and notably in transport, the notion of hypothecation of taxation is gaining ground and may hold the key to resolving some policy problems which require a combination of regulatory and fiscal interventions.

References

Bailey, N., Turok, I. and Docherty, I. (1999) *Edinburgh and Glasgow: Contrasts in competitiveness and cohesion*, Glasgow: University of Glasgow.

Boddy, M., Lambert, C. and Snape, D. (1997) *City for the 21st century: Globalisation, planning and urban change in contemporary Britain*, Bristol: The Policy Press.

Bramley, G. (1996) *Housing with hindsight: Household growth, housing need and housing development in the 1980s*, London: Council for the Protection of Rural England.

Bramley, G. (1998) 'Measuring planning: indicators of planning restraint and its impact on the housing market', *Environment and Planning B: Planning and Design*, vol 25, no 1, pp 31-58.

Bramley, G. (1999a) 'Housing market adjustment and land supply constraints', *Environment and Planning A*, vol 31, no 7, pp 1169-88.

Bramley, G. (1999b) 'The influence of planning on housing supply and economic performance', paper presented at the Housing, Property and Competitiveness Colloquium, University of Reading, May.

Bramley, G. and Lambert C. (1998), 'Regulation entrenched: Planning for housing', in P. Allmendinger and H. Thomas (eds) *Urban planning and the British new right*, London: Routledge.

Bramley, G., Pawson, H. and Third, H. (2000) *Low demand housing and unpopular neighbourhoods*, report of research for DETR.

Bramley, G. and Watkins, C. (1996) *Steering the housing market: New building and the changing planning system*, Bristol/York: The Policy Press/Joseph Rowntree Foundation

Breheny, M. (1991) 'The renaissance of strategic planning?', *Environment and Planning B: Planning and Design*, vol 18, pp 233-49.

Breheny, M. (1999) *The people: Where will they work?*, London: Town and Country Planning Association.

Breheny, M. and Hall, P. (1996) 'The people: Where will they go?', national report of the TCPA regional inquiry into housing need and provision, London: Town and Country Planning Association.

Champion, A.J., Atkins, D., Coombes, M. and Fotheringham, S. (1998) *Urban exodus*, London: Council for the Protection of Rural England (CPRE).

Cheshire, P. and Sheppard, S. (1989) 'British planning policy and access to housing: some empirical estimates', *Urban Studies*, vol 26, no 5, pp 469-85.

Cheshire, P. and Sheppard, S. (1997) 'Welfare economics and land use regulation', Research Papers in Environmental and Spatial Analysis No. 42, London: Department of Geography, London School of Economics.

Cheshire, P., Marlee, I. and Sheppard, S. (1998) 'The microeconomic structure of British housing markets', paper prepared for DETR seminar on 'Development of a microsimulation model for analysing the effects of the planning system on housing choices', 26 June.

CRU (Scottish Office Central Research Unit) (1994) *A review of the use classes order*, London: HMSO.

Cullingworth, J.B. and Nadin, V. (1997) *Town and country planning in the UK* (12th edn), London and New York: Routledge.

Danielsen, K., Lang, R. and Fulton, W. (1999) 'Retracting suburbia: Smart growth and the future of housing,' *Housing Policy Debate*, vol 10, no 3, pp 513-40.

DETR (Department of the Environment, Transport and the Regions) (1998) *Land use change in England No 13*, London: DETR.

DETR (1999) *Towards an urban renaissance*, final report of the Urban Task Force under the chairmanship of Lord Rogers of Riverside, London: TSO.

DETR (2000) *Planning policy guidance note 3: Housing*, London: HMSO.

DETR (2001) *Planning policy guidance 13: Transport*, London: TSO.

DoE (Department of the Environment) (1996) *Household growth: Where shall we live?*, Cmnd 3471, London: HMSO.

Downs, A. (1997) 'Challenge of our declining cities', *Housing Policy Debate*, vol 8, no 2, pp 359-408.

Evans, A.W. (1991) 'Rabbit hutches on postage stamps: Planning, development and political economy', *Urban Studies*, vol 28, no 6, pp 853-70.

GCVSPJC (Glasgow and Clyde Valley Structure Plan Joint Committee) (1997) *Survey of industrial and business floorspace*, Glasgow: GCVSPJC.

Gerald Eve and the University of Cambridge (1992) *The relationship between house prices and land supply*, DoE planning research programme. London: HMSO.

Grant, M. (1992) 'Planning law and the British land use planning system', *Town Planning Review*, vol 63, no 1, pp 3-12.

Hall, P., Thomas, H., Gracey, R. and Drewett, R. (1973) *The containment of urban England*, London: Allen and Unwin.

Healey, P., McNamara, P., Elson, M. and Doak, J. (1988) *Land use planning and the mediation of urban change*, Cambridge: Cambridge University Press.

Healey, P., Purdue, M. and Ennis, F. (1993) *Gains from planning? Dealing with the impacts of development*, York: Joseph Rowntree Foundation.

Hooper A., Dunmore K. and Hughes M. (1998) *Home alone: The housing preferences of one-person households*, Amersham: Housing Research Foundation.

House of Commons (1996) *Housing need: Report of inquiry by the environment committee*, HC22, London: HMSO.

Imrie, R. and Thomas, H. (eds) (1993) *British urban policy and the urban development corporations*, London: Paul Chapman.

Jenks, M., Burton, E. and Williams, K. (1996) (eds) *The compact city: A sustainable urban form?*, London: E&FN Spon.

JSPTU (Joint Strategic Planning and Transport Unit in the former Avon area) (1998) *Joint replacement structure plan.*

Krugman, P. (1995) *Geography and economic development*, Cambridge, MA: MIT Press.

Kumar, A. and Paddison, R. (2000) 'Trust and collaborative planning theory: the case of the Scottish planning system', *International Planning Studies*, vol 5, no 2, pp 205-23.

Lloyd, G. (2000) 'New agendas for economic development and planning in Scotland, *Town and Country Planning*, vol 69, no 10, pp 304-5.

McKinsey (1998) *Driving productivity and growth in the UK economy*, McKinsey Global Institute.

Monk, S. and Whitehead, C. (2000) *The use of housing and land prices as a planning tool: A summary document*, Cambridge Housing and Planning research report No 1, Cambridge: Department of Land Economy, University of Cambridge.

Panel Report – South East (1999) 'Regional planning guidance for the south east of England', public examination, May-June, report of the panel. Guildford: Government Office for the South East.

Panel Report – South West (2000) 'Regional planning guidance for the South West region', public examination, March, report of the panel, Government Office for the South West

SERPLAN (1992) 'Housing land and structure plan provisions in the South East', RPC 2220.

SERPLAN (1996) 'Housing land and structure plan provisions in the South East', SERP 128.

SERPLAN (1998) 'Housing completions and commitments in ROSE 1996 to 1998', SERP 506.

Tewdwr-Jones, M. (1996) *British planning policy in transition: planning in the 1990s*, London: UCL Press.

Thompson, R. (1995) 'Innocent by-stander mown down by council review?', *Planning*, 14 July.

Turok, I. and Edge, N. (1999) *The jobs gap in British cities: Employment loss and labour market consequences*, Bristol/York: The Policy Press/Joseph Rowntree Foundation.

US Department of Housing and Urban Development (1999) 'The state of the cities 1999: Third annual report', report to the President by HUD.

Wootton-Jeffreys Consultants Ltd and Bernard Thorpe (1991) *An examination of the effects of the use classes order 1987 and the general development order 1988*, London: HMSO.

FOURTEEN

Conclusions and policy implications

Iain Begg

Why some cities prosper while others decline is a complex question. Location, inheritance, governance and sheer luck all play a part in shaping the capacity of a city to nurture, attract and retain economic activity. Opportunities for expansion, regeneration or transformation will depend on the mix of ingredients and how well they are combined, even if no single recipe can be guaranteed to work. Certain urban areas appear to find it easy to reinvent themselves and to accommodate new trends in the labour and product markets, but many struggle to adapt, and become caught in a vicious circle of decline accompanied by growing social exclusion (for a recent review of British cities, see Robson et al, 2000).

Cities devote considerable effort and resources to encouraging the 'right' sort of economic development, often in a race against near neighbours, and many policy initiatives are aimed at improving the attractiveness of the city. They are, too, frequently judged by how well they 'perform' in league tables of indicators as diverse as income, crime, cost of living, unemployment, environmental quality or excitement of night-life. That cities compete with one another ought, consequently, to be undeniable and the notion of urban competitiveness is a conceptual approach that brings together these various determinants of performance and competition. Yet there are many – Krugman (1996) is particularly associated with this standpoint – who would argue that only firms compete and that it makes little sense to apply the term to territorial units.

What the different contributions to this volume demonstrate, however, is that there is indeed value in looking at competitiveness from the perspective of the city, but that it encompasses a wide range of influences (as I have argued elsewhere – Begg, 1999) and needs to be approached with care in applying it to policy. The starting-point is to flesh out what can and cannot be measured. This chapter then looks at factors that shape urban competitiveness and at the policy issues raised. The concluding sections look at how some of the techniques discussed in earlier chapters might be applied for policy purposes and at possible directions for further research.

The trouble with competitiveness ...

One of the strongest messages to emerge from the work reported in this volume is that there is no simple or unambiguous way of measuring competitiveness, especially at the level of the city. It manifestly includes how well a city's economy is functioning and is influenced by the panoply of variables that bear on the costs of doing business in a particular location, but also has to encompass dynamic elements. The effects of structural change and of new technologies are especially salient, and manifest themselves in a new international division of labour, as pointed out by Lever.

The chapters by Deas and Giordano and by Kresl question some of the more nebulous readings of competitiveness, which tend to view the concept as synonymous with economic performance, broadly conceived. Such conceptions are alarmingly pervasive, witness the plethora of crude attempts by policy makers to rank cities and regions according to their competitiveness. Many of the most obvious variables commonly used to measure 'performance' reflect years, even decades, of urban development and structural change. Indicators such as GDP per capita, unemployment or employment rates, or stocks of vacant or derelict land are all affected by long-term processes. However, they probably tell us relatively little about current performance or future prospects, or what needs to be remedied to make the city more competitive. Indeed, one of the most thorny issues for policy makers is to how to set targets for long-term change to alter the trajectory of the local economy. This requires taking a step back from the day-to-day imperatives to consider what has to be done if the economy is to achieve a step-change.

Urban assets matter, but they can be hard to identify or to relate to performance. The chapter by Deas and Giordano puts forward an innovative approach in which they select and monitor a range of 'hard' and 'soft' assets that bear on both current and prospective economic success. Their assets-outcomes model provides a first attempt at moving beyond the crude 'league table' approaches to urban competitiveness. Their approach could be seen as more akin to attempts at measuring educational performance not just in relation to crude exam performance, but taking account of pupil or student abilities at the outset of their education in order to estimate 'value added'. In other words, what are the raw materials

– the assets – which firms in a given city can harness, and how effectively do they do so? Their ranking of cities attempts to enumerate and measure the asset bases of different cities, and to view competitive outcomes in light of them. The result, as is evident, is a rather different ranking of cities.

A related concept is that of social capital which also suffers from problems of definition. The evidence from several chapters suggests that cities which have well-developed social networks or which are characterised by greater social cohesion tend to have better prospects, especially in the 'new' industries. Equally, several of the contributions to this volume demonstrate that cities that have failed to nurture their social capital are the most vulnerable to structural change. Developing a better understanding of urban assets and social capital can, consequently, be valuable in improving the analysis of competitiveness and in articulating a policy response. The relationships between social cohesion and competitiveness are, however, complex and are not easy to translate into proposals for action. Moreover, as Potts shows, the traffic is not all one way. Well-developed social networks can also exclude new talent and inhibit innovation if they create barriers to entry.

Factors shaping urban competitiveness

The research in this volume provides many insights into the factors that shape the competitive advantage of cities. Though by no means exhaustive, four broad explanatory strands that are examined in the research on which this volume is based can be distinguished. They are:

- the impact of broad structural changes in the economy and in the location requirements of different stages of production;
- technological developments and the growing significance of 'knowledge' as a factor of production;
- how land, property and key regulatory decisions about planning affect the attractiveness of a city and its scope for balanced economic development;
- the inter-linkages between social cohesion and competitiveness and the parallel relationships between the performance of the city and social exclusion.

The consequences of economic change

The industrialised countries exhibit rich histories of rise and decline of regional and urban economies. In the past, this was due to such factors as the deterioration or irrelevance of a raw material or a change in transportation patterns. The findings of Begg, Moore and Altunbas show that the long-run patterns of urban development in Britain have been shaped by such structural change, with persistent decline in 'older' industrial cities and a steady rise in the fortunes of cities that are identified with newer industries and services. The contrasts identified between Glasgow and Edinburgh by Bailey, Docherty and Turok tell a similar story.

The advantages of specialisation and diversity feature prominently in the literature as an explanation for urban performance (Duranton and Puga, 2000, for instance, summarise work on this theme). Interest in this question has been given a new momentum in recent years as economists have sought to test alternative theories of economic growth, particularly endogenous growth models, by examining differences in urban growth performance rather than cross-country growth differences. One particular focus of research has been the issue of whether specialisation favours the growth of an industry in a city or whether growth is encouraged by industrial diversity (Glaeser et al, 1992; O'Donoghue, 1999). Such a view of the foundations of competitiveness suggests that long-term efforts to adapt the economic structure and to sustain the factors contributing to productivity growth are more relevant than short-term actions aiming at increasing the efficiency of the operation of specific markets.

The balance between specialisation and competition is a second issue. Insights from industrial economics (see, for example, Baumol, 1992) suggest that achieving a healthy degree of rivalry has a positive effect on company performance, a notion that provides an important part of the rationale for privatisation. Equally, there are circumstances in which cooperation also makes sense. A parallel could well be drawn with competition between cities, not just in the limited sense of government awarding funds from national urban regeneration programmes to the best applicants, but in much broader ways.

The challenge is, however, to make the area more competitive overall, rather than to pursue a particular cluster or specialisation. Cities might also gain from specialising in those activities that best suit their current mix of attributes, but it is the dynamics of changing advantage that are arguably more important in the contemporary economy. Rosentraub and Przybylski (1996), for example, suggest that attempts to boost the *comparative* advantage of an area are unlikely to bear fruit in an era of rapid technological advance, and that the focus of policy should, instead, be on boosting *competitive* advantage. Global competition will mean that however successful an urban economy is in lowering factor costs, it will always risk being undercut from elsewhere. Seeking to achieve economic advantage by stimulating competition is seen as less vulnerable to efforts by rivals to react by subsidising their own productive sectors.

Technology, knowledge and competitiveness

With an increasingly open and interconnected global economy, as the chapter by Kresl shows, the focus of attention has to shift. He argues that the keys to competitive success now are the availability and quality of factors of production, the rate of start-up of new firms, and the ability to coordinate the activities of several economic entities and urban amenities. Lever, similarly, observes that many cities of the developed world have lost the competitive edge they owed, historically, to access to large pools of cheaper labour, raw materials and capital. Instead, developed nations and their cities can only sustain their competitiveness by using their superior access to the knowledge base. However, innovation is highly concentrated in a minority of regions or states in both Europe and North America. The rate of innovation in the South East of England, for example, has been considerably higher than that for any other region in the UK since at least the 1940s.

The implication is clear: knowledge 'production' has to be seen as a key factor in underpinning competitiveness. Not all knowledge is equally valuable in this respect – tacit knowledge, often transmitted face to face, confers a competitive advantage on highly accessible places, whereas the much more ubiquitous codified knowledge does not. Unlike other factors of production such as labour, space and capital, it is relatively difficult to measure the quantum of knowledge available at a particular location. However, it is through research and development leading to innovations in both products and processes that competitive positions are strengthened. As the chapters by Simmie, Sennett and Wood (highlighting the dominant position of the London area) and by Lever show, there are marked differences between cities in the rate at which innovations arise. What is clear is that big disparities in propensities to innovate, in turn, bear on the comparative 'success' of cities. Thus, Lever finds that the most knowledge-intensive and competitive European cities are London, Paris, the Randstad, Copenhagen, Munich, Frankfurt and Stockholm.

Knowledge production in such cities is facilitated by a wide range of factors, pointing to areas that policy makers might examine. Lever focuses on the availability and price of telecommunications, the number of R&D establishments, the scale of university research in terms of students and publications, the connectivity of the local airport(s) and the scale of local exhibitions and fairs. Simmie, Sennett and Wood argue that the conditions conducive to product innovation are greatest in core metropolitan regions such as London. The sheer numbers and densities of other relevant firms provide endless opportunities for discontinuities and new recombinations of factor inputs to innovation on an irregular 'pick and mix' basis. The London region, with its long history of international trade, functions as a major gateway and frontier with international customers and suppliers. It is the ability of innovative firms in the region, albeit a minority of all firms in the region, to sell large proportions of their new products into international markets that is the key indicator of the competitiveness of the region. Key inputs to the innovation process are social investment and social capital. These consist of such phenomena as education and training, the production of new knowledge, and the development of a highly educated professional and technical workforce.

Property markets and planning

Land and property have long been at the heart of urban economic analysis, are readily identifiable as 'hard' assets of cities that shape the business environment, and are typically viewed as important 'drivers' of urban economic performance. Gibb, Mackay and White argue, however, that the role of property within the urban economy is often inadequately linked to other facets of competitiveness and that its propensity to trigger vicious or virtuous cycles of economic development, in particular, is not sufficiently explored.

Hill and Nowak argue that particular attention should be paid to the operation of property markets in distressed cities as a marker of regeneration for two reasons. First, well-functioning property markets are essential to integrating cities into regional housing, labour, and business location markets. Second, property markets are where economic regeneration leaves its most lasting footprint – in the effective demand for housing and commercial properties. Cities have a limited set of assets to trade in the economy for income: they have land and they have labour. While labour is mobile, land is not.

An important feature of the London region that makes high rates of innovation possible is the presence of highly qualified pools of technical and professional labour. This is shown by Simmie, Sennett and Wood to be the most significant prerequisite for innovation. Because of the higher incomes and therefore higher degrees of residential locational choice of this type of labour, innovation needs to be examined not just from the point of view of firms and the economy but also in terms of quality of life choices by high quality labour. The attraction and retention of such key labour is an important reason why firms tended to rate quality of life features as making significant contributions to their innovative capabilities. The ability to offer highly paid key staff the kinds of homes, schools, public services, leisure facilities and environments that they like is an important external advantage to firms located to the arc west of London.

Hence, questions of urban form, design and the environment also bear significantly on how well a city is able to adapt to economic change. A substantial part of the urban economic development effort in Britain and (as Hill and Nowak show) in the US has related to the urban property sector. Indeed, as Gibb, Mackay and White point out, a variety of property initiatives formed the mainstay of British urban policy for much of the last 20 years, although the rationale for intervention has not always been clear or thoroughly argued. Nevertheless, a key policy question is how much emphasis should be given in a competitiveness-orientated strategy to land and property.

The significance of social cohesion

The interplay between social conditions and competitiveness is shown in the chapters by Boddy and Potts to be a complex and poorly understood one. To the extent that there is a received wisdom, it is that cohesive societies are likely to be more competitive, but firm evidence on this is conspicuously hard to find. Nevertheless, there are good reasons for being concerned about the extent of the gulf in so many cities between the affluent and the excluded.

Much recent research has stressed the multifaceted nature of the outcomes of social exclusion, captured in multidimensional indicators of social conditions. Research has also focused on the dynamics of exclusion over time. Such longitudinal studies emphasise the fact that for many, exclusion persists over time and that early experiences of childhood poverty, family disruption and low educational attainment are strongly associated with social exclusion and its outcomes later in life. It follows that if a high incidence of social exclusion is a characteristic of a city, its impact on competitiveness will be an enduring one. Hence, the social dimension is potentially an important one in shaping urban competitiveness. In particular, tackling childhood poverty, educational failings, and problems with employment and family structure in order to counter long-term social exclusion later in life has implications in terms of unemployment, poverty and deprivation.

High levels of social exclusion might, in theory at least, impact adversely on competitiveness and business success. The adverse image or anticipated costs associated with social exclusion might deter business investment in some locations while expectations in terms of quality of life, schooling or crime might make it more difficult to recruit more mobile technical, professional or managerial staff. If however, this simply shifts investment and economic activity around, it implies differential spatial impacts but no overall impact in terms of the competitiveness of the economy as a whole. Evidence as to the adverse impacts of social exclusion on competitiveness for the UK at least is inconclusive.

Competitive success would on the face of it seem likely to counter social exclusion. Levels of unemployment and social deprivation are, unsurprisingly, lower in economically more buoyant cities and regions. On the other hand, there remains persistent and in many respect worsening social deprivation and polarisation of economic and social circumstances within UK cities and the gap between the best and worst areas within UK cities would appear to have widened in recent years. There is moreover persistent poverty and deprivation in the most buoyant urban areas as well as the more depressed economically. Processes of labour market change and the adverse impacts of the educational system would seem to be a factor here.

Towards a toolkit for enhancing urban competitiveness

Urban policy, narrowly defined, has tended to focus on the regeneration of individual cities or dealing with particular problems, often in a piecemeal manner. However, lasting solutions can only come from looking at the individual city in the context of changes in the urban system as a whole. There are varied explanations for why individual cities have done well or badly, and this suggests that a single policy formula is not the answer – see the chapters by Begg, Moore and Altunbas, and by Bailey, Docherty and Turok. Quick fixes are unlikely to work and nor are initiatives that address only certain facets of a city's economy. Equally, the balance between social, economic or environmental priorities will vary both between cities and over time, yet all three can be adjudged to bear on competitiveness. Moreover, the relevance of national programmes to individual cities will be uneven.

Several of the chapters in this volume shed light on how an approach to economic development rooted in analysis of competitiveness can be constructed. A first step is diagnosis. The methodologies put forward by Kresl and by Deas and Giordano offer ways of calibrating where a city stands in relation to actual or potential competitors. By looking at a range of assets, for example, a city can ascertain whether it has significant gaps that need attention. The categories of assets advocated by Deas and Giordano provide a useful starting point, covering a range of quantifiable variables, but it is the principle that matters and it is clear that many other variables could be considered.

There can be little doubt that the quality and availability of property affect the ability of a city to attract and retain investment and to achieve a better economic performance. Property also has the peculiarity that there may be long-term market failures that require policy interventions. Gibb, Mackay and White stress that a well-functioning land and property sector is at least a necessary condition for a durable competitive urban economy. But they also argue that it is essential to adopt a broader strategy that encompasses other, often 'softer' attributes of the local economy, rather than looking at these markets in isolation. Thus, while a property market failure framework is a useful element in the toolkit for promoting competitiveness, it needs to be complemented.

Kresl argues that urban economies can gain a better understanding of their competitive position and then use this information to design strategies to enhance their competitiveness by looking simultaneously at quantitative and qualitative information. Each has its advantages and its limitations, but together they allow the position of the individual urban economy to be categorised and the elements of an effective strategy to be developed. What is common to both approaches is the understanding that an urban economy can consider its situation only in comparison with other similar economies. Kresl's approach is more demanding in some respects, but can also be more easily tailored to the circumstances of an individual city.

Lessons can be learnt from the recent history of Montreal, one of North America's most interesting urban economies. The city has undergone a series of external structural changes, such as creation of the St Lawrence Seaway, the continental shift of economic activity to the west and the south and the Canada–US Free Trade Agreement, which have dramatically altered its economic position and its competitiveness. However, it has been Montreal's development of a focus on strategic planning, involving all levels of government, which has brought it from an economy that was gradually being marginalised to one of Canada's most competitive urban economies.

In the UK, 24 urban areas have been identified by DTLR as 'partner' cities in which, inter alia, there will be an attempt to quantify the extent of any progress towards the varied and disparate aspirations set out in the urban White Paper, *Our towns and cities* (DETR, 2000). Although the broad thrust of the White Paper arguably paid scant attention to economic concerns at the city level, there may be an argument for applying an asset-outcome model in the context of the planned 'partner' towns and cities, measuring changes in competitiveness across the 24 places in relation to the assets each has at its disposal. The 'partner' cities are supposed to embody exemplars of good and bad practice with regard to attempts to revitalise city economic bases (*Regeneration and renewal*, 2001), and there may be scope to extend the asset-outcomes approach to identify both under- and over-performing places.

The benchmarking exercises implicit in these approaches also allow for a more nuanced understanding of local strengths and weaknesses. In industry, benchmarking has become an important management tool, but its value goes well beyond the provision of a target or some notion of 'best practice'. Correctly deployed, the real advantage of benchmarking lies in examining *why* the company falls short of a benchmark, and in identifying and correcting the processes that are deficient in order to improve performance. Much the same approach could be applied to urban economies through an audit of the various components of the supply-side of the economy.

The quality of available data is plainly a problem. Bailey, Docherty and Turok conclude that, despite their extensive efforts to obtain and validate comparable statistics, official data for Britain's cities suffer from poor reliability, so that the validity of some of the measures used as indicators of economic performance or competitiveness is open to question. The implication is that an effort by statisticians to develop appropriate indicators would be valuable.

Issues for policy makers

Cities are, and will continue to be, the mainspring of mature economies such as the UK or the US, so that their economic health is a vital matter for public policy. Hitherto, the discourse on how to assist cities has focused on regeneration of declining urban economies facing acute structural change, or dealing with specific social and environmental problems. Although there have been many shifts in emphasis over the decades (see Amin et al, 2000), policy has tended to concentrate on the individual city and on instruments labelled 'urban'.

From the viewpoint of competitiveness, a rather different policy approach can be put forward. A first element of this is to recognise that support need not be a zero-sum gain in which advances by one city are invariably at the expense of another. The key to this is to understand that it is productivity, the underpinning for competitiveness, which has to be enhanced if a city is to transform its performance. The efficiency of firms and the rate at which they invest are a first and crucial constituent, but a sizeable contribution to the overall productivity of an economy comes from the stimulation of innovations it is important that this is recognised as a source of productivity gain and, moreover, one that affords greater scope for adaptation to change, (see the chapter by Simmie, Sennett and Wood).

As local economic development strategies have become more comprehensive, the question of how to attract and retain industrial investment has also come to the fore. This evolution in development policy has been reinforced by changes in regional policy. Direct subsidies for companies have given way to horizontal measures aimed at enhancing the economic environment, while increasing attention has been paid to institutions, the promotion of innovation and the development of knowledge-based industries (OECD, 1997; Cooke and Morgan, 1998; Fagerberg et al, 1999). In part, these changes are the result of budgetary pressures to reduce public spending and to allow competition more free rein – the EU, for example, has been pushing hard to curb the use of 'state aids' to industry. But the growth in decentralised industrial policy has also been stimulated by the growing belief that local actors are better placed to carry out such policies. What policy makers now have to confront is how to turn this into routine practice.

Much recent work has focused on the 'industrial district' and the potential gains from harnessing local energies to promote 'milieux innovateurs'. One of the consequences of Porter's (1998) work on the underpinnings of competitive advantage and of studies on 'clusters' is that there has been growing interest in how clustering can reinforce competitiveness. This has led to considerable efforts within economic development strategies to promote clusters of activity, although as Gordon and McCann (2000) show, the term 'cluster' has been used in three distinct ways that complicate articulation of an appropriate policy package. They distinguish between agglomeration of firms in the original Marshallian sense, what they call the industrial complex model in which the clustering is of related industries, and networks in which the creation of shared social capital is the core of the model of clustering. The analysis of social ties by Potts shows, moreover, that the social links that are believed to underpin clustering need to be looked at with care.

Nor are clusters necessarily a 'good thing' that policy ought to be seeking to nurture. Gordon and McCann emphasise that the different forms of clustering give rise to differing types of externalities, and the consequences of these for local economic development are not always evident. As Potts points out, it is possible for the networks based on social ties to exclude certain actors in a way that is detrimental to competitiveness, as well as damaging to cohesion. Simmie, Sennett and Wood suggest that, in core metropolitan regions, clustering of suppliers, collaborators or customer linkages and networks is not the main reason for the concentration of innovations in them; instead, international connections with clients and customers play a much more significant role in the development of innovations. They point to the significant role played by regional infrastructure (such as Heathrow airport in the London area) in facilitating the multiple personal contacts that are required to develop innovations.

In policy terms an important conclusion about the interplay between competitiveness and social exclusion is that competitive success and economic buoyancy is not in itself sufficient to address issues of social exclusion. This emphasises the need in policy terms to focus on the factors and processes whereby people find themselves unable to participate in society and the economy and are cut off from the life chances available to the mainstream.

It is necessary to address the specific mechanisms of social exclusion rather then rely on so-called trickle-down effects of the effects of a rising economic tide. Addressing the dynamics of social exclusion and the persistence of such effects over time and across generations would appear to be particularly crucial.

Policy 'integration'

Bringing these elements together, it becomes self-evident that policy to support the competitiveness of cities has to be more than urban policy as traditionally understood. Regulatory and fiscal policies will shape the local economic environment, both setting limits to what is feasible and shaping opportunities. The vagaries of land-use planning are a case in point. As Bramley and Lambert show, there are systematic variations in the stance of planning between more and less affluent areas, with the latter tending to apply a greater degree of planning restraint.

A consequence of this is likely to be a growth of inter-regional/inter-urban disparities in housing and other property markets, together with a more general up-market shifting in the economic and social profile of already successful areas. In that sense planning may be reinforcing the market, but it also leads to problems of housing exclusion in successful areas, and does nothing for less favoured areas. There is also evidence of differential attitudes to the development of housing as opposed to employment-related development, with the latter less likely in practice to be resisted, leading to problems of labour supply/scarcity in constrained areas and/or a growth of longer distance commuting.

Hill and Nowak, looking at the ostensibly different circumstances of US cities, make a closely related point. They argue that regeneration is not about public policies directed at poverty alleviation: it is about re-establishing the competitive viability of distressed central cities. They discuss potential public policies that can reconnect fiscally distressed cities to their regional economies through the fundamentals of economic development: improving assets values in the land, labour and business location markets. The reason for this focus is that cities can help relieve the poverty of their residents only if they foster economic opportunity.

The problem facing too many central cities and fiscally distressed older (formerly) industrial and residential suburbs in the United States is that they have institutional structures, redistributive practices, and political cultures that are more appropriate to the market positions they had in the 1940s and 1950s when most business transactions had to be completed within their municipal boundaries, then the economy of today. Distressed cities must become competitive in terms of tax costs and the bundle of services they offer to residents and business in order to regain their historic role as generators of opportunity, income, and wealth – these are the foundation of a competitive future. If changes are not made, city governments will continue to be managers of decline, their competitive position will continue to erode, and connections to their regional economies will remain tenuous.

Some more affluent city-regions may for local political reasons be particularly reluctant to make explicit a long-term vision for how growth should be managed. This undermines their ability to make proper provision for infrastructure and adds to the risks of jobs/housing imbalance. Thus, as Cooke, Davies and Wilson show, in innovative environments such as the knowledge-intensive economic centres of Oxford and Cambridge, pressures to reconcile sustainability with economic dynamism have led to calls for a new concept of 'planning for growth' rather than traditional 'planning for containment'. A challenge for policy, therefore, is how to overcome the tendency in land-use planning for local political interests opposed to growth to undermine strategic responses to growth and its management, and to implement measures that promote a more integrated understanding and consideration of the links between economic development, employment, labour supply and housing.

Various forms of institutional development can also be envisaged as a means of overcoming blockages, notably in the planning arena. Bramley and Lambert point to stronger regional planning machinery as one way of trying to secure a commitment to longer term plans allied to spatial development strategies. The solution Cooke, Davies and Wilson canvass, in a context where growth and sustainability seem to be in opposition, is to moderate conflict between them through the development of urban networks. They argue that this constitutes a 'third way' approach between unfettered market-led development and strongly interventionist state planning under which groups of nearby towns and cities cooperate and work up a consensus about areas that can rationally develop and those that ought not to if residents and representatives do not seek it. The key is to foster partnership and collaboration among hitherto competing jurisdictions, so that groups of urban centres located distantly from major metropolitan areas are able to generate a 'city-effect' or economies of agglomeration to counter the 'urban overload' or agglomeration diseconomies often suffered by giant cities. By pooling funding and expertise, networks can support a collective facility that individual towns would not be able to afford.

The research reported in the chapters by Hill and Nowak and by Bramley and Lambert shows that, at the level of the city-region, institutional fragmentation, notably in terms of local government boundaries, can severely inhibit the development of plans for areas that make sense in economic terms. It is always tempting to suggest local government reorganisation as an answer, but such a suggestion is unlikely to attract much political support. Instead, a much more promising approach is local strategic partnerships, which may in the longer term provide vehicles for consensus building and the development of more integrated policy responses at the level of the city region. It is in this sort of context that social capital and the role of civic society assume a greater prominence.

Several sorts of interaction between governance and the potential for economic development can be envisaged. They include, how rapidly the planning system functions, the responsiveness of government agencies in dealing with prospective investors, and the fiscal arrangements in an area. Incoherence in governance may also be a problem. The degree to which different agencies with a remit in a territory combine to promote economic development or inward investment will also be important.

Concluding remarks and suggestions for further work

Is the concept of competitiveness a useful one for analysing economic change in cities and constructing economic development strategies? The research summarised in this book clearly concludes that it is, but also that the concept needs to be used with care and that it is prone to overly simplistic interpretations. That competitiveness is the outcome of many diverse influences is testified to by the broad range of topics shown to bear on it. Some are amenable to policy action at the local level, while others require policies from different tiers of government acting jointly or separately. Investment in infrastructure, provision of training and other labour market interventions, the incidence of planning policies and the promotion of inward investment and innovation are all manifestly of importance in shaping urban economic performance.

There are, nevertheless, dimensions of urban competitiveness that are much more difficult to pin down. In particular, the links between social conditions – however defined – and the competitive position of cities are not easily understood. Perhaps the most prominent is the salience of social cohesion for economic success. Weak economic activity and a dearth of jobs will, generally, aggravate social exclusion, but an economic boom does not necessarily trickle down to the socially excluded to create a more cohesive society. Nor is it immediately obvious either how a more cohesive society contributes to improved urban performance or how an increased 'accumulation' of social capital can be engineered. In both respects, as the chapters by Boddy and Potts imply, the presumption is that there is, indeed, a link, but how to translate this into policy prescriptions remains elusive. The two chapters examine the many channels through which social conditions can influence competitiveness, but there is a lack of solid empirical evidence on mechanisms at work and how policy could affect them.

Although the work reported in this volume, together with other research conducted under the ESRC 'Cities' programme, has advanced understanding of urban competitiveness, it is clear that significant gaps in our understanding remain. The concept of competitiveness can lead to a richer definition of the goals of economic development, encompassing social and environmental aims, as well as economic ones. As Bailey, Docherty and Turok note, there are differing growth paths that affect trade-offs between different interest groups and thus require a political input. There is scope for much greater debate about these strategic issues in local and regional economic development policies. Similarly, to reap all the benefits promised by the diffusion of ICTs and to redistribute them efficiently and effectively across society, a variety of social and institutional innovations might be required, including a reduction of working time. These might be issues for further research.

In the policy arena, there is encouraging evidence of fresh thinking on how to deal with urban problems. The White Paper on urban policy published in 2000 in the UK and the Rogers report highlighted some of the big questions, while intensive efforts have been made in the US to develop new approaches, some of which are mentioned in the chapters by Hill and Nowak and by Kresl. Urban policy has, moreover been identified as one of ten key cohesion objectives within the EU. The message from this volume is that a focus on competitiveness is likely to facilitate the move from diagnosis and analysis to effective action.

References

Amin, A. Massey, D. and Thrift, N. (2000) *Cities for the many, not the few*, Bristol: The Policy Press.

Baumol, W.J. (1992) 'Horizontal collusion and innovation', *Economic Journal* vol 102, pp 129-37.

Begg, I. (1999) 'Cities and competitiveness', *Urban Studies*, vol 33, no 5/6, pp 795-809.

Cooke, P. and Morgan, K. (1998) *The associational economy: Firms, regions, and innovation*, Oxford: Oxford University Press.

DETR (Department of the Environment, Transport and the Regions) (2000) *Our towns and cities: The future – delivering an urban renaissance*, London: HMSO.

Duranton, G. and Puga, D. (2000) 'Diversity and specialisation in cities: why, where and when does it matter?', *Urban Studies*, vol 37, no 3, pp 533-55.

Fagerberg, J., Guerierri, P. and Verspagen, B. (eds) (1999) *The economic challenge for Europe: Adapting to innovation based growth*, Cheltenham: Edward Elgar.

Glaeser, E.L., Kallal, H.D., Scheinkman, J.A. and Shleifer, A. (1992) 'Growth in cities', *Journal of Political Economy*, vol 100, no 6.

Gordon, I.R. and McCann, P. (2000) 'Industrial clusters: complexes, agglomeration and/or social networks?', *Urban Studies*, vol 37, pp 513-32.

Krugman, P. (1996) *Pop internationalism*, Cambridge, MA: MIT Press.

O'Donoghue, D. (1999) 'The relationship between diversification and growth: some evidence from the British urban system 1978-1991', *International Journal of Urban and Regional Research*, vol 23, no 3, pp 549-66.

OECD (1997) *Industrial competitiveness in the knowledge-based economy: The new role of governments*, Paris: OECD.

Porter, M.E. (1998) *The competitive advantage of nations*, London: Macmillan.

Regeneration and Renewal (2001) 'Partner cities picked to help speed up urban programme', 30 August, p 1.

Robson, B., Parkinson, M., Boddy, M. and Maclennan, D. (2000) *The state of English cities*, London: DETR.

Rosentraub, M.S. and Przybylski, M. (1996) 'Competitive advantage, economic development, and the effective use of local public dollars', *Economic Development Quarterly*, vol 10, pp 315-30.

Index

NOTE: Page numbers followed by *tab* indicate information in a table, those followed by *fig* in a figure, those followed by *n* in a note. Headings refer to the UK unless qualified by (US).